A NEW EMBASSY ALONG
AN ANCIENT ROUTE
IN UZBEKISTAN

ADST MEMOIRS AND OCCASIONAL PAPERS SERIES
Series Editors: Lisa Terry & Margery Thompson

In 2003, the Association for Diplomatic Studies and Training (ADST), a nonprofit organization founded in 1986, created the Memoirs and Occasional Papers Series to preserve firsthand accounts and other informed observations on foreign affairs for scholars, journalists, and the general public. Through its book series, its Foreign Affairs Oral History program, and its support for the training of foreign affairs personnel at the State Department's Foreign Service Institute, ADST seeks to promote understanding of American diplomacy and those who conduct it. Henry Clarke's personal account as the first U.S. ambassador to Uzbekistan explains the country's immediate post-Soviet history and its relations with the U.S. embassy in Tashkent.

RELATED TITLES FROM ADST SERIES

THOMPSON BUCHANAN, *Mossy Memoir of a Rolling Stone*
CHARLES T. CROSS, *Born a Foreigner: A Memoir of the American Presence in Asia*
JOHN GUNTHER DEAN, *Danger Zones: A Diplomat's Fight for America's Interests*
PETER D. EICHER, *Raising the Flag: Adventures of America's First Envoys in Faraway Lands*
BRANDON GROVE, *Behind Embassy Walls: The Life and Times of an American Diplomat*
DONALD P. GREGG, *Pot Shards: Fragments of a Life Lived in CIA, the White House, and the Two Koreas*
CAMERON R. HUME, *Mission to Algiers: Diplomacy by Engagement*
DENNIS JETT, *American Ambassadors: The Past, Present, and Future of America's Diplomats*
WILLIAM MORGAN and CHARLES STUART KENNEDY, eds., *American Diplomats: The Foreign Service at Work*
DAVID D. NEWSOM, *Witness to a Changing World*
RAYMOND F. SMITH, *The Craft of Political Analysis for Diplomats*

For a complete list of series titles, visit <adst.org/publications>

A NEW EMBASSY ALONG
AN ANCIENT ROUTE
IN UZBEKISTAN

Henry L. Clarke

MEMOIRS AND OCCASIONAL PAPERS SERIES
ASSOCIATION FOR DIPLOMATIC STUDIES AND TRAINING

NEW ACADEMIA PUBLISHING   VELLUM

Washington, DC

New Academia Publishing/VELLUM Books, 2022

The views and opinions in this book are solely those of the author and do not necessarily reflect those of the Association for Diplomatic Studies and Training or the Government of the United States, including the Department of State.

Printed in the United States of America

Library of Congress Control Number: 2021902779
ISBN 978-1-7359378-6-1 paperback (alk. paper)

VELLUM An imprint of New Academia Publishing

New Academia Publishing
4401-A Connecticut Ave. NW, #236, Washington DC 20008
info@newacademia.com - www.newacademia.com
NEW ACADEMIA
PUBLISHING

CONTENTS

List of Illustrations   vii
Acknowledgements and Sources   viii
Map of Central Asia   xii
Map of Uzbekistan   xiii

Prologue—A New Path to Tashkent, without the Silk   1
    Route
1 – Learning Karimov's System   11
2 – Why Should Uzbekistan Be Independent?   25
3 – Dangerous Neighborhood   37
4 – Islam—the Context or the Enemy?   49
5 – Visitors as Mixed Blessings, Yet Necessary for   55
    Bilateral Relations
6 – Big Changes in U.S. Relations, without Domestic   69
    Reform
7 – Lost Economic Opportunities   83
8 – Water, Air, and Karakalpakstan   97
9 – Military Contacts Open Up   105
10 – Staffing Up   115
11 – "Club Med" and the "Best Little Embassy" in   123
    Central Asia
12 –How Much Physical Security?   135
13 – Creating a Clinic   151
14 – Language Hazards   157
15 – Inspectors Have Their Say   169
Epilogue – Will Independence Endure?   173

Appendix A—Letter of Instruction from President   188
    George H. W. Bush

Appendix B – Principles for Security at New Posts   192

Appendix C – Press Conference, U.S. Secretary of De-   196
fense William Perry, Tashkent, Uzbekistan, 6 April
1995

Appendix D – Remarks by Ambassador Henry Clarke   199
about the Central Asian–American Enterprise
Fund, Tashkent, February 3, 1995

Appendix E – Remarks by Ambassador Henry Clarke   201
at the Kokdumalak Signing Ceremony, Tashkent,
April 12, 1995

Appendix F – Remarks by Ambassador Henry Clarke   203
at the Meeting of Experts on Security and Cooperation in Central Asia, Tashkent, September 5, 1995

Notes   205
References   213
Index   215

LIST OF ILLUSTRATIONS

Map of Central Asia xii
Map of Uzbekistan xiii
President Karimov 29
Map of Fergana Valley 36
Registan Square, Samarkand 48
Foreign Minister Kamilov 68
Foreign Minister Saidkasymov 82
1992 U.S.-Uzbekistan Agreement Signing 91
Aral Sea 96
Biplane 98
Defense Secretary Perry 111
U.S. Embassy Tashkent 128
Presidential Letter of Instruction 188

ACKNOWLEDGEMENTS
AND SOURCES

Establishing the first U.S. embassy in a country the size of Uzbekistan had to be a team effort, and I am especially grateful to the embassy employees who worked with me, both Americans and locally hired staff. Many people outside the embassy assisted us in critical ways, starting with the Department of State in Washington, the New Post Support Unit in Bonn, and many other American civilian and military agencies. Also indispensable was support from the Government of Uzbekistan, from its president and ministries, the city of Tashkent and our local Chilanzar Rayon (District). Some of their help (and occasional lapses) will be obvious from the following pages. Our needs were extensive, and those who helped meet them cannot all be mentioned—in some cases I did not know them—but are greatly appreciated.

Regrettably, I have not stayed in touch with all of the people who worked with me during the first three years of U.S. Embassy Tashkent, 1992–95. I am sure they could have helped make this story a better one. I did receive help from several colleagues in reviewing all or parts of the draft and contributing their points of view and anecdotes. Sylvia Babus, Delia Barnohodjaeva Valente, and my son Edwin "Dobby" Clarke contributed particularly useful and colorful experiences. Arthur Downey made many helpful editorial suggestions. I also thank Muhammad Babur Malikov for his views on the Soviet cotton purge in Uzbekistan and the events leading to his request for asylum as ambassador to the United States. The book as a whole attempts to reflect my personal understanding of what happened in U.S. relations with Uzbekistan, 1992–95, so any omissions and errors are my mistakes.

The opinions and characterizations in this book are mine, and do not necessarily represent official positions of the United States Government.

While in Tashkent I was too busy to think about writing a book, so I have no journal and little written material from that period. I did retain my desk and pocket calendars, which not only recorded the dates of meetings but often included names of participants. In the text below, where I have given a specific date, it is based on those calendars or other written material. If only the month is given, then I established that from memory or by reference to other events, which might be fallible.

My son Christopher Clarke prepared the map of Central Asia, and I drew the maps of Uzbekistan and the Fergana Valley, all three based upon information from maps produced by the Office of the Geographer, Department of State, and the Nations Online Project.

The English spelling of names and places, in the maps and in the text below, are as we used them in the embassy in 1992–95 and are mostly transliterations from Russian. The spellings differ somewhat from Uzbek written with the Latin alphabet, which was adopted gradually after 1992.

I asked the State Department to declassify certain telegrams from U.S. Embassy Tashkent, mostly written and classified by me between 1992 and 1995, and mostly reporting meetings with President Karimov. Unfortunately, the department declassified only a few, for reasons not explained to me. I have cited the declassified telegrams in the endnotes in the form "95 Tashkent 0000," showing the year and the serial number of the telegram. Although my classified notes from high-level meetings were destroyed, in a few cases I kept an unclassified list of points for follow-up.

Some of my views about being ambassador to Uzbekistan have been included in interviews with me in 1998 and 1999 by Stuart Kennedy, archived in the Foreign Affairs Oral History Collection of the Association for Diplomatic Studies and Training.* I did not know his questions in advance, so my replies were spontaneous and in some cases not the best choice of words, but most are consistent with this book. I am grateful to Mr. Kennedy and the association for the oral history collection's major contribution to the history of American foreign relations by recording the views of so many participants, and for including me. Finally, Lisa Terry and Margery Thompson of the association assisted me in preparing this book for publication.

I hope this book will also be a useful addition to the history of American foreign relations. It may be of practical value when new American diplomatic and consular posts are established abroad. I also hope it will be of interest to people of Central Asia, and to those who study this fascinating region, to have the perspective of a foreigner who lived and worked in Tashkent for three of the first four years of Uzbekistan's independence.

Henry L. Clarke

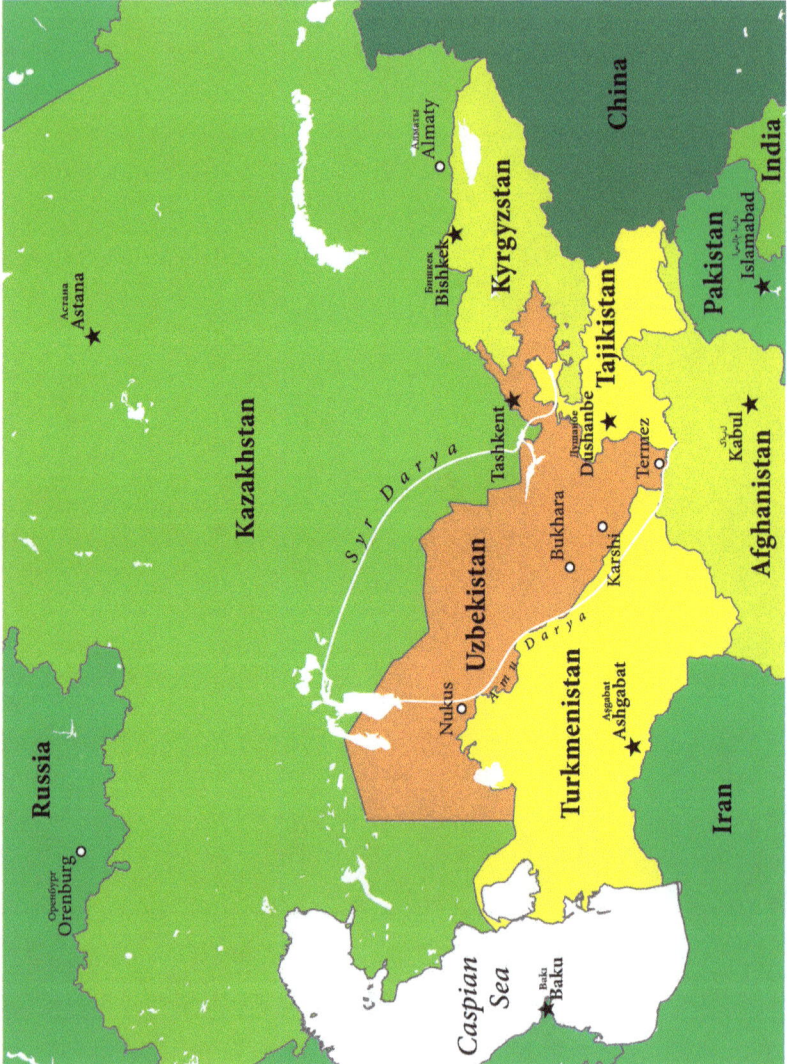

Source: Christopher Clarke

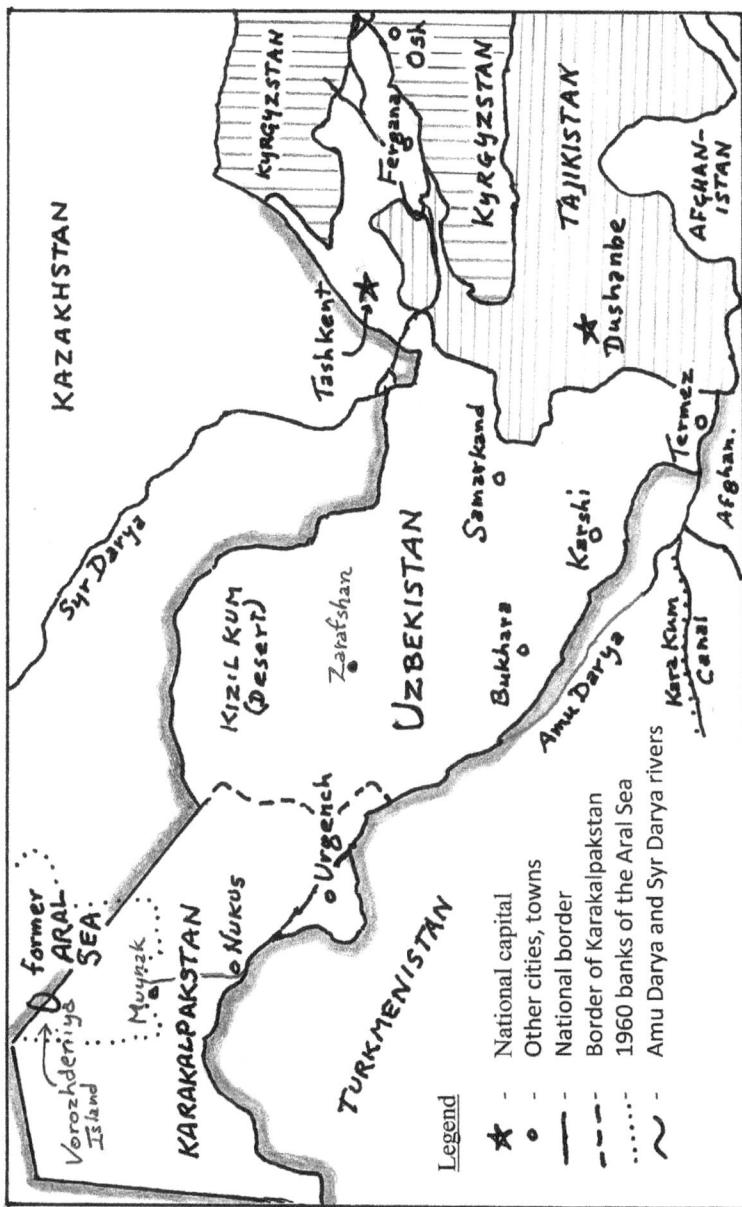

Source: Henry Clarke

PROLOGUE

A NEW PATH TO TASHKENT, WITHOUT THE SILK ROUTE

The Peaceful Collapse of an Empire

By 1990 the unity of the Soviet Union was being seriously challenged by its Union Republics. Early in that year Lithuania declared independence. By the end of October 1990 all fifteen Union Republics, including Russia, had declared either their "sovereignty" or full independence from the Soviet Union. Efforts to form a new union treaty among the Union Republics did not succeed. In August 1991 a failed coup against President Mikhail Gorbachev convinced most of the remaining Union Republics to declare full independence and secure their own futures.

American diplomats had worked hard to negotiate the end of the Cold War, and certainly supported East European countries in regaining their full independence from the Soviet Union. But the United States had taken no action to promote the collapse of the Soviet Union, other than to urge President Gorbachev not to use force against Lithuania and other republics seeking independence. The KGB (Committee on State Security) tried to claim publicly that the United States was subverting the Soviet Union,[1] but their claim had little credibility, because political developments in the republics took place in the full view of the Soviet press and television, which under Gorbachev's *glasnost* were reporting accurately for the most part. The United States and many other Western countries had never recognized *de jure* the incorporation into the USSR of the three Baltic Republics, which had been independent countries before World War II. But even in those three republics the United States took no action against Soviet authority. Some American officials, fearing internal conflict and instability, including possible loss of responsible control over nuclear weapons, did not favor the Soviet Union's collapse. Those American officials who welcomed the collapse saw that it was not in America's interest, nor in the interests of the Soviet peoples, for the United States to be involved in causing it.

The collapse became final in December 1991 and was entirely peaceful. The decisive blow came at a meeting in Belarus of the leaders of three republics, two of which would have been essential to any continuation of the Soviet Union: Boris Yeltsin for Russia, Leonid Kravchuk for Ukraine, and Stanislav Shushkevich for Belarus. Kazakhstan's Nursultan Nazarbayev was invited but did not come. The three organizers signed an Agreement on Creating a Commonwealth of Independent States that would be open to all former Union Republics of the Soviet Union. This new international organization would not be a state or have a government other than coordinating bodies to be located in Minsk, Belarus, nor would it limit the sovereignty, territory, or independence of member states. All of the former Soviet Union Republics, except the three Baltic republics and Georgia, adhered to the Commonwealth of Independent States on December 21, 1991. The Soviet Union was gone.

The State Department Responds to the Creation of Independent States

Realizing that the Soviet Union was falling apart, and expecting to need additional embassies and staff to establish and maintain contacts and reporting from the increasingly independent republics, the State Department sent out an inquiry worldwide asking Foreign Service personnel who spoke Russian and other languages spoken in the USSR for expressions of interest in serving in the former Soviet Union. I responded from my post in Tel Aviv, saying I spoke two relevant languages: Russian from my three-year Moscow assignment, and Romanian, spoken in Moldova,[2] from my two Bucharest assignments totaling six years. There was no response, and I did not know what posts the State Department expected to open.

Secretary of State James Baker decided that the United States would establish an embassy in every newly independent republic of the former Soviet Union—and ordered those not already open to be opened on March 16, 1992. (Embassies had already been established in Ukraine and the Baltic republics.) The European Bureau had cautiously recommended opening regional embassies to cover several countries each. But Baker was right. We did not know what was going to happen in these new states, and we would need a full-time presence in each country, dealing with the new governments on a daily basis, if we hoped to understand and perhaps influence their future direction. The new posts opened on time and were kept open by a series of temporary personnel—some borrowed from U.S. Embassy Moscow, others from Washington and posts around the world. The State Department set about assigning permanent staff, including ambassadors.

It typically takes a long time to appoint an American ambassador. In the early 1990s, the White House would ask the State Department to provide candidates for those embassies to be headed by career diplomats, including all of the new posts in the former USSR. The deputy secretary chaired a committee to consider lists of potential candidates. In late February of 1992 the European Bureau asked me whether I would be willing to serve as ambassador to Moldova, if I were chosen. I said yes, thanks for putting me on your list. Weeks of silence followed. Meanwhile, I became the full-time but temporary deputy chief of mission (DCM) in Tel Aviv.

Then came "the call" from a deputy director general: "Congratulations, you are the department's candidate to be ambassador to Uzbekistan, but you must treat that fact as confidential until the president announces you." Having visited both Moldova and Uzbekistan, I knew how different they were. I would have been pleased with either appointment, but I wondered if there had been a mistake, so I asked what had happened to the European Bureau's proposal for Moldova. My caller cheerfully replied along the lines of, "Well, we don't talk about committee decisions, but I can say that Uzbekistan is one of the republics with a real economy, and an economic officer like you might be useful there." I felt pleased by the honor and humbled by the responsibility, not just to help launch a new embassy, but to launch one in a country of over 20 million people, the third largest former republic of the Soviet Union by population, after Russia and Ukraine.

Next I filled out a stack of paperwork about my background, which some unfortunate White House lawyer would examine to see whether I might be a liability to the president if he appointed me. Although tedious, this process was not difficult for anyone who had been a career public servant with a security clearance, no political affiliation, and no private business on the side. More weeks of silence followed. The Government of Uzbekistan was asked and agreed to my assignment. The White House public announcement on May 28 came as a relief.

The price to be paid for such a unique and challenging professional assignment was family separation. There was no accredited English-language high school anywhere near Uzbekistan. With the kind permission of both the Israeli Foreign Ministry and the U.S. State Department, my family stayed for another year in Israel so my children could continue to attend the American International School there. After my daughter, Marie, graduated in 1993, she went off to Occidental College, and my wife and son moved to California for the remainder of my assignment in Tashkent. Though we could visit each other, the distance became enormous – halfway around the globe.

The Senate Acts

The Senate's reaction was not typical for giving "advice and consent" to the appointment of ambassadors. 1992 was an election year, President George H. W. Bush was a Republican, and the Democrats had a majority in the Senate. A typical senatorial reaction would have been a slow roll. Instead, the Senate Foreign Relations Committee seemed as enthusiastic as the State Department to be sending Foreign Service officers as ambassadors to the far corners of the former Soviet Union. They scheduled two hearings for August, five at one time going to Central Asia, and four going to Azerbaijan, Belarus, Georgia, and Moldova on another day.

My close cousins Jim and Cathy Fort, longtime Washington area residents with whom I had often stayed during my trips in and out of Washington, were determined to attend the hearings.

Jim had been general counsel and chief lobbyist for United Parcel Service for many years. He knew the workings of the Congress in detail and actually liked watching them in action. Instead of calling me, he called the Senate Foreign Relations Committee directly to ask about the hearings. The staffer on the telephone never heard of me. Jim persisted, until the staffer finally said, "Oh, you mean he is one of those mud-hut ambassadors!"

The Senate Foreign Relations Committee did not expect much of a crowd or any press. Instead of the committee's huge hearing room in the Dirksen Senate Office Building, for our hearing by the Subcommittee for European Affairs on August 5, 1992, they chose the small, historic Foreign Relations Committee room inside the Capitol building. We five would-be ambassadors to Central Asia sat on one side of the table, with various senators coming and going on the other side, and everyone else—staff, friends, relatives— squeezed into corners or left out in the hall. The senator in the chair welcomed us warmly by observing that we five nominees each had an average of twenty-five years of diplomatic experience and each spoke a language appropriate for his post.[3]

The senators did not hesitate to ask substantive questions, and as professional diplomats we were fully prepared for them. My friend from graduate school, Senator Larry Pressler, had, as expected, questions for me about human rights in Uzbekistan. He had visited Tashkent only a few weeks before the hearing. On June 29, Abdurahim Pulatov, Chairman of the Birlik political movement, was severely beaten and his skull fractured on the street near the entrance to the State Prosecutor's Office in Tashkent, where he had just been questioned. Larry had visited Pulatov in the hospital. The senator seemed unsurprised that I responded forthrightly that the beating was a violation of Pulatov's fundamental rights. We all knew advocating for human rights would be a substantial part of my job in Uzbekistan.

Near the end of the hearing, Senator Joe Biden gave a lengthy and obviously well-briefed presentation on the importance of drug trafficking in Central Asia (opium and heroin from Afghanistan were transiting Central Asian countries, en route to Russia and the rest of Europe).[4] A few days later the full Senate voted its consent to our nine appointments, including those for Azerbaijan, Belarus, Georgia and Moldova.

Even late in an election year, both the executive branch and the Senate, representing different parties, were united on the importance of quickly establishing a separate embassy, a permanent official presence, in each of the newly independent countries of the former Soviet Union, and agreed on appointing ambassadors from the career Foreign Service.

On to Tashkent

I thought it important that the first U.S. ambassador to Uzbekistan not arrive via Moscow, as American diplomats would have done only a few years before. It would have been colorful and romantic to arrive by camel, using the ancient Silk Route, but I was eager to get on with my new job. So I was glad to have a nonstop flight from Istanbul to Tashkent on Turkish Airlines.

Uzbek officials had complained that there was no U.S. ambassador, not understanding that by American standards the process of appointing me had moved quite fast. Although I could not be released early from Tel Aviv, I did get some leave with my family before reporting to Washington for briefings and the hearing. The other ambassadors to Central Asia had served at their new posts as chargés d'affaires before the Senate's confirmation procedure began. Once confirmed, they took some leave before going back to their posts.

So by chance, when I arrived in Tashkent on September 7, 1992, I was the first credentialed U.S. ambassador to arrive in Central Asia, which pleased the Uzbek officials. Starting with Turkish Ambassador Erdogan Aytun, who had arrived at least six months earlier, and who became dean of the Ambassadorial Corps by seniority, some nine ambassadors from other countries had beat me to Tashkent.

Shifting to a Permanent, Sustainable Embassy

I chose my flights to arrive late on Monday, U.S. Labor Day, hoping that meant that my small staff could take some time off on the weekend, since I knew they would be very busy once I arrived. A big round of formal and informal meetings would ensue with government officials of all kinds, plus individual meetings with the other ambassadors. I guessed wrong—the embassy staff had worked hard all weekend preparing for my arrival.

Their work wasn't just in my honor: the American staff had been in the habit of working seven days a week since temporary employees had opened the embassy over five months earlier. By September permanent American employees were starting to arrive and this habit could not continue. At an early staff meeting I made clear that I really valued their work, that I understood that we had more work than people to do it, but that staying late in the evening and then working through the weekends and holidays was unsustainable. I cared more about the quality of our reports and our management than I cared about quantity, so we would set priorities. Reporting quality was simple: as long as our reporting was as good as we had come to expect from U.S. Embassies like Paris, Tel Aviv and Moscow, it would be fine with me. We could not possibly implement all the State Department regulations for embassies at once, so we would decide which were most important for managing our situation, and implement those first.

As for working hours, I said I would come in on Saturday mornings, read the cables that were sent Friday evening from the State Department (which helped me organize the next week), keep my door open if someone wanted to see me, perhaps tend to other tasks, and go home. I would not come to the embassy on Sundays except in an emergency. Everyone else could choose: they could follow my example, or if they liked working in the quiet of Sunday, they should not come in on Saturday. I suggested that the American staff should find out what recreation was available, or just go out into the city and meet ordinary people. If they wanted to take the whole weekend off, or travel out of town, great. We had a lot to learn about Uzbekistan that we would never learn from behind our desks, or even in weekday meetings with officials.

This instruction worked. The Americans just needed me to say it, and abide by it myself, which I did. I enjoyed Sundays off in Uzbekistan. A small staff can sometimes be more efficient, or adjust more quickly to new situations, than a large one, and we accomplished a lot working only five or six days a week.

With a new embassy in a newly independent country, the most urgent question for me was not how to manage our own affairs, though I was responsible for that too. The critical questions had to be, who are the people running this country, and how are they doing it? What will Uzbekistan make of its independence? How can we develop a new relationship between Uzbekistan and the United States?

Goals for this Book

The first few years of Uzbekistan's independence were a formative period in its history, both internally and in its relations with foreign countries. My delayed decision to write this book reflects my realization that American diplomats living in Tashkent during that period might have insights that were worth recording for others, both in Uzbekistan and abroad. Thus I have tried to present Uzbekistan, the way in which the United States established our bilateral relationship, and the early formation of the U.S. Embassy in Tashkent, as my colleagues and I saw them from 1992 through 1995, even if we were sometimes wrong. I have tried hard not to have those views blurred by what we have learned since that time, in the hope this story will be more useful to future research. The exception is the Epilogue, in which I offer a limited retrospective and comments on the future.

This book is not a chronological record, which I think would be confusing. I saw the major issues faced by our new U.S. Embassy in Tashkent as separate and continuing themes, which often had to be dealt with simultaneously. The first six chapters deal with the political context, domestically and internationally, including the role of Islam. Parts of Chapters 2 and 6, and all of Chapter 7, deal with the economic situation, and with Uzbekistan's largely unsuccessful efforts at economic reform, despite America's willingness to help. Chapter 8 is about the environment. Chapter 9 deals with the changes in U.S.-Uzbekistan military relations, 1992-95.

Administrative challenges to the establishment of a new embassy so far from the United States (nine or ten time zones, depending upon the time of year) affect the quality of work the embassy can do, so there are separate chapters dealing with personnel, our offices and homes, our security, and our medical support. Chapter 14 describes the challenges we and the Uzbeks faced with the Russian, Uzbek, and English languages, as Uzbekistan began to change its official language and alphabet.

The goal of the Epilogue is not to explain all that has changed since 1995, but rather to ask, looking back now, what have we learned about Uzbekistan's independence, and its chances for survival in the future?

Finally, for readers who are interested, there are appendices: (A) President George H. W. Bush's instructions to me as ambassador; (B) my views on principles for security of new posts; (C) Defense Secretary William Perry's press conference in Tashkent; (D) my short speech at the beginning of the Central Asian–American Enterprise Fund; (E) another citing the contribution of an American-financed project to Uzbekistan's energy independence; and (F) my remarks to experts on security and cooperation in Central Asia. Hopefully these samples will give some flavor of the way we conducted our diplomacy in Tashkent in the early 1990s.

1

LEARNING KARIMOV'S SYSTEM

A First Impression of the President

In most capitals, including Washington, a newly arrived ambassador has to sit around for days, sometimes even weeks, before the host government finds time to receive him and to accept his credentials at the head of state level. Until it does, in most capitals tradition expects that the new ambassador will not be out meeting any other government officials, or otherwise engage in public activity. But I had no time to sit around: foreign ministry officials dealing with the United States met me at the airport on a Monday evening, my appointment with the acting foreign minister was the next day, and President Karimov received me on Wednesday, less than forty-eight hours after my flight landed. I took it as evidence of the interest and importance Karimov attached to relations with the United States. Later, as I got to know more about the bureaucracy surrounding the president, it became clear that this would never have happened so quickly without his personal instruction.

The foreign ministry's building in 1992 had an open, spiral staircase leading from the ground-floor lobby to a second-story lobby, and the foreign minister's office was just off the latter. This stone staircase looked nice, but was deceptive: not all the stairs were the same height. Hastening up the stairs to meet acting Foreign Minister Ziamov, with President George H. W. Bush's letter of my credentials in my hand, I tripped—and caught myself with both hands, but the envelope with the letter was caught between my hand and the stairs, and was obviously bent. I had been so careful with it in my hand baggage for more than a week, and here on the last day before delivering it, I have to fall on it. This did not visibly bother Deputy Foreign Minister Ziamov, who read the letter and returned it for me to give President Karimov the next day. At that ceremony, on September 9, with top officials of the government and the embassy's ranking diplomats, President Karimov held up the slightly beat-up envelope, looked askance at it, but said nothing.

Then followed the first of many meetings with President Karimov, this one in a small office. (Most of our meetings would be in a conference room with other officials present.) I wanted to include my deputy, Michael Matera, for the benefit of his opinion and his notes, but protocol officials insisted that the meeting would be just between the president, his interpreter, and me. Soon it became clear why he wanted the meeting to be one-on-one: the main thing on Karimov's mind was to complain about our embassy's activities, including Michael's own actions as chargé d'affaires. It was a rather blunt way to get my attention to the president's priorities.

President Karimov did not like the U.S. Embassy's contacts with dissidents, former politicians, or human rights activists, and he led our dialogue by making clear that he did not think such contacts were legitimate. He specifically accused Michael of sneaking around at midnight to meet with one of them. Karimov's take on this meeting did not remind me of any reports I had read in Washington, so I wondered if the meeting had happened while I was on my way to Tashkent. Since I didn't know about the incident, I could only point out that we in the American Embassy hoped to meet with Uzbek citizens of all persuasions, as we did in many other countries. I said I would look into the specific case.

Afterward, Michael confirmed that his meeting with the dissident took place, but at noon and not midnight. And he had been driven to the meeting by a locally hired embassy driver in an embassy car, which remained parked nearby. So he had done no sneaking at all. I was starting to learn about the extent and poor quality of official Uzbek reporting on our activities, and on people opposing Karimov, or at least how Karimov was interpreting such reports. It was also my first example that Karimov, for all his intelligence and strength, was not always adept at using meetings to advance his purposes effectively. He had used my first impression of him to put me on guard, without actually having a convincing case. It was an old-school, Soviet-style meeting. After six years in Nicolae Ceauşescu's Romania, and three in Moscow at a frigid time in the Cold War, I was not intimidated. The embassy's contacts with dissidents continued without pause, usually done by our political officer, Daria Fane, while Michael or I carried out most of the human rights discussions with officials.

Although this first meeting was not the last in which Karimov was ham-handed enough to be self-defeating, it probably reflected his inexperience in dealing with American diplomats. Later meetings in his offices remained rather formal but became more productive. Perhaps he realized that our courteous manners did not imply ignorance or weakness in pursuing U.S. policies. He never expressed any personal animosity toward me. Gradually I understood that he wanted a good working relationship with the United States, whether or not we accepted the harsher aspects of his rule.

For a new embassy, it was critical for us to learn the system through which Karimov was governing Uzbekistan, and it did not take long to figure that out. We knew how the Soviet Union had been organized and governed, so the first question was, what had changed?

Swift Changes from the Soviet System

The Soviet system relied on two parallel structures: (a) the government, which functioned at the USSR, republic, oblast, and various local levels, with varying degrees of centralization, and (b) the Communist Party, which guided all levels of government. The party centralized control in Moscow, through its Central Committee, which had a large staff but did not often meet as a full committee. The Communist Party Politburo and especially the general secretary made all the key decisions for the party and for the USSR as a whole. Some governmental "organs," such as the defense and foreign ministries, the Committee for State Security (KGB), Central Planning Committee (GosPlan), among others, administered the entire Soviet Union directly from Moscow; whereas agriculture, light industry, and many other activities had ministries at both the Soviet and republic levels.

Before the Soviet Union collapsed, Islam Karimov was first secretary of the Communist Party of Uzbekistan, and thus the most powerful person in Uzbekistan. Yet even within Uzbekistan he could not consider that the KGB, or the Defense Ministry's factories and installations, or the gold or uranium mines and their processing plants, actually worked for him. President Karimov once remarked to me and others that when he had been Uzbekistan's finance minister he had no knowledge of the actual value of Uzbekistan's gold production. That amount was secret: it was considered production of the Soviet Union, controlled by a Soviet ministry in Moscow, and not subordinate to, or coordinated with, the Uzbek Soviet Socialist Republic.

Karimov did not cause Uzbekistan's independence, but he knew what to do with it. He lost no time in seizing levers of power that had been controlled from Moscow. Uzbekistan established new ministries of defense, foreign affairs, state security, and other formerly Moscow-centered functions, each with new headquarters in Tashkent. Many officials of European origin in the government and in the Communist Party left Uzbekistan, voluntarily or otherwise. Karimov moved more cautiously with professionals who could not be replaced easily or quickly, such as army officers or border guards.

In the process, the Communist Party of Uzbekistan disappeared. Party officials who remained, mostly ethnic Uzbeks, found work in Uzbekistan's governmental organizations. Party buildings were taken over by the newly expanded, Tashkent-centered ministries.

Karimov held an election for president in 1991, which he won without much effective opposition, confirming his authority over the entire governmental structure. Much of his reorganization took place during the year, September 1991 through August 1992, after declaring independence, and before my arrival. It was not a public process, and it was deliberate.

Much later, in 1994, Karimov was quoted by *Time* Magazine that he considered the "possible re-emergence of the Communist Party" a "major danger for us in Uzbekistan."[5] Since Karimov had been, as first secretary, the head of the Communist Party of Uzbekistan before independence, why should he have judged his former party as so dangerous? My assumption was that he saw a reinvigorated

Communist Party as one of the most likely instruments Russia would use if it wished to reverse Uzbekistan's independence. Since Karimov had been a high-level survivor of the great "cotton affair" purge of the 1980s, he would have seen at close hand just how harshly a Moscow-centered Communist Party could deal with Uzbek officials (as described in Chapter 2 below).

Washington took a while to absorb these changes. The State Department objected to our drafts of the Uzbekistan portion of the department's annual human rights report for 1992 and 1993, disbelieving that the Communist Party was gone.[6] At first I wondered too, where is Karimov's own political party? The nominal parties of the 1991 election, including Karimov's own National Democratic Party, seemed to have faded out of sight. Two opposition parties in the election, Birlik and Erk, were driven out of active politics through persecution of their leadership—including, for example, the June 1992 severe beating of Abdurahim Pulatov, Chairman of Birlik, which Senator Larry Pressler had raised at my confirmation hearing (Prologue, above). Party politics in Uzbekistan was being replaced by repression and human rights cases.

It became clear that Karimov intended the entire government at all levels—that is, the ministries, parliament, mayors, and other local officials—to support him, both officially and personally. Thus he didn't need a party, or an ideology, and did not permit others to have parties either. He would make all key decisions, including appointments and candidates for future elections. Everyone else would implement them. Some officials looked for opportunities to praise him.

Our embassy and the State Department had no doubts that we were dealing with an authoritarian government, one that could deal harshly with any opposition. As elsewhere in the world, we had doubts about the legitimacy and stability of such regimes, and knew that severe human rights violations would make it difficult for the American political system to improve bilateral relations. So how did we represent American views, especially those that were contrary to President Karimov's?

Managing Our Human Rights Cases

Whether or not you believe that human rights cases should have taken such a high priority in the new relationship between the United States and Uzbekistan, in fact our embassy's agility in staying in close touch with the modest number of dissidents and former opponents of President Karimov was absolutely vital to the embassy's credibility, on human rights or any other subject. State Department officers following Uzbekistan were, like me, all cold warriors—our desk officer had served in Poland after the rise of Solidarity, her boss had served in Moscow and in Bucharest. Department officials seemed to expect that since human rights had made major gains in Russia and in the Baltic republics, and apparently also in Kyrgyzstan, there was less excuse than ever for continued violations of basic human rights in the other newly independent republics.

I thought American observers sometimes underestimated the difference between Russia's recent, largely self-induced liberalization, and the unbroken history of dictatorship in most of Central Asia, yet I did not quarrel with our policy. If we could somehow persuade Uzbekistan to change course on human rights in its first few years of independence, it could start a process of reform from which Uzbek citizens, and our long-term relationship with Uzbekistan, could only benefit.

Karimov's opponents were not just in contact with us; they had contact with various human rights organizations in Moscow and elsewhere, which they could reach by telephone. Those organizations in turn remained in contact with the U.S. Embassy in Moscow, and with nongovernmental organizations there and in the United States. We were glad these private channels worked, but our embassy did not want some atrocious event in Uzbekistan to be reported first out of Moscow (inevitably suggesting we were clueless or slow), or worse yet, first reported to us as an instruction from Washington, based on facts that had been relayed several times and possibly misunderstood. I expected to be instructed to raise every serious incident with the Uzbekistan government, and I wanted to be sure of our facts. If the news came from Moscow or Washington, we had to choose between complaining promptly (and perhaps ineffectively) and delaying our approach until we had checked out the facts locally. This could become difficult if the dissident or other victim had been taken into custody by the police, or was hiding and afraid to meet with us.

Instead, if we could first learn the facts from the victims or their friends ourselves, I could go directly to the Foreign Ministry without waiting for Washington to instruct us. Generally the ministry would have heard nothing from the security services, but would have to accept our inquiry, and our talking points. Then we could report to Washington on the incident, on my meeting, and include our recommendations about what to do next, if anything. We avoided both overreactions and awkward delays. We were not modest: we thought we could manage these issues best because we were directly in touch with both sides of the problem, the dissidents and the government. Despite Washington's long experience with the Soviet Union, no one in Washington had ever worked in Uzbekistan beyond a visit or two, or knew the dissidents better than did our political officer, Daria Fane. Being a new embassy in a "new" (to us) country was, in this and other matters, sometimes an advantage.

Results?

What did all our righteous zeal accomplish? It did not change Karimov's system of internal security. Beatings remained routine. As Senator Larry Pressler had seen before the Senate hearing, we often saw the victims' injuries first-hand or learned about them from credible witnesses. Information reported from the security services to the foreign ministry or to the president continued to be different from what we heard from dissidents or their friends and relatives. Yet by raising human rights cases at high levels we did several things, well short of generating reform: (1) officials from Karimov on down knew that close relations with the U.S. would be affected by human rights issues, and our specific concerns were continuously being put on the record; (2) while we could not protect dissidents, I am sure they felt our support and sympathy; (3) some less important cases may have been treated more leniently, although I cannot prove that; (4) we learned a lot about the Karimov regime and its internal control system by following specific cases closely;

and finally (5) if Karimov had wanted to reform his internal security system, we were giving him some examples of what that would require. When nothing changed, we established beyond doubt that he did not intend to liberalize his security system.

Karimov's would-be rivals felt the consequences of his system most acutely. First priority for repression went to the leaders of the Birlik and Erk parties, and other activists who had opposed Karimov in the 1991 elections, in public demonstrations in 1992, or in other ways. Punishment took various forms: prohibition of party publications, prosecution of people found with copies of such newspapers, people being fired from their academic positions, public beatings, beatings while in police custody, an assassination attempt against former Vice President Shukrullo Mirsaidov,[7] and criminal charges with imprisonment. When there were no plausible excuses for criminal charges, police and security officials would charge the former activists with possession of narcotics and weapons. While our embassy had no means to investigate, other than talking with people who were willing to talk, over time the pattern became obvious that the "evidence" was planted to convict and jail people who had broken no law.

Our embassy and its contacts in the early 1990s never found convincing evidence of any serious threat to Karimov's rule. The most significant political opposition was perhaps the attempt in the spring of 1992 to form an "alternative parliament" (Melli Majlis), which met only once before being blocked and having several participants arrested.[8] In a democratic country such an event might be considered radical politics, but hardly treasonous. After lengthy detention, some of the leaders were convicted of treason and then received an amnesty. Mohammad Solikh, the leader of the Erk Party, who had won over 12 percent of the vote in the 1991 presidential election, was also charged with treason for his role in the Melli Majlis, and he fled Uzbekistan before he could be brought to trial.[9] For known political rivals who remained in Uzbekistan, the pain did not stop: one beating was seldom enough, and criminal charges could be imposed at any time.

I found it difficult to understand the motives behind the repeated punishment of former rivals, as well as their friends, relatives, and spouses, once these people no longer had the ability to challenge the regime. I suspected that internal security officials sometimes deliberately "discovered" would-be problems in order to advance their careers, or to demonstrate their own importance. Over time the pattern was repeated so often that there could be only one conclusion: President Karimov himself, or those around him who wanted to curry his favor, sought the continued and senseless physical punishment of former rivals.

If we were right that there was no plausible threat to Karimov's rule, was he paranoid? Never once did I hear him speak, publicly or privately, as if he were fearful of threats against him personally. He did show disproportionate concern about Muslim extremists, discussed in Chapter 4, but as a threat to Uzbekistan, not as a personal threat.

In trying to understand Karimov in Tashkent, I recalled that Romania's Nicolae Ceauşescu had become increasingly paranoid the longer he remained in power, reportedly fearing various forms of assassination. Both Karimov and Ceauşescu had come to power through the Communist Party, and they had inside experience with brutal regime change. Although both initially enjoyed some popular support for their deliberate independence from Moscow, neither expected to be protected by public support. Neither would accept any form of opposition, no matter how limited that opposition might seem by American standards. Both admired medieval predecessors who were renowned for their brutality — Amir Temur (Tamerlane) for Karimov, Vlad the Impaler for Ceauşescu.

By the mid-1990s we could see that Karimov's regime was losing popularity, for a variety of reasons, not just heavy handed police action. Yet the loss of popular enthusiasm was not enough to create instability or weaken Karimov's personal power. People in Uzbekistan were used to the Soviet system, and when it came to police, Karimov's system hardly differed, except perhaps in the greater frequency of physical beatings. Most people in Uzbekistan did their best to avoid trouble. Uzbeks generally became active dissidents only after they, or someone close to them, had been treated unjustly. Thus through their harshness, Karimov and his internal security apparatus gradually increased the numbers of Uzbeks and other ordinary citizens who turned against the system, and against Karimov.

Loyalties, and Early Defections

Any leader might expect, rightly or wrongly, the personal loyalty of his subordinates, especially from those he entrusts with functions important to him. Yet dictators typically demand a total personal commitment, greater than one's loyalty to the well being of one's country. In Karimov's Uzbekistan, this was certainly the case. Over a period of three years, I met with President Karimov as often as any other ambassador. In my discussions with him and separately with his subordinates, I understood that Karimov believed he alone could and would decide what was best for Uzbekistan. At one meeting he said that there was no one in Uzbekistan qualified to discuss the country's future with him; that might happen someday when big businessmen were running important parts of the economy, but not in the early 1990s.

Consequently, officials would want to know what Karimov thought before proposing a different course of action. Often it would be safest to tell Karimov what he wanted to hear. While Karimov may not have completely trusted anyone, those top officials who demonstrated sufficient personal loyalty seem to have had a degree of tenure. They might be transferred from one job to another, but were not likely to be dismissed. For examples, two very able foreign affairs professionals, Sadyk Safaev and Abdulaziz Kamilov, served as foreign ministers, ambassadors to the United States, and in other jobs that the president considered critical.

Uzbekistan did not inherit a large cadre of qualified foreign affairs professionals from the Soviet Union, but it did have the good fortune to bring a few outstanding officials back to Uzbekistan from various Soviet institutions. No doubt some of these officials were able to influence Karimov to some degree on some subjects, based on their experience, their insight, and their loyalty. At the same time, they were able to encourage a positive attitude toward Uzbekistan and its policies in their interactions with foreign officials, including me. President Karimov did not quickly create a lot of new embassies and ambassadorships, and I was led to believe he took care in his choice of Uzbekistan's ambassadors to important countries.

In the fall of 1992, President Karimov chose his Justice Minister, Muhammad Babur Malikov, as Uzbekistan's first ambassador to the United States, one of his first appointments overseas. By that time Malikov had already had a distinguished career in the justice system, including service as a judge and ultimately as chairman of the Supreme Court of the Uzbek Soviet Socialist Republic. He was widely and favorably known in Uzbekistan for his work in rehabilitating some 3,500 people who had been convicted in the purge following the great "cotton affair"[10] (described in Chapter 2).

I met Ambassador-designate Malikov in his office in the Justice Ministry in December 1992, and was favorably impressed. Considering the lack of knowledge about the United States in Uzbekistan, and that most of such information had been filtered through Soviet propaganda, I thought that having an effective ambassador from Uzbekistan reporting accurately from Washington could only make my job in Tashkent easier. He and his family joined me at my temporary dacha for dinner, February 23, 1993. It was a cordial evening, and I concluded that Uzbekistan would be very ably represented in Washington. He left for Washington a few days later, and his wife and daughters joined him in May.

During my consultations in Washington in 1993, I met Ambassador Malikov for lunch at a restaurant, just to find out how he was getting along and his impressions of the United States. We again had a very friendly conversation, without a hint of any dissatisfaction or problems with his job.

Although Karimov had originally appointed him as minister of Justice, Ambassador Malikov eventually came to the conclusion that his next appointment, to Washington, was really an exile—to get him out of the justice ministry. Perhaps Karimov distrusted Malikov's independent attitude while serving as a minister. Perhaps Malikov's popularity among Uzbeks, independent of Karimov, was a factor.

A disagreement over instructions in June 1993 may have led, or at least contributed to, Ambassador Malikov's removal. Deputy Minister of Foreign Affairs Teshabaev called Ambassador Malikov from Tashkent, at 3 a.m. Washington time about an incident at the Tashkent airport in which a U.S. embassy employee was beaten by border guards after she'd crossed a control line. Teshabaev "demanded" that Malikov go to the Department of State and seek an explanation for the incident, under the assumption that the embassy employee was at fault. Thinking as a professional judge, Malikov told Teshabaev that there must be an investigation first, before assuming or assigning blame.[11] Tashkent's leading Russian-language newspaper, *Pravda Vostoka*, then published an article blaming the embassy employee, an Uzbek woman hired in Tashkent.

The State Department, however, decided that even if the employee had violated the border guards' control line, by crossing it with a departing visitor, the guards had no right to beat her. In retaliation for the reported beating, the State Department sent a note asking a visiting high-level parliamentary delegation from Uzbekistan to break off their program and leave the United States. The delegation tried to reach Foreign Minister Sadyk Safaev for instructions. When they were unable to do so, they asked Ambassador Malikov for advice, and he told them they should comply with the department's request.[12]Apparently authorities in Tashkent found fault with their ambassador's actions in this case, and it is likely that Teshabaev was acting under instructions from the president or the president's staff.

Malikov's belief that he had been sent into exile was reinforced when he and his wife and daughter (who were helping in his embassy) discovered that his deputy chief of mission, Ulugbek Ishankhodjaev, seemed to be secretly undercutting him with unauthorized appointments in Washington, and was reporting separately to the president's powerful advisor, Timur Alimov, and the new foreign minister, Saidmukhtar Saidkasymov (Safaev had just been sent as ambassador to Germany). It appeared to the Malikovs that the deputy was collecting material with which to discredit Ambassador Malikov.[13]

Ambassador Malikov was asked to return to Tashkent for consultations. In Tashkent, one of President Karimov's advisors, Alisher Azizkhodjaev, informed him that he would be transferred from Washington to become deputy chairman of the State Control Committee. Malikov met with that committee's chairman, who had no objection to his return to Washington to collect his family and close his accounts. Malikov expected that the State Control Committee would be shut down. Yet a presidential aide strongly objected to his plan to return to Washington, even though in normal diplomatic practice, a permanently departing ambassador has farewell meetings with his most important contacts in the host country. Malikov realized he was about to be arrested, and caught the next available flight to Russia, which was to Samara. From there he traveled to Moscow and bought a Delta Airlines ticket to Washington, using his diplomatic passport. In Washington he requested asylum for himself and his family.[14]

The shock of his request for asylum reached me in Tashkent in the fall of 1993. On one hand, I regretted the loss of an able counterpart, but on the other, I understood he must have had very strong reasons for giving up both his job and his country.

It is rare for an accredited ambassador to request asylum, and embarrassing to his country that someone of that rank would want to do that. I expected complaints and accusations from Uzbek officials, and I had a couple of meetings with Deputy Foreign Minister Teshabaev in November 1993 that dealt with the subject. Yet the meetings were not especially difficult, and the asylum request did not interfere with my work in Tashkent. My instructions were to say only that the U.S. Government would process Malikov's request for asylum just as they would any other under U.S. law. That meant he would have to show that he had a reasonable fear of persecution if he returned to Uzbekistan, and in the end the circumstances showed that his fear of arrest was reasonable. I concluded that the Government of Uzbekistan had found no excuse for blaming the U.S. for its self-inflicted injury.

President Karimov named Ubaidulah Abdurazzakov as ambassador to Turkey about the same time that he assigned Malikov to the United States. Abdurazzakov was a veteran of the Soviet diplomatic service. When he was foreign minister of Uzbekistan in 1992, I had frequently met with him on such matters as the civil war in Tajikistan. Turkey was eager to have good relations with all the newly independent states in Central Asia, and Abdurazzakov seemed to me an excellent choice as ambassador. Yet problems cropped up when Uzbek dissidents sought and obtained asylum in Turkey. The Turkish government did not agree to punish or extradite the refugees. According to Malikov, Karimov never forgets anyone who has opposed him and likes to take revenge.[15]A more pragmatic policy, even for a dictator, might have been to forget the dissident exiles, rather than call attention to them.

Ambassador Abdurazzakov telephoned Malikov in Washington to show his support for Malikov's decision to remain in the United States. Abdurazzakov said that he too "will not return to Uzbekistan." But he was called back for consultations, and he went. When he landed in Tashkent, he was met by officials who immediately took his passport, so he could not leave again.[16]

If there were any real examples of disloyalty to Uzbekistan by either Abdurazzakov or Malikov, I did not hear of them. It would appear that two able and prominent Uzbeks were removed as ambassadors by the presidential staff, acting with the approval of President Karimov.

One can argue whether these incidents (and others, some to be described below) were the natural result of Karimov's internal security system and the people who implemented it, or whether personal decisions by the president himself exacerbated the conflicts. I think that both answers are correct, and that Karimov's highly centralized and repressive system was dysfunctional for both reasons.

2

WHY SHOULD UZBEKISTAN BE INDEPENDENT?

While our embassy's first task was to understand the government we had to deal with, there was a much larger context—what was Uzbekistan like as a country? Who were the Uzbeks who made up a large majority of the population, and what about the minority ethnic groups? It can certainly be argued that the Russian occupation, the Russian Revolution, and the economic development of the Soviet Union brought the area that is now Uzbekistan out of a medieval society and into a wider and better world. Then the Soviet Union fell apart from its own internal failings, and the breakup was driven by demands in other Soviet Republics. But was there also a legitimate basis for Uzbekistan's own independence? Even though their government was still authoritarian, what would the people have wanted if they had a voice?

Uzbek Nationalism under Soviet Rule

Although the breakup of the Soviet Union must have come with surprising swiftness for most residents of Central Asia, Uzbeks at various levels of society had reasons to welcome it. Uzbekistan was one of the most ethnically homogeneous republics in Central Asia, with ethnic Uzbeks estimated in the early 1990s as approaching 75 percent of the population. Russians, with about 8 percent and Tajiks at 4.7 percent were the most important minorities, and smaller minorities came from all parts of the USSR.[17] Non-Uzbeks living in Uzbekistan reacted in different ways to independence, but I do not recall a single Uzbek expressing regret at Uzbekistan's independence. Uzbeks had a completely different language, history, and cultural and religious background from Russians, and they looked different, which made discrimination by other Soviet citizens against Uzbeks easier. They even used disparaging names for each other.[18]

Uzbeks held resentments toward imperial Moscow, and often against the dominance of European-origin residents in jobs and government in Tashkent. A Russian could spend his entire life in overwhelmingly Uzbek Uzbekistan without feeling obliged to learn the Uzbek language. Yet any Uzbek who wished to succeed in the Communist Party or in a highly educated profession would have to speak Russian fluently and would attend Russian-speaking schools and universities. At higher levels, the "glass ceiling" for Uzbeks was clear: none could rise above two-star general in the Soviet military, or be appointed to the Supreme Court of the USSR, or take supervisory positions in the Interior Ministry, for example. Within Uzbekistan, although the first secretary of the Communist Party was Uzbek, the second secretary had to be of Slavic origin, and the pattern of ethnic control continued at lower levels too.

None of this surprised me when I arrived in Tashkent in 1992. Ten years before, while stationed at the U.S. Embassy in Moscow, I had read Hélène Carrère d'Encausse's book, *Decline of an Empire*,[19] predicting that ethnic-based nationalism would tear the Soviet Union apart. While in the early 1980s I thought the threat to Soviet unity was somewhat overdrawn in that book and did not expect a collapse of the USSR during my career, I was keenly interested in the persistence of nationalism in the Soviet republics. Part of my job as economic counselor was to travel in various parts of the USSR, including Central Asia, and write reports on their diversity as well as their economy. Uzbek nationalism did not show me the same fierceness that I noticed in Estonia, but it had a natural history, stretching back to the Basmachi rebellions of the 1920s and '30s, that lasted, some said, into the 1940s.

Several conflicts between the Soviet leaders and the Uzbek Republic in the 1980s had strengthened Uzbek nationalism. The scale of the great Uzbek "cotton affair" amazed us at the U.S. Embassy in Moscow, when Uzbekistan was by far the largest cotton producer in the USSR and one of the largest in the world. Through falsification of reports at every level, from the farm up to the republic level,

Uzbekistan officially claimed to produce 6 million tons of cotton per year while actually producing less than 4 million tons.[20] During a trip with my family to Uzbekistan in 1983, I managed to buy a Statistical Yearbook of the Uzbek Republic that confirmed the six-million-ton claim. According to a Soviet prosecutor, from 1978 to 1983 over one billion rubles had been paid by the state in Uzbekistan for cotton that was never produced.[21]

General Secretary Andropov ordered an anticorruption campaign in the Uzbek SSR, and the KGB made its first arrests in the "cotton affair" or "Uzbek case" in April 1983 in Bukhara Oblast. At the request of the KGB, special investigators Tel'man Gdlyan and Nikolay Ivanov came from Moscow, and soon afterward Uzbek SSR interior minister Ergashev shot himself. The powerful and long-serving first secretary of the Uzbek Communist Party, Sharaf Rashidov, had a four-hour, one-on-one meeting with USSR Politburo member Geydar Aliev and died of an apparent heart attack a few days later.[22]

General Secretary Chernenko continued the anticorruption campaign by sending a large number of Communist Party and law enforcement officials to Uzbekistan to replace those officials being removed at various levels, and Uzbeks saw them as acting like conquerors. By 1986, only three out of thirteen oblast party first secretaries remained, and more than three-fourths of the Uzbek Communist Party Central Committee had been replaced. James Critchlow argues that many Uzbeks, who saw the padding of statistics and reports as a way to offset exploitation by the Moscow-centered economic system, then saw the purges of their leaders and the loss of funds for use in their communities as further exploitation by Moscow.[23] On the other hand, Babur Malikov, who was a judge in the Uzbek SSR during those years, says that ordinary Uzbeks did not protest against Moscow's actions, believing that "all the evil was in the leadership of the republic itself."[24] In any event this had been the most comprehensive and highest-level purge in the Soviet Union since purges under Stalin in the 1930s, removing a large part of the Uzbek elite and decisively changing the relationship between Moscow and Tashkent.

Huge numbers of Uzbeks were killed in World War II, and as in the rest of the Soviet Union, there are monuments to the fallen all over Uzbekistan, even in state farms. Uzbeks were proud of their contributions to the Soviet victory. By the 1970s and '80s, the declining birth rate in the European part of the USSR, together with high birth rates in Central Asia, meant that an increasing share of all Red Army draftees had to come from Uzbekistan. Yet many young Uzbeks from rural areas did not speak Russian well enough to be fully integrated into an army that depended more and more on communications. The practice of hazing draftees by older, professional soldiers became more noticeable and led to more reported casualties and deaths. Following a recruit murder scandal in 1989, Uzbek families perceived the hazing as ethnic persecution.[25] These tragedies came on top of the casualties suffered by Uzbek families, like families elsewhere in the USSR, during the war in Afghanistan. Unlike World War II, the justification for the war in Afghanistan was widely but not publicly questioned.

Non-Uzbeks living in Uzbekistan generally did not share in Uzbek nationalism. Many Russians, Ukrainians, and other Soviet citizens of European origin had moved into Uzbekistan as part of industrialization or modernization of agriculture and were more likely to supervise Uzbeks than work for them. Whole factories had been moved, together with all their machinery and all their workers, from European Russia to Central Asia at the outset of World War II to protect their production from invasion. The huge Chkalov aircraft factory in Tashkent was one of these, initially building the U.S.-designed C-47 for the war effort.

By the early 1990s the Chkalov factory produced large Soviet-designed jet transports, such as the IL-76. The employees continued to be mostly (but not exclusively) Russians, including children of the original work force, proud of the quality of their products. For them, the end of the USSR was followed by the realization that their big transport aircraft were no longer commercially viable, due to their high operating costs.

For many non-Uzbeks in Uzbekistan, independence meant the loss of privileged or protected jobs, and many qualified workers looked for jobs in Russia. Non-Uzbek military officers who remained in Uzbekistan to become part of the new army of Uzbekistan could, like their counterparts in Russia, be nostalgic for the days when they served in the Soviet Army, defending a great power.

Yet among ordinary Uzbeks and their higher officials, I sensed only pride that they now had their own country. I think it enhanced the warmth of their hospitality toward me as the first American ambassador to their country. Following President Karimov's example, every *hokim* (mayor or governor) of a major city or *oblast* (major territorial subdivision of Uzbekistan) that I called on for the first time would dress me in a black Uzbek hat with silver embroidery and a traditional Uzbek robe, so that I acquired a large number—all the same basic Uzbek form, but with colors or decorations specific to the local area.

President Islam Karimov dresses me in a traditional Uzbek robe, September 14, 1993.
Source: Author's collection, probably a U.S. State Department photo.

Uzbeks enjoyed showing and explaining their customs to Americans, some specifically Uzbek, others shared with other Central Asian ethnic groups. Whether it was ceremonial or everyday *plov* (with regional variations, but still *plov,* a slowly cooked rice stew*),* green tea, other foods, or handicrafts such as *suzane* wall hangings, we were never in doubt that there was a strong Uzbek sense of ethnic and national identity. The ancient celebration of the spring equinox, *Navruz,* was reintroduced, and together with Uzbekistan's new Independence Day on September 1, these became two favorite holidays, comparable to New Year's Eve or Victory Day on May 9. In Uzbekistan's mild climate, both new holidays were to a large extent celebrated outdoors. In Tashkent, sidewalks and squares were filled with people, many buying food and drinks, notably Coca-Cola, from kiosks and open grills.

Independence Comes with a Few Russian Issues

Uzbekistan declared its independence shortly after the failure of the military coup against Soviet President Gorbachev in August 1991. Islam Karimov, as first secretary of the Communist Party in Uzbekistan and a few months later as president, took a strong interest in defining a new relationship with Moscow and the other newly independent republics. In December 1991, Uzbekistan and the rest of Central Asia became members of the new Commonwealth of Independent States (CIS), recognizing that there were many issues that needed to be coordinated, especially with regard to defense and economic relations, regardless of their degree of independence. From a Russian perspective, the CIS became a means to try to manage the process of devolution and to retain some of Moscow's leadership, if not hegemony.

Border guards. One of Moscow's early and ongoing priorities for its own security was to maintain a common Russian-defended border regime all along the former Soviet external borders.[26] I saw evidence of that in two cases in Tashkent's international airport, one affecting an American military aircraft in 1992,[27] and the other affecting a U.S. embassy employee in 1993.[28] In both cases, high Uzbekistan authorities did not appear to have full authority over their border police. The logic of the Russian position was obvious: they already had facilities and personnel along the entire former Soviet border, but the internal borders among the former Soviet republics had neither. Especially in Central Asia, displacing Russian border guards from the formerly Soviet border to the Russian border would be a huge undertaking for Russia itself, and could create new vulnerabilities in the Central Asian states if they were unable to replace the Russian guards.

In a meeting on December 12, 1994, with visiting U.S. ambassador to Tajikistan Stan Escudero, Foreign Minister Kamilov, and me, President Karimov asserted that Uzbekistan was the only Central Asian state to have its own border guards, making clear he did not want the Russians involved. He cited Russian agreements with all the other Central Asian states on guards and mentioned that the Russian Caspian fleet protected the coastal borders of Turkmenistan and Kazakhstan.

Apparently by late 1994 Karimov had managed to disengage Moscow's control over the border guards. Uzbekistan had one of the shortest and most manageable borders with the world outside the CIS: just something over 100 kilometers of border with Afghanistan, along the Amu Darya river and including one major crossing at Termez, and the Tashkent international airport. It was a very modest burden compared with the tasks of controlling all the other Central Asian countries' lengthy borders with Iran, Afghanistan, and China.

Bases and the Russian Presence in Tajikistan. Unlike Russia, Kazakhstan, Ukraine, and Belarus, Uzbekistan had no Soviet nuclear weapons; the Soviet military withdrew to Russia everything it considered sensitive. Uzbekistan had no Russian bases or troops; the former Soviet bases, some conventional weapons, personnel, and other military activities left behind became Uzbekistan's.

Russian border guards remained deployed along Tajikistan's border with Afghanistan and were backed up in Tajikistan's interior by the 201st Motorized Rifle Division. Given the political instability in Tajikistan, Uzbekistan's officials did not quarrel with that presence as far as I knew. Like other foreign observers, some Uzbek officials, including President Karimov, did question privately whether those troops were an effective barrier to infiltration of heroin and Islamic radicalism into Central Asia.[29]

Russian forces, acting in the name of the CIS, played a role in moderating and ending the civil war in Tajikistan, from late 1992 into 1993. Uzbekistan supported the CIS and therefore the Russian position, fearing a spillover of conflict. Uzbekistan's alleged military involvement, together with the Russians or separately, seems to have been very small—reported as an occasional individual aircraft and very few vehicles. I considered most of the reports plausible but unconfirmed at the time. I would not have been surprised if Uzbekistan's role had included Russian use of air bases in Uzbekistan and other logistical support, considering the geography of the region.

Viewed from our embassy in Tashkent, the conflict in Tajikistan seemed to be mainly among major regional clans, fighting for power in Tajikistan, and ideological or religious differences were at best secondary. Uzbek officials, including President Karimov, had opinions about the various Tajik politicians and their positions regarding Islam, yet the most serious concerns expressed to me about the civil war in Tajikistan were over the Tajik refugees fleeing to Uzbekistan, some of whom had relatives and friends to stay with, so their numbers were not easy to estimate. Russian and CIS efforts to stabilize Tajikistan did not seem to me, at the time, as much affecting Uzbekistan's independence.

Dual Citizenship was another important bilateral issue between Russia and Uzbekistan. Soviet and Uzbekistan passports listed each person's nationality in addition to citizenship, so it could be fairly clear who might qualify for dual citizenship. Kazakhstan, with a large Russian population all along its lengthy Russian border, allowed dual Russian and Kazakhstan citizenship to ethnic Russians. So did Kyrgyzstan, with a smaller Russian percentage of its population but great economic dependence upon Russia.

President Karimov strongly opposed dual citizenship in Uzbekistan. I assumed that he considered dual citizenship a path to weakening the integrity of the state, potentially creating opportunities for Russia to intervene on behalf of Russian citizens. In addition to Russians there were also Ukrainians, Armenians, other Central

Asians, and smaller numbers from other Soviet republics. If Tajiks, the largest non-Uzbek Central Asian ethnic group in Uzbekistan, could claim dual Uzbekistan and Tajikistan citizenship, what would the population of Bukhara, Samarkand, and the border areas near Tajikistan look like? Karimov's family roots were in Samarkand, so he would have known and distrusted the implications. In any event, Karimov did not waver in not recognizing dual citizenship, and he did not claim it for Uzbeks living in neighboring countries.

Everyone with an Uzbekistan passport could travel to Russia without a visa and potentially get a Russian passport, yet it is not clear that ordinary Russians in Russia were eager to absorb "immigrants" from Uzbekistan of any ethnicity. Some ethnic Russians from Uzbekistan had difficulty obtaining documentation from local authorities when they resettled in Russia. Without dual citizenship, some Russians and other minorities felt an additional incentive to leave Uzbekistan, while others had roots only in Uzbekistan. Moscow may not have been happy with Karimov's decision on dual citizenship, but it was a stabilizing factor, strengthening Uzbekistan's sovereignty and Karimov's control over Uzbekistan's population.

Apart from border guard problems, I did not see many signs of interference by Russia in Uzbekistan's internal affairs from 1992 to 1995. There may have been issues I did not see, but I would have been alert to signs of them, as I considered Uzbek-Russian differences one of our embassy's basic reporting responsibilities. Some Russians in the Yeltsin administration would have preferred more formal CIS coordination and control of defense issues, but in general Russia appeared satisfied with bilateral agreements with Uzbekistan governing such issues as use of air bases. Among the Central Asian states, Russia would have been much more sensitive about defense issues involving Kazakhstan, Tajikistan, or Turkmenistan.

Independence Prevails

In 1992 it was reasonable to ask whether the independence of Central Asian countries would last, yet by the time I left in 1995 the question had gradually and quietly been answered "yes," especially for Uzbekistan. Of course these countries can, even now, come under pressure from larger countries and make concessions to their sovereignty that larger countries might not make, but on the whole, the international community and the former Soviet republics, including Russia, accepted the basic idea of independence. From my perspective, Russia made few overt efforts to reestablish bilateral political control over Uzbekistan during the early 1990s, and other outside powers had no opportunity to do so.

International recognition became the norm. The number of foreign embassies in Tashkent continued to increase. Uzbekistan joined the United Nations, and the U.N. and its associated agencies established a major mission in Tashkent. The World Bank and International Monetary Fund sent representatives and staff. From an American perspective, Uzbekistan's adherence to the Final Act of the Helsinki Conference on Security and Cooperation in Europe and its membership in the Organization for Security and Cooperation in Europe (OSCE) represented an acknowledgment of European and American standards for human rights and economic relations, even if Uzbekistan did not fully observe those standards.

Why did Uzbekistan join? These multilateral organizations represented international legitimacy for Uzbekistan's independence and might be important sources of financial or other resources in some future crisis. The United States and other countries welcomed these multilateral ties, and since all the former Soviet states did too, these ties established a structure of legitimate independence and a platform for conveying international standards to the newly independent states.

Even a Good Measure of Economic Independence

In the early 1990s Russia had no interest in continuing the economic burdens of the Soviet empire, such as subsidized trade or transfer payments, so Uzbekistan's already limited dependence on Russian finances simply evaporated. A critical moment came in 1993, when Uzbekistan found Russian terms for continued participation in the ruble zone unacceptable, and Uzbekistan created its own currency. Whether the Russian leadership intended it or not, and whether or not Uzbek leaders would have preferred to remain in the ruble zone, the creation of the Som was a major step toward independence for Uzbekistan's economy, and especially for the government's ability to manage its own economic policies.

Bilateral trade with Russia continued, as with all other countries, whenever there was sufficient mutual interest to overcome the obstacles in transportation. Some new obstacles arose. The post-Soviet railroads and their customers, for example, suffered large-scale losses from theft and armed robberies, though countermeasures (such as welding containers shut) also began.

Uzbekistan had little opportunity to become a big energy exporter, compared with Turkmenistan or Kazakhstan, but it had enough natural gas and oil resources to give it a measure of energy independence, and it could take advantage of world markets for its large cotton and gold exports. To be sure, the marketing advantages of world trade were offset by exposure to major price swings, a source of uncertainty for Uzbekistan's leaders to which they were not accustomed.

Even the world's largest economic powers have various economic dependencies on other countries, which they must manage. Arguably, the many aging Russian textile mills that depended upon cheap, guaranteed supplies of Uzbek cotton were more vulnerable than Uzbekistan's producers and more dependent upon the bilateral trade. Selling Uzbekistan's production of monetary gold involved little or no dependence on others, except perhaps for developing the expertise to handle the timing of sales.

I had the feeling in the early 1990s that many foreign observers, and some Uzbeks, underestimated the degree of economic independence that Uzbekistan had already achieved, and could assert in the future, even though it had just emerged from a huge state that had been centrally planned, supplied, and controlled. In only two years, Moscow's controls were gone, and Uzbekistan had emerged from the ruble zone.

The Fergana Valley, in green, and surrounding mountains, in brown, showing national borders and three enclaves. Source: Henry Clarke

3

A DANGEROUS NEIGHBORHOOD

As peaceful as Uzbekistan seemed from the beginning of my assignment in September 1992, our embassy could not ignore the ongoing conflicts in Afghanistan and Tajikistan, and the latter soon turned into a civil war of great concern to the Uzbekistan government. Perhaps it was natural for a newly independent government to feel insecure, not only with respect to nearby conflicts but also vis-à-vis more powerful countries such as Russia and Iran and the interest of Muslim groups in other countries in an Islamic revival in Uzbekistan. Viewed from Tashkent, Uzbekistan was in a dangerous neighborhood.

Russian Army troops still guarded Tajikistan's border with Afghanistan, but given the mountainous terrain and the Tajiks living on both sides of the border, there was considerable leakage of people and narcotics from Afghanistan. Uzbekistan's own short border with Afghanistan along the Amu Darya River was less of a concern and easier to patrol. Yet Afghanistan's Uzbeks were also fighting in northern Afghanistan.

In the fall of 1992 there were no effective controls on the borders between former Soviet republics in Central Asia. In the Fergana Valley the borders between Kyrgyzstan, Tajikistan, and Uzbekistan were especially confusing. Although supposedly drawn to reflect ethnic lines between villages, the borders were practically invisible, difficult to locate on the ground unless you were a local resident. Some created enclaves of Uzbek villages within what would otherwise be Kyrgyzstan, and there was at least one Tajik enclave. During the Soviet period people crossed republic borders freely and sometimes relocated across them—for example, to newly established collective farms or factories—blurring whatever original ethnic basis the boundaries might have had. Certainly the Soviets never intended that these would become borders between independent states.

Uzbekistan did begin to establish some checkpoints at road crossing points with Tajikistan and Kyrgyzstan as early as 1992, tightened these controls afterward, and later established controls on the borders with Kazakhstan and Turkmenistan. But in the early 1990s, if you wanted to cross borders between former Soviet republics without being checked, the most you had to do was leave the road and walk, and some roads had no checkpoints. Inside Uzbekistan, Tajiks were the largest Central Asian minority, especially in Bukhara and Samarkand and along the Tajikistan border, so an infiltrator who spoke Tajik and Uzbek could easily blend in. During Tajikistan's 1992–93 civil war, many Tajiks did seek refuge from the violence by fleeing to Uzbekistan, demonstrating the point that the border was no obstacle.

Thus Uzbek officials, including President Karimov, had practical reasons to care about the potential for infiltration by radical Islamists from Afghanistan, Iran, or elsewhere, whether or not they actually came. While our embassy was not likely to be the first to know if they did, eventually we would learn of any serious trouble they caused, and for three years we found no evidence of that.

I also had some difficulty imagining the motivation that would bring such troublemakers to Uzbekistan during my time in Tashkent in 1992–95. Afghans had enough ethnic conflict at home; anyone ready to fight was needed there. Iran had plenty of radicals, yet any Shia in Uzbekistan were too few to support outsiders. Rumors about radical Sunni Wahabis from the Arabian Peninsula did not result in credible incidents during 1992–95. I had not heard of al-Qaeda in the early 1990s; the embassy had no information about any specific groups that would attack Uzbekistan, nor did we learn of any threats against the U.S. Embassy in Tashkent, a soft target.

Helping Evacuate U.S. Embassy Dushanbe

Our best information about the conflict in Tajikistan came from our embassy in Dushanbe. That embassy was awkwardly housed, with both offices and living quarters on one floor of a hotel, just above the floor occupied by the Russian embassy. Since the Russians had troops and many other ties in Tajikistan, I imagined the advantages and disadvantages of such close proximity probably balanced each other. Ambassador Stan Escudero, his deputy Ed McWilliams, and their colleagues were prolific reporting officers with lots of contacts. We in Tashkent were getting copies of their reports to Washington, and in September and October 1992 we followed the deteriorating situation. One side in the conflict moved its forces closer and closer to Dushanbe. Unfortunately, these forces were coming up the same valley that U.S. Embassy Dushanbe had planned as its evacuation route by land to Uzbekistan. In mountainous Tajikistan, other, more circuitous land routes through steeper valleys did not look to me like practical alternatives, and apparently our colleagues in Embassy Dushanbe felt the same way.

Finally the State Department called me to alert us that they had decided to evacuate Embassy Dushanbe by air. The U.S. Air Force could fly a C-141 round-trip from Germany to Dushanbe, but if they did, it would mean landing and taking off from Dushanbe with a heavy load of fuel. That required using more runway and a slower rate of climb when taking off. In an emergency, what about using Tashkent airport? As I remember the conversation, I suggested staging the evacuation from Tashkent's airport, where neither refueling nor runway length would be a problem. The largest Soviet aircraft used it, and foreign airlines were routinely refueling there. I saw no reason why Uzbekistan would object, having met Rafikov, the director general for civil aviation, and Foreign Minister Abdurazzakov. I promised to confirm their support right away, and did.

While I had the State Department on the line, I asked them to attach one officer from Dushanbe to my embassy to report on the continuing situation in Tajikistan. I knew Washington would not lose interest in Tajikistan just because we closed the embassy, and Tashkent was the closest and most obvious listening post. I assumed, rightly, that Stan Escudero would not be happy to leave his post; he would be eager to remain up-to-date and return to reopen Dushanbe as soon as possible. My staff was already busy dealing with developments in Uzbekistan; we would be hard pressed to effectively cover a neighboring country with a raging conflict, a task I saw as a fulltime job.

Everything worked smoothly at first. The C-141 landed in Tashkent on October 23, thence to Dushanbe, and the evacuation proceeded over the weekend of October 24–25. As required by standard procedures, U.S. Embassy Dushanbe destroyed their communications equipment, including the only hard drive for the computer that could prepare classified documents and telegrams. The Russian Army took Embassy Dushanbe's handful of Americans in armored vehicles to the airport, where they were joined by a number of other Americans and Europeans who happened to be in Dushanbe and wanted to leave. They took off in the C-141 without difficulty and landed in Tashkent.

Once they arrived at Tashkent's airport, the smoothness ended. Some of the unofficial passengers were not pleased to learn that they would have to pay for their flight. Some who did not want to go to Germany left the group to go into Tashkent or to catch other flights. Billing them and collecting their money was not my issue; it was one to be worked out when they got home.

More seriously, the Tashkent airport border guards wanted to inspect the aircraft. The U.S. Air Force said no. Knowing that the Air Force was not facing such a request for the first time and would not yield, I appealed to Foreign Minister Abdurazzakov. I claimed that the C-141 was a "state aircraft" and was exempt from any inspections. Non-diplomatic passengers getting off, and their luggage, could be inspected as they entered Uzbekistan, but not the aircraft itself. Refueling was not a problem, but the standoff about inspections continued for hours.

It became clear to me, from the foreign minister's inability to resolve the issue quickly, that Tashkent's border guards were working for the Russian border guards in Moscow, not Uzbekistan. Most of the border guards in Tashkent were ethnic Slavs, not Uzbeks. While the flight crew would have to stay on board the aircraft, I began wondering about finding hotel rooms for the passengers that wanted to fly on to Germany.

It was not a happy moment for Foreign Minister Abdurazzakov. Uzbekistan had agreed to assist our evacuation without conditioning the aircraft clearances on an inspection. The Russian border guard headquarters in Moscow, at some level, would have known the U.S. Air Force policy. The Soviet, now Russian, Air Force probably had a similar policy about inspecting their aircraft abroad. So somewhere in the guards' chain of command they were playing with Uzbekistan's foreign minister (and me)—or they just wanted to see whether their gambit would work. Eventually they released the aircraft and it flew the evacuees safely to Frankfurt. For me it was a lesson that Uzbekistan's sovereignty was not complete, or at least not yet.

No permanent damage was done. I continued to discuss the situation in Tajikistan and its effects on Uzbekistan (such as refugees) with the foreign ministry, including the minister, in the months to come.

Our designated Dushanbe reporting officer, Ed McWilliams, had brought his pocket telephone book, full of contacts to call in Tajikistan, and he began turning out an impressive, steady flow of reports. In shanghaiing him to Tashkent, I had made one mistake: we needed that secure computer he left in Dushanbe, and I should have asked for it before the hard drive was destroyed. Incredible as it may now seem, we only had one computer for preparing classified messages in Tashkent, and Tashkent's reporting officers (including me) were lining up to use it every day. If a message included a comment that we did not want to become public, or if we wanted to protect a source, the whole message had to be classified. Ed offered to save any work that he didn't urgently need to prepare on the computer until after hours, and I encouraged the Tashkent staff to type their reports as early as possible. We were already preparing all unclassified messages on other computers. We just had too many good reporting officers, with too much material, for one machine.

After the fighting in Tajikistan stopped, there were questions in the new Clinton administration about whether the U.S. Embassy in Dushanbe should be reopened. I later learned that high officials in the Office of Management and Budget felt that a good way to reduce the State Department budget was to have fewer U.S. embassies in less important countries. Somehow the European Bureau managed to reopen Dushanbe, perhaps because it was so inexpensive, and perhaps by arguing, as I would have, that the fate of the former Soviet Union was still unclear, and we needed representation in every newly independent country to follow that larger issue.

Afghanistan

After the Soviet military withdrawal from Afghanistan in 1989, Afghanistan slid into a multisided civil war. Each ethnic group had at least one warlord, each seeking more power and more territory or defending what they had against the others. The U.S. State Department declined to reopen the embassy in Kabul, which had been closed years before—on grounds that the U.S. interest in keeping the Soviet Union out, which had included arming various groups fighting against Soviet occupation, was now gone. Not only had the Soviet Army left, but the Soviet Union itself disintegrated in 1991, and the newly independent Central Asian states were no threat to anyone. A senior executive in the State Department's South Asian Bureau, responsible for Afghanistan and other countries, told me during my consultations that their policy was "to let Afghanistan return to the obscurity it deserves." Fighting among the warlords provided a further reason not to reopen the embassy, because there was a danger of periodic fighting in Kabul.

I strongly suspected there was a further, perhaps decisive consideration: the State Department's budget was being cut. The new embassies in the former Soviet Union had been created by cutting budgets and personnel positions elsewhere in the European Bureau, including embassies in Western Europe. In order to reopen in Kabul, the South Asian Bureau, which covered Afghanistan, would have had to cut money and positions from such sacred cows as posts in India, Pakistan, and Bangladesh. There was practically no "lobby" within State for the importance of Afghanistan. We still had a building in Kabul and a few local employees to look after it. The United States participated in meetings of a group called "friends of Afghanistan" at the United Nations in New York, and perhaps occasionally elsewhere, but apparently the group was ineffective in influencing the deteriorating conflict on the ground. Reporting on Afghanistan continued to come from the U.S. Embassy in Islamabad, and from our Consulate General in Peshawar, where there were still lots of Afghan refugees.

Ed McWilliams, who had served in Afghanistan, added a new perspective in his reporting from Dushanbe, especially on the northern parts of Afghanistan, and continued to do so from Tashkent while in our embassy. Our political officer, Daria Fane, also took particular interest in Afghan affairs, having worked there before joining the Foreign Service. The Afghan embassy in Tashkent did its best to interest our embassy, including me, in Afghanistan, by inviting us to their embassy from time to time for delicious meals and to discuss their concerns. Having a full agenda in Uzbekistan and having had no previous experience with Afghanistan, I was wary of becoming too captivated by the complex events and personalities there, but gradually I was also drawn into learning about the unfolding warfare in Afghanistan.

Uzbekistan's government could not ignore Afghanistan. There seemed to be little danger of the internal conflict spilling over directly into Uzbekistan; the border along the Amu Darya River seemed reasonably secure. From time to time questions arose about the sources of arms and materiel for Afghan Uzbek troops, and Uzbekistan was suspected of providing them. Our embassy had little light to shed on the accusation. The various factions in Afghanistan had quantities of weapons and munitions left over from the war with the Soviets, and for much of the Soviet occupation the Afghan Uzbeks had sided with the Soviet Union, so they would have been well armed. Since Uzbekistan had been a major part of the Soviet supply line to Afghanistan, we also assumed that plenty of Soviet conventional weapons remained in Uzbekistan. They had become property of the Uzbekistan Army and Air Force, but apart from a few parades and demonstrations it was not clear to us how much was in useable condition. No doubt some could have been shared with fellow Uzbeks in Afghanistan, if in fact they needed them.

The unquestioned leader of the Afghan Uzbeks, General Abdulrashid Dostum, asked to meet with me during one of his visits to Tashkent, and I was happy to agree. It turned out to be a courtesy call, with no requests for assistance. Perhaps the general wished to reassure himself that the U.S. government had no lingering grudges against him for his role during the Soviet occupation of Afghanistan. My attitude was to try to meet with anyone who might someday be a useful contact or source of information, especially independent warlords from nearby countries, unless there was a specific reason not to meet.

General Dostum was certainly a colorful character. With one bad eye and thought to be largely illiterate, he was nonetheless believed to be an effective combat leader. We tried to make him feel at home: one of my staff offered to stand by, refilling half-teacups continuously throughout the meeting. Dostum spoke several Afghan languages, but since I spoke none of them, we used his Uzbek-English interpreter. At one point, one of his staff brought out a map, and, literate or not, the general seemed to have no difficulty reading it. I had been warned by my staff NOT to refuse any gifts, and sure enough, at the end of the meeting his men brought in a huge red and black Afghan carpet. I cheerfully accepted it on behalf of the embassy, knowing that my residence had no carpet at all in the main reception room, and would not be getting one soon. I was happy to write the necessary memo to the State Depatment about the gift, and add the carpet to the inventory of U.S. government property in the residence. If General Dostum intended his visit to be memorable, he could not have done it better—I crossed that carpet every day, every guest saw it, and it looked great.

As I learned more about Afghanistan, I wondered how it remained one country during the continuous domestic fighting, most of it between ethnic groups. Wouldn't at least one or two of the factions want to be a part of a more peaceful neighboring state, with which they had ethnic and linguistic ties? The largest Uzbek diaspora was in Afghanistan, and during my three-year tour I heard no word about any Uzbek desires for *Anschluss* on either side of the border. I finally accepted the conclusion of other observers: Afghans are Afghans first, with their ethnicity and language second. It still seems remarkable to me that people can retain that loyalty throughout decades of bitter fighting with each other.

What about Uzbekistan's ambitions in Afghanistan? I didn't see or hear of any, despite the rumors about President Karimov's links with General Dostum. I concluded that Karimov's policies were largely hands-off in Afghanistan. The Soviet Union fought a long war there, and lost, even with Dostum's Uzbeks fighting on the Soviet side much of the time. For many families in Uzbekistan, that war had been too close to home, and its casualties had been too bitter. Most Uzbeks in Uzbekistan would have opposed renewed involvement in an Afghan civil war. Karimov may have taken the reasonable view that there was nothing to be gained by involvement, and the risks would be greater for Uzbekistan.

Outside the Immediate Periphery: Iran, Israel, and China

Although initially it was not clear to me why Iran should have been considered, objectively, a threat to Uzbekistan, President Karimov had his reasons, and for him they were not trivial. Karimov was an Uzbek from Samarkand, a city still heavily populated by Tajiks and with centuries of Persian cultural influence. Karimov represented post-Soviet secular rule, and he had a deep aversion to the idea of a government controlled by a Muslim clerical hierarchy. Iran might be taken as a model for an Islamic state, and he wanted no part of that. Religious Uzbeks and Tajiks in Uzbekistan were Sunni, not Shia, Muslims, and thus had no allegiance to Iran's religious leadership; but that distinction was just not comforting enough for someone as secular as Karimov.

Presumably in order to refine his judgments about Iran, President Karimov made an official visit to Tehran—and came back with negative impressions. Iran opened a cultural center in Dushanbe and reportedly wanted to do the same in Uzbekistan, perhaps in Bukhara or Samarkand; but during 1992–95 Karimov would not agree. He did accept an Iranian ambassador and an embassy in Tashkent.

President Karimov wholeheartedly supported American efforts to discourage Russia from providing nuclear technology and equipment to Iran. He did not think it was in Russia's interest to have a nuclear-armed regime such as Iran in the region, and he was certain it was not in Uzbekistan's interest.

With the breakup of the Soviet Union, Turkish truckers established a major route from Turkey, across Georgia, Azerbaijan, the Caspian Sea, and Turkmenistan, to Uzbekistan, Kazakhstan, and Kyrgyzstan, as an alternative to importing through Russia.

A third route for imports to Central Asia was established later: from ports in the Persian Gulf , across Iran and Turkmenistan. The trans-Iranian route became very competitive for goods from Asia as well as Europe. These routes amounted to branches of a new "Silk Route" for shipping all kinds of non-silk consumer goods to Central Asia. Tashkent was a leading destination of both the Turkish and Iranian routes. If there was a political dimension to this commercial activity I missed it, though it did enable Iran to more easily market Iranian consumer goods in the region.

Neither Karimov nor other Uzbeks I met expressed any hostility toward Israel, which established an embassy in Tashkent. Israel assisted in starting a small model dairy, and demonstrated drip irrigation techniques on a farm, both near Tashkent. Bukharan Jews had lived in Uzbekistan along the Silk Route for centuries, and Israel hoped at least some of them, as well as Russian Jews, would emigrate to Israel. The Jewish state also looked for opportunities to develop friendly relations with Muslim countries, not least with those having secular governments. Uzbekistan Airways operated nonstop flights between Tashkent and Tel Aviv. This was handy for me and my family, which remained in Tel Aviv during my first year in Tashkent, 1992–93.

China was extremely cautious in dealing with independent Uzbekistan. I assumed that Beijing's hesitation arose from concern about China's Turkic-language minorities in Xinjiang Province. Although some Uzbeks, Kyrgyz, and Kazakhs lived there, the largest ethnic group in Xinjiang was Uighur, who surely must have envied the independent states of the former Soviet Union, especially Uzbekistan. In October 1992 a Chinese embassy opened in Tashkent, and at some point a Chinese restaurant opened near Samarkand. Cheap Chinese consumer goods poured into Uzbekistan, as into other former Soviet countries.

A Nuclear Weapons–free Zone for Central Asia?

Near the end of my assignment, Uzbekistan began promoting the idea of a nuclear weapons–free zone in Central Asia, with the thought that since nuclear weapons had been withdrawn from the area with the collapse of the Soviet Union, such a zone might prevent them from being reintroduced. Considering that there were nuclear powers in all directions—Russia, China, India, Pakistan, and potentially Iran—I thought the idea had some merit, if we really supported the independence of the post-Soviet republics and opposed proliferation of nuclear weapons.

The U.S. policy position, however, was opposed to a nuclear weapons–free zone. We did not like such zones anywhere, we argued. No doubt that was true, although I believed that was largely a U.S. Navy doctrine to permit its vessels freedom of movement, and Central Asia was landlocked. Russia would have been opposed, and I think some of our senior officials found it easier to oppose Uzbekistan's idea than to oppose the Russians. Perhaps this was a reflection of "sphere of influence" thinking about Russia's role in Central Asia. The zone would have been difficult to enforce, especially against Russia, but that argument was not made to me— the United States just wished to avoid a precedent. I do not know whether the Russians offered to support our position against such zones in the Pacific Ocean or elsewhere.

Given the firm U.S. position, I had no opportunity as a U.S. official to explore the idea in any depth, so I cannot say what kind of scenario Uzbek officials were trying to prevent. Uzbek officials would say that such weapons were not welcome from any source and avoided pointing fingers. I thought that the only power likely to introduce nuclear weapons was Russia, and the territory most likely to receive them was Kazakhstan (where intercontinental ballistic missiles had been based), not Uzbekistan. The Russian decision to withdraw nuclear weapons from a region of fragile, new states seemed very sensible, and the United States had strongly supported that. So why should any be returned to Central Asia?

Registan Square, Samarkand, with three madrasas built in the fifteenth and seventeenth centuries. Source: Author's photo, April 1983.

4

ISLAM—THE CONTEXT OR THE ENEMY?

The Historical Legacy

President Karimov had a high regard for ancient civilization in what is now Uzbekistan. That history is, for him and for many Uzbeks, part of their national identity. Never mind that the language probably spoken—and certainly written—in Samarkand or Bukhara in the fifteenth century was closer to Indo-European Persian or Tajik, than to Uzbek, a Turkic language. In a meeting with me and others, Karimov proudly claimed to have told visiting Russian prime minister Chernomyrdin that Uzbeks in Samarkand were studying astronomy while Russians were still wearing animal skins and living in caves.

Karimov was particularly interested in the fourteenth century's Amir Temur, or Tamerlane, whose empire was based in Samarkand, Karimov's hometown. He promoted Amir Temur's memory through a monumental equestrian stature in the center of Tashkent and later established a nearby museum. A new historical study, *Amir Temur in World History*, by a collection of authors in cooperation with UNESCO,[30] also included Karimov's speeches about Amir Temur.

Uzbekistan has some of the world's finest examples of ancient Muslim architecture, fortunately spared from earthquakes and from Soviet secularism. The Soviet Union protected the most impressive buildings for their historic value, and Intourist even advertised to attract foreign tour groups to the three highlights of the Silk Route—Samarkand, Bukhara, and Khiva. Karimov's regime gradually expanded restoration to more sites of religious or cultural significance, often working with UNESCO. Yet Karimov's interest in Muslim architecture remained historical and nationalistic, not religious.

The Aga Khan held a magnificent twilight ceremony in Samarkand's Registan Square on September 19, 1992, to honor the winners of the Aga Khan Award for Architecture, an annual competition to promote Muslim architecture. President Karimov and prominent guests from many countries attended—the nine winners were all from different countries, from Burkina Faso to Indonesia. Surrounded by the three madrasas, the winners' impressive works were projected onto a giant screen after sundown. After the ceremony we fortunate guests were treated to a banquet in the courtyard of the oldest madrasa. I could not imagine a more sophisticated presentation of the modern architectural expressions of an ancient culture.[31]

Secular Rule vs. Religious Practice

The Russian Revolution brought a secular revolution to Central Asia. Soviet rule forced Muslims to accept that governments, and especially the Communist Party, would be strictly secular. While the Soviet system could be brutal, it was hardly more brutal than life under the emirs before the Russian conquest of Central Asia. Soviet education was secular, girls went to school, and young people could not practice Islam if they wanted to pursue a modern career in the Soviet system.

General Secretary Gorbachev did not initially intend for either *perestroika* or *glasnost* to liberalize the practice of religion. In 1986 and 1987, following his visit to Uzbekistan, fifty-three members of the Uzbek Communist Party were expelled for "organizing and participating" in religious rituals. But Gorbachev took a more affable tone toward religion during a visit to Uzbekistan in 1988, and Uzbek Party officials were no longer chastised for taking part in Muslim funerals.[32] With independence and the disappearance of the Communist Party, government officials seem not to have been restricted from participating in Muslim events, yet I did not know of any who practiced Islam seriously on their own.

In the 1980s, only very few Uzbeks or Tajiks living in Uzbekistan knew Arabic, so most Muslims could not read the original Koran. Very few prayed five times a day, and not many attended services at a mosque. A tiny percentage of the population undertook the pilgrimage to Mecca. A much larger number would participate in a brief traditional prayer following a meal. Some would refrain from drinking alcohol. Pork was not available. A visitor to most cities in Uzbekistan would not think the people were more religious than in other parts of the former Soviet Union.

A Haven for Practicing Islam?

During the Soviet era, the Fergana Valley of Uzbekistan was known as the Soviet region that retained the most overt Islamic practices and traditions. The valley floor, surrounded almost completely by mountains (with an outlet of the Syr Darya River to the west) is mainly Uzbekistan but includes irregular border areas of Kyrgyzstan and Tajikistan, borders which had little ethnic or commercial significance during the Soviet period (see map of Fergana Valley on page 36).

When I visited the town of Margilan in the Fergana Valley in 1983, there were no women in the market, either as buyers or sellers, and a man objected to my taking pictures. Women who went out of their homes in Margilan were well covered and wore dark colors. This contrasted dramatically then and later with Uzbek women in most of the rest of Uzbekistan. Such women dominated the markets both as buyers and sellers and wore their brightly colored silk dresses everywhere, with their faces and often their hair exposed. Muslim worship was discreet, but in the early 1980s the Fergana Valley reportedly had more working mosques than in other parts of the USSR. In the Fergana Valley I saw an occasional man saying his daily prayers on his mat in the street, generally a rare sight in the Soviet Union.

Starting in the very last years of the Soviet Union and continuing with independence, religious activity increased in Uzbekistan. Korans and other Islamic religious assistance flowed into Uzbekistan, and especially into the Fergana Valley. The number of working mosques expanded dramatically, by reopening some that had

been closed or used for other purposes and by building completely new mosques. Teaching boys Arabic and to read the Koran re-
sumed, usually associated with local mosques. In Bukhara an old
madrasa continued more advanced Islamic education in the fash-
ion of pre-Soviet Central Asia. The Karimov administration toler-
ated this activity initially and then moved to reduce the external
Muslim assistance, including the inflow of funding and Korans.
This slowed construction and perhaps other activity, but left the acceptable practice of Islam at a higher level than it had been during
the Soviet era.

President Karimov showed no interest in changing the basic Soviet concept of secular government, and public schools remained
secular. He distrusted any political expression from those practicing Islam, and in late 1991 he banned religious political parties.
In March 1993 the mufti of Uzbekistan, Mohammad-Sadiq Mo-
hammad-Yusuf, was replaced by a less politically oriented mufti,
Mukhtar Abdullaev, the leader of the Naqshibandi Sufis of Bukhara.[33]

Karimov reportedly completed the Hajj, combined with an official visit to Saudi Arabia, in one of his first foreign trips as president.[34] Yet he never mentioned the Hajj, an element of Muslim faith,
in conversations with me. Perhaps he considered making the Hajj
a diplomatic way of introducing himself, as the leader of a tradi-
tionally Muslim country, to the ruling Saudis. Saudi Arabia was
considered the source of funding for the inflow of Korans and other
aspects of the revival of Islam in Uzbekistan, and Karimov may
have wanted to make his own assessment of the country and its
rulers—as he later did in visiting Iran.

A Threat from Radical Islam?

Officials of the secular government, especially the internal security apparatus, remained suspicious of the revived religious activity.
As during Soviet times, rumors circulated about alleged Wahabis
in the Fergana Valley—either resident in Uzbekistan or infiltrat-
ed from Kyrgyzstan or Tajikistan—who were supposed to have
learned this more radical form of Islam in Saudi Arabia and who
intended to use violence to advance their goal of reestablishing the

rule of Islamic law.[35] President Karimov frequently mentioned the threat of radical Islam in meetings with Americans. While we were awaiting the arrival of a visiting head of state in the VIP pavilion of Tashkent's airport, President Karimov specifically cited the threat of Wahabis to me as if it were a fact, supporting his argument that Uzbekistan, and the U.S., should be more vigilant against Islamic extremists.

An example of excessive vigilance, and the way in which the security services' repression of Muslim believers could create opposition to Karimov's regime, occurred in the Fergana Valley in 1994 and 1995. When worshippers in a Kokand mosque held a sit-in to protest the detention of their religious leaders, officials claimed to find weapons and drugs in the detained leaders' homes and put the leaders on trial,[36] further alienating their Muslim followers, who believed the charges were absurd.

By the time I left Tashkent for a new assignment in fall of 1995, tolerance of routine religious practices was undoubtedly higher than during the Soviet period. Most Uzbeks accepted, and many welcomed, that their government, public education, and other aspects of public life would remain secular. The Uzbekistan government did support some aspects of Islam: Mukhtorkhon Abdullaev, the mufti and chairman of the Muslim Religious Organization Movaroulmmakhr, told me during my farewell call on September 28, 1995, that the government had offered to fund half of the construction of a new $5 million Islamic Center for Learning in Tashkent, the city mayor had provided the land for it, and the remaining costs were to be paid through donations. The mufti, who generally defended government positions on Muslim extremists, forcefully argued to me that women should not be covered or obliged to stay at home, and that both girls and boys should receive education as Muslims.[37]

Yet I did not feel that there was a new social contract on the role of Islam in Uzbekistan's society—too much tension remained. Despite President Karimov's contributions to historical preservation, such as the Naqshiband architectural complex in Bukhara,[38] believers had reason to fear repression, and security officials distrusted believers, leading to friction. Valuable time had been lost for initiating and building more constructive relationships between the religious and secular societies in Uzbekistan, especially in the Fergana Valley.

While I saw little evidence of violent, extreme forms of Islam in Uzbekistan during 1992–95, such threats as the violent Islamic Movement of Uzbekistan would become greater in later years. President Karimov and his security services may have exaggerated the threat in those early years, but I also sensed that he was genuinely concerned about the potential threat. After all, Islamic extremists had assassinated Ulugbek, the famous ruler and astronomer of Samarkand in the fifteenth century and grandson of Amir Temur.

5

VISITORS AS MIXED BLESSINGS, YET NECESSARY FOR BILATERAL RELATIONS

Most embassies get plenty of visitors, official and unofficial, not least U.S. embassies. Supporting official visitors affects nearly everyone at a small embassy. With our tiny staff in 1992, U.S. Embassy Tashkent could not afford to spend all of its time shepherding visitors, but sometimes we did.

Yet we needed visitors too—not just those who helped us, like the Seabees who replaced our bad wiring, or the USAID officers who ran programs for Uzbekistan, but also visitors from various agencies at various levels in Washington who needed to learn firsthand the context from which we were reporting. Tashkent embassy officers and I had occasional consultations in Washington, but visitors sometimes provided further insight into what was going on, in Washington or elsewhere in the world, that the embassy needed to know. High-level visitors sometimes had meetings with high-level Uzbek counterparts that brought out new, reportable information.

Every U.S. embassy has the right, in principle, to refuse specific official visits and is expected to give the reasons—inability to support the visitors logistically, or perhaps political timing. But it is a hammer you cannot swing often. At best it will irritate the people who had taken the time to prepare to visit you. At worst, it can build a negative reputation for the embassy in Washington. And the embassy may miss the benefits of a useful visit if it cannot be rescheduled.

If No Treasury Visit, Then No Financial Reform Agenda?

My first decision about a proposed visit was a mistake, although at the time it seemed right. The Treasury Department proposed to send a small team of officials to Kazakhstan and Uzbekistan and probably other posts to meet with finance officials. Deputy Chief of Mission Michael Matera and our political/economic officer Sylvia Babus asked me about it very soon after my arrival in Tashkent. The timing conflicted with several USAID visits, people Sylvia would need to work with for the rest of her tour, and Michael had other visitors then too, all of whom had already been given clearance to come before we heard about Treasury's plans. Coming at the end of September or beginning of October suggested that spending end-of-fiscal-year money might be more a factor in the timing than any urgency for the visit. So I decided we would ask Treasury to re-schedule, pleading insufficient staff to support them properly.

Treasury never rescheduled. Over the following months I became concerned that while we had a fairly clear and specific political agenda for my discussions with Uzbek officials, there was no similarly specific agenda for economic reform. I came to regret that I had not taken on the Treasury visit myself, in order to learn some of whatever knowledge the visitors might have on the reform process in other parts of the former Soviet Union. Michael and I did not think an ambassador should be the "control officer" for such a visit—juggling changes in schedules, arranging cars, hotels, entertainment, and so on—when higher priority demands might crop up. We had no American secretary to help with it, and our handful of locally hired employees had little experience. Yet later I felt no one in the embassy had more experience with being control officer for every rank and description of visitor than I did, so I should have used the Treasury visit to train one of our locally hired employees in managing visitors, and accompany the visitors myself to key meetings when I could.

After a few months I tried to get some instructions from Washington on economic reform in Uzbekistan. Realizing that a simple, open-ended request for instructions would probably go nowhere, I commandeered our one and only classified computer and drafted a long cable proposing some ideas about how to proceed, and asked for Washington's comments and instructions—specifically from Treasury. There was no response, not even after I leaned on the State desk informally to prod them. It just didn't work. Perhaps if I had proposed something outrageous, that would have provoked a response. I was left with my own unanswered proposals, until the World Bank published its much more comprehensive *Uzbekistan: An Agenda for Economic Reform* in 1993.By the time I learned about the World Bank's agenda, their office in Tashkent was taking the lead in policy discussions on economic reform with the Government of Uzbekistan.

It took a visit to Washington by Deputy Prime Minister Chzhen on May 5, 1994, for me to understand Treasury a little better. I happened to be in Washington on consultations and accompanied Chzhen to a meeting with Under Secretary Lawrence Summers. It started badly: no one had forewarned the gatekeepers that Chzhen was coming, so he was left cooling his heels at the 15th Street entrance while I and others tried phoning people to get him in. After an agonizing delay he did meet with Summers. Chzhen was typically resistant about economic change, and Summers was diplomatic, saying there was no single formula for the transition to a market economy. After Chzhen left, I met with the assistant secretary for international affairs, who had sat in with Summers. He contradicted Summers, saying that in fact there was only one way to a market economy. I was not successful in drawing him out for more details about that path. But by that time it was becoming apparent that Uzbekistan, and Chzhen in particular, were not, or not yet, committed to making a further transition to a market economy, and therefore finding a specific formula was not so urgent. All we had, really, were individual USAID programs, some of which worked, and some, such as tax reform, that didn't have a chance.

Another Unnecessary Beating

In late May 1993 retired ambassador Roger Kirk and his wife came to Uzbekistan on a trip sponsored by United States Information Service (USIS) to meet and talk with various groups about the process of international diplomacy. Roger had been my ambassador in Bucharest, 1985–89, and it was a pleasure to spend some time at dinner with them on at least two evenings. While I was on a short trip to Tel Aviv to pick up my son, the Kirks left Tashkent by air.

Our embassy was in a full-fledged crisis when I returned on June 23. Dildora Yusupova, an Uzbek who worked for USIS, had accompanied the Kirks to the airport and past the immigration official's desk to the waiting room beyond, part of the transit area for departing passengers only. Unbeknownst to the Kirks, on her return to the immigration control area she said she was grabbed by the border guards, taken to another room, and beaten. She may, or may not, have insulted the guards in the process. The guards were angry that she had slipped past them—something they are not supposed to allow. It did not help that she was an Uzbek woman showing disrespect for Slavic-origin male border guards. In addition to being understandably very upset, she was visibly bruised and scratched but fortunately without serious injuries.

The embassy's report of her beating aroused understandable outrage in Washington. The timing could not have been worse. A group of Uzbek parliamentarians was just arriving for an extended tour in the United States, financed by USIS or USAID. Someone high ranking decided to retaliate by sending the parliamentarians home. The visitors did not know anything about the incident, could not have been remotely responsible for it, and could not understand our action. I was disappointed, because the group had taken months to organize, and I doubted that it could be organized again for the foreseeable future. An opportunity for prominent Uzbeks to learn about the United States was simply lost. The beating certainly required us to react quickly and negatively on the diplomatic level, but retaliation against the wrong people was the wrong call.

Next steps fell to me. The U.S. wanted an apology and an investigation, and punishment for the border guards involved. Uzbek officials expressed regret about the beating but pointed out that it was not acceptable for Yusupova to evade the border control point, and she surely knew that. I did not know in 1993 that the border guards were still under Moscow's control, but I sensed the same Uzbek reluctance to take any action against them that I had observed with high Uzbek officials and the airport border guards less than a year before, during the evacuation of Embassy Dushanbe (Chapter 3).

I called on President Karimov the next day, June 24. He too re-gretted the incident and said he would order an investigation. He wanted a letter from us, which I delivered the following day to the Foreign Ministry. I had no great expectation that the investigation would accomplish much, but it was correct to ask for it, and it could be a lesson in accountability. Our protest showed again that the U.S. cared about beatings, especially beating our employees. USIS, concerned about Yusupova's further safety, found her a scholar-ship and sent her to the United States.

Ordinary Uzbeks tended to admire our embassy for defending the Uzbek woman against Slavic-origin officials. Others questioned whether Yusupova had exaggerated the incident. But by the time I heard those questions, Washington and I had already acted under the assumption she was at least approximately correct.[39]

A couple of months later Uzbekistan's official investigation was completed, confirming what we already knew about violating the immigration control border and the beating. One or two border guards would be transferred. Not much punishment, but at least it was a conclusion. I found the result of the investigation more sat-isfactory than when we protested beatings of dissidents, probably because Yusupova's mistreatment was just the visceral, immediate reaction of the guards involved, and not a deliberate decision by higher authority. Dissidents who were beaten were usually more seriously injured.

Human Rights, Uzbek Dissidents, and Democratic Development

Strobe Talbott, the special representative for the Newly Indepen-dent States (S/NIS), the czar within the State Department for rela-tions with all of the former Soviet Union, and therefore my most important superior for most issues, visited Tashkent September 13–14, 1993. Though he remained concerned about the Yusupova incident and questioned me closely about it, he had a larger agenda for human rights and other issues.

At Washington's request, Daria Fane and I organized a meeting at my house between selected dissidents and Talbott on the evening of his arrival. Two came, and two were prevented from coming; one was under house arrest and the other was detained to prevent her from coming. Talbott used that as his basis for raising human rights in general with Foreign Minister Saidkasymov the next morning. Saidkasymov objected to my organizing the meeting; Talbott said he wanted the meeting to learn about Uzbekistan's political life prior to the next election. In a contentious discussion of the importance of human rights and movement toward a more democratic society, Talbott mentioned he had sought a similar meeting with dissidents in 1980, with almost identical results.

Human rights were not Talbott's sole agenda. He discussed economic cooperation with Deputy Prime Minister Hamidov and other economic officials, stressing that this depended mainly on U.S. companies, not the U.S. government. Nicholas Burns, then on the National Security Council staff, emphasized the need to sign three agreements to support the private sector: a trade agreement, an agreement on bilateral investment, and one to avoid double taxation.[40] Hamidov agreed.

President Karimov led off his meeting with the Talbott delegation by expressing his dissatisfaction with relations with the United States. In particular he wanted much more participation by U.S. firms in Uzbekistan, asserting that the Europeans, especially European bankers, were doing better. To become more like the U.S., attitudes would have to change among Uzbekistan's 22 million people, and they would need U.S. help to do that, Karimov said.[41]

Karimov then gave a lengthy lecture, which took about an hour with translation. It ranged from Uzbekistan's history and resources to his views on relations among the newly independent states. He stressed his concerns about stability, mentioning earlier violence in the Fergana Valley, and problems in Tajikistan. Karimov was concerned that during the civil war and under Iranian influence, Tajikistan had moved toward an Islamic state (although it still had a secular government). For Uzbekistan, the threat was Islamic fundamentalism, and the best response was to open up society and move toward democracy, Karimov said, and a greater U.S. presence in Uzbekistan would help. Talbott had just come from Dushanbe and said his views on Tajikistan were close to Karimov's. Talbott also said the U.S. was not satisfied with the bilateral economic relationship. Under instructions from President Clinton, he and Burns were committed to improving it.[42]

There followed a give-and-take on third countries, including Turkey and India, which as Muslim or Asian countries might be partial models for democracy in Uzbekistan. Talbott emphasized the importance of human rights to democracy and assured Karimov of America's respect for Uzbekistan's sovereignty and its right to choose its own future. He mentioned that President Clinton's interest in Central Asia dated back to his time as a Rhodes scholar and said he would report their meeting to him. The meeting and visit ended on a positive note.[43]

By presenting U.S. views forcefully, the Talbott visit added credibility to my own positions in meetings with these officials. It was not an easy visit, but it was a useful one from my perspective.

Senator Arlen Specter

When I learned that Senator and Mrs. Specter would visit Tashkent in June 1994, I welcomed it. They had visited Bucharest while I was chargé d'affaires there and had stayed at my DCM residence. So I invited them to stay with me again, and they agreed. In Romania, Specter had been mainly interested in international affairs, and his dialogue with President Nicolae Ceaușescu on the Middle East had been the highlight.

In Tashkent Specter had a different agenda, oriented toward human rights. Anita Hill, who had accused Supreme Court candidate Clarence Thomas of sexual harassment, had come under sharp questioning by Specter during Thomas's Senate Judiciary Committee hearing. TV coverage of the hearing had given Specter the image of being hostile to women's rights, even to constituents in his home state of Pennsylvania. He was looking for opportunities to counteract that image, and he wanted meetings with dissidents in Tashkent, preferably female, in addition to meetings with the president and other high officials.

We knew we had to make the meetings with dissidents as informal and low key as possible, or risk cancellation of the official meetings. A meeting with the president would not be confirmed until nearly the last minute, so it might not happen. There would also be a risk to the dissidents themselves. Our solution, facilitated by having the Specters stay at my residence, was to invite several dissidents to a buffet breakfast with us there. It could be early enough not to interfere with the rest of the schedule. If a dissident decided not to come or couldn't make it, the format was flexible — Senator Specter could move around and talk with each one who came. Our political officers contacted the guests to set it up.

Uzbek police had detained our female dissident guest the day before. At breakfast time, only one dissident arrived — apparently the authorities missed him. Specter was disappointed not to meet the woman, but at least Specter had a conversation with the man who came and asked him about the woman who could not come.

After breakfast the senator wanted to write a letter of complaint to President Karimov about his government's treatment of the dissidents, and we did our best to support him. He took quite a while to draft it but expected a final letter, with copies and a translation into Russian, in no time flat, while we went on with his schedule. When the embassy's only copier failed, someone tried to get it fixed, and the senator lost patience with me, accusing me of sabotaging his letter. Key to his suspicion was his inability to believe we had only one copier in the "whole" embassy. I began thinking differently about the senator, who was blaming us for resource shortages his Congress would not appropriate. He could have had the same experience of only one copier at most of the newly established embassies, not just ours. Later I learned that the senator was known in Washington for being irascible — his loss of patience with me was not unusual.

To his credit, Senator Specter cared about his issues and made the points on human rights to Uzbekistan's high officials that otherwise we would have had to make. Our political/economic officer, Sylvia Babus, was with him when he suddenly demanded they stop at the Ministry of the Interior, where he had no appointment. He asked the guard at the door to speak with someone about a person he was supposed to meet but who was being held by the Interior Ministry. An officer on duty came to the door, politely denied knowing about the case, and said he would look into his question and inform the U.S. Embassy. But he did not get back to us. Specter also mentioned the same woman to Defense Minister Akhmedov, who laughed about it. He apparently confused the name with someone else who had complained about hazing in the military.

In the end, of course, the senator got his letter, his copies, and even his meeting with President Karimov, which I attended. I never found out whether Specter was able to make political use of his letter to President Karimov with his constituents, but I assume he tried.

After sending him off, we went on with the unhappy task of finding out how much harm had befallen our dissident contacts. The woman that Specter was particularly concerned about met with Sylvia in the park behind our Embassy after her release from detention. She had a scar on her wrist from her attempted suicide while being held outside the city and seemed most upset by officials' efforts to harass and alienate her husband.

Lessons in Patience

For an established embassy, it is often hard to see that the benefit from a stream of visitors outweighs the burdens of time spent and the expenses. It is just part of an embassy's job in the modern world. Congressional visits can be serious, as Specter's was in both Bucharest and Tashkent, or just glorified, taxpayer-financed shopping and entertainment tours (I was control officer for one such tour in Munich, my first post). Each embassy must do its best to help them, even with frivolous matters, because congressional attitudes toward the State Department will suffer if it doesn't. And it must do so patiently and silently. Ambassador Arthur Hartman, one of the most broadly experienced professional diplomats of his generation, warned us in Moscow after a huge and rather loose congressional delegation departed, "Don't talk about it. At all. We can only lose" if the delegation's misdeeds or foibles were exposed.

To be fair, an embassy is not always in the best position to judge the value of a visit to overall U.S. interests. For example, the National War College (NWC), which teaches national security strategy to military and civilian officers at the colonel or lieutenant colonel level, has annual trips abroad to various parts of the world for all its students, led by faculty members. I have been involved in receiving NWC groups in practically every assignment abroad, and for a long time I tended to think of the trips as boondoggles, as do many Foreign Service officers. Then I was assigned to the faculty of the

NWC, and it opened my eyes. Many of the most promising military officers, those who would go on to become admirals and generals, reached the NWC without the slightest experience in foreign affairs beyond warfare. Yet at flag rank in the military some sophistication in foreign affairs is really essential. For them, no amount of reading and lecturing was as educational and memorable as these study trips—and the students did prepare in advance. If their questions seemed sometimes off the mark, that often reflected genuine curiosity and readiness to learn. At the NWC I was faculty advisor for three such groups, and concluded that the study trips—usually to two or three countries in the same region—were well worth their considerable expense (faculty and student salaries, plus the travel and accommodations) in preparing our future military leadership.

In Tashkent, an NWC group visited in May 1993, and a second came in 1994, led by Ambassador David Mack. In addition to a big reception, at which the officer-students could talk more directly and candidly with Uzbek military and civilian officials, we were able to get military appointments, including Defense Minister Akhmedov, which we were finding difficult to arrange for our Moscow-based defense attaché at that time. In Samarkand one of the groups visited a military driving school, in addition to the world-class Muslim architecture and monuments there. Another group came in May 1995, not long after Defense Secretary Perry's visit. By then it was not difficult to arrange another useful schedule and to help these officers develop a firsthand understanding of what the collapse of the Soviet Union meant in Central Asia.

No Russian Sphere of Influence

When Strobe Talbott was promoted to deputy secretary of state, former ambassador to Moscow James Collins replaced him as the senior official in charge of relations with the Newly Independent States (S/NIS), as the former Soviet republics were increasingly referred to, and therefore effectively my boss, as Talbott had been. This meant visiting all of his new "client" states for high-level discussions. On November 4–6, 1994, more than a year after the 1993 Talbott visit, Collins brought a strong U.S. government delegation with him to Tashkent. They met with the ministers of foreign affairs and defense, and on economic matters with the prime minister and his deputies. In the latter meeting, the Uzbek officials made an effort to point out ways in which they were changing economic policy, including privatization without "shock therapy," and the American delegation was supportive.

President Karimov, accompanied by top officials of his government, met with Collins and his delegation, and used the meeting to try to increase official American interest in Central Asia and Uzbekistan in particular, apparently assuming that Collins would be preoccupied with Russia. Collins replied that President Clinton and the State Department did not recognize a Russian sphere of interest, not in Central Asia nor elsewhere in the Newly Independent States (NIS). It was the first time I had heard such a categorical statement by a senior American official, and it was very reassuring. Collins pointed out that the non-Russian NIS took more of his time than Russia did.

Collins also found common ground with Karimov on terrorism in general, pointing out that "some of our friends" were taken hostage in Tehran in 1979, and others were killed in the bombing of the U.S. Embassy in Beirut.

Threats from Iran and, Potentially, Russia

After meeting with the entire American delegation, President Karimov asked to meet separately with S/NIS Collins and me, to discuss Russia's relationship with Iran in confidence. He said that the Russian arms export organization *Rusoruzheniye* had visited Turkmenistan several times, and he concluded that they were selling modern weapons to Iran and perhaps other countries, and just using Turkmenistan as a bridge. Karimov expressed great concern, asking against whom the weapons would be used. He accused the Iranians of imperial ambitions in Turkmenistan, and even in Bukhara and Samarkand, saying that Iran would claim "50,000 Iranians in Samarkand," referring to ethnic Tajiks who lived there, to put pressure on Uzbekistan.[44]

Karimov said he could not understand why it was in Russia's interest to play an "Iran card," unless increasing the Iranian threat to Uzbekistan would force Uzbekistan to seek Russia's help.

Collins suggested several possible motives: Russia wanted the money from selling weapons, Russia had historically considered Iran important and wanted to have influence there. And intelligence chief Primakov was also dealing with Iraq, as he had before, and perhaps Russia just wanted to keep its options open. Collins stressed that Russian weapons sales to Iran were a serious issue in U.S.-Russian bilateral relations, on which agreement had not been reached.[45]

Karimov asserted that Iran was stirring up the civil war in Afghanistan, dividing the factions. He also cited supplies of Russian weapons and aircraft fuel transiting Turkmenistan and Tajikistan to Afghan warlord Ahmad Shah Masood. Karimov said he had asked Primakov why he would support Masood but got no answer. Collins agreed with Karimov that Iran was playing an unhelpful role in Afghanistan. He understood the seriousness of these concerns for Uzbekistan and promised to discuss Karimov's concerns with the secretary and deputy secretary of state.[46] In my comment at the end of the reporting telegram, I emphasized (to other readers in Washington) that Karimov's concerns that Iran would expand its influence in Central Asia, perhaps with support from Russia, were quite serious. Others in Uzbekistan's secular elite also tended to identify theocratic public life in Iran with the evils and brutality of the pre-Soviet period in Uzbekistan.[47]

Karimov saw Central Asia's problems with Iran as related to the rest of the Middle East. Consequently, Uzbekistan would be opening embassies in Saudi Arabia and Egypt and had even invited Arafat to visit Tashkent.[48] (Uzbekistan already had diplomatic and civil aviation relations with Israel.)

Collins saved the subject of human rights for the end of the meeting; he raised it quite clearly but diplomatically, expressing appreciation for the way Uzbekistan had held a CSCE Seminar in Tashkent, including the human rights aspects. Human rights problems would take time to resolve; institutions had to be developed. But serious human rights problems would be an impediment to the bilateral relationship. Karimov said he appreciated Collins's "delicacy," and insisted that he was jealous of Western European countries, where people lived and voted with greater freedom. He asserted that he did what was necessary in Uzbekistan, not what he would want. He had seen the Fergana Valley when hundreds of people had been slaughtered on the Uzbekistan-Kyrgyzstan border at Osh, and called it "medieval fanaticism." People in Uzbekistan were gradually changing, but much of Uzbekistan was still made up of "stone-age" country people.[49]

Although I firmly believe that professionally experienced ambassadors can effectively represent the United States abroad, Jim Collins's meetings reminded me of the value of periodic high-level meetings, especially in countries like Uzbekistan, where so much of the decision-making authority is concentrated in few hands, or even just one. Karimov used high-level meetings with Americans to try out his own thinking on international relations, and that was surely in U.S. interest.

Foreign Minister Abdulaziz Kamilov and me at the U.S. Embassy third anniversary reception, March 1995.
Source: U.S. Government photo.

6

BIG CHANGES IN U.S. RELATIONS, WITHOUT DOMESTIC REFORM

A New Working Environment

Every day in Tashkent I was reminded how much easier it was to function as a normal embassy in Uzbekistan than in Ceaușescu's Romania, or in Moscow during the transition years from Brezhnev to Gorbachev. We hired or fired local staff without interference. We paid employees in U.S. dollars, shielding them against the ruinous inflation underway in the ruble and later in the som. We went out looking for houses, and when we found one we liked, we could rent or buy it from the owner, as in a normal country.

Did we want to announce a new U.S. scholarship program? Just call the TV station and the newspapers, they would happily bring their gear over to the embassy, ask reasonable questions, and not cut out what we wanted to say. At first I was surprised, at the entrance to an official event, to have a microphone appear under my nose and have a journalist ask me to comment on the occasion, sometimes with the journalist's colleague pointing a video camera at me. I learned to have a few friendly phrases in mind. The media were not free to criticize the Government of Uzbekistan, but the idea that they should so frequently report on what the American Embassy was doing was totally post-Soviet.

Could we Americans talk with junior officials or ordinary citizens, without worrying about the consequences for the interlocutor? Yes, and we did. This did not apply to dissidents, with whom we needed to be discreet. Otherwise the freedom to meet new people and make friends throughout the country was most unlike my tours in Bucharest and Moscow.

Businessmen from a variety of countries, led by the Turks, had begun flowing in before my arrival. On October 9, 1992, the chairman, president, and other officials of Newmont Mining arrived in my office from Denver. Instead of asking me for help or information, they offered to help the embassy, which was newer in Uzbekistan than they were. As a former commercial officer, this was a first for me. Newmont was negotiating a direct investment to launch a major gold extraction project near Zarafshan and was getting close to an agreement on product sharing that would have been impossible a few years earlier.

A few days later, on October 13, representatives from the Peace Corps were in my office, determined to set up a program in Uzbekistan. I signed the bilateral agreement for the Peace Corps on November 4,[50] and the Peace Corps staff soon began preparing for the first group of volunteers to arrive in early 1993 for in-country training. Coordination between the Peace Corps and the embassy was not always ideal, and the first group of volunteers had some problems that could have been avoided, but the very fact of young Americans from the Peace Corps working with ordinary Uzbeks in several different cities amazed me. To be sure, some and perhaps all were suspected of being spies, and the first cohort may have had to work harder than in other countries to become accepted. But they were accepted, and they multiplied the number of Uzbeks who had a chance to meet and get to know Americans.

Did I want to visit another city, meet with a mayor, or see a factory? We could just call them up and work out a schedule. And they seemed almost as delighted with the idea of a visit as I was. Unlike the USSR, where diplomats had struggled with travel restrictions, diplomats in independent Uzbekistan did not face formal travel restrictions. One attempt to impose such restrictions, before my arrival, was either rebuffed or ignored by Western embassies, and our chargé d'affaires, Michael Matera, stated publicly that the U.S. Embassy would not comply with them.

I was also determined to be vigilant in preventing travel restrictions. When the Peace Corps agreed in writing to some restrictions on travel by its personnel without consulting me, I formally denounced that agreement in consultation with the Department of State.

We were welcomed wherever we went, surely a change as important as the absence of formal restrictions. Unlike the USSR that I remembered, our appointments did not evaporate when we arrived in another city, and neither Intourist nor obvious KGB minders tried to track our moves.

When I mentioned to Foreign Minister Saidkasymov in 1993 that I wanted to visit Termez, on the Afghan border near Tajikistan, he objected, saying it was unsafe for me to go there. I protested that my safety should be up to me, not him, and he became upset, saying if something happened to me, the Government of Uzbekistan would be held responsible. If he had a specific reason for his objection, he did not say, and I never found out; perhaps it was just the proximity to the unsettled situation in Tajikistan or some local issue in Termez. Without agreeing to delay, but also not eager to escalate an argument that might lead to formal restrictions, I changed the subject. I did put off traveling to Termez, but later made the trip together with Defense Minister Akhmedov in 1995.[51]

Meanwhile, on March 1, 1994, I signed a Memorandum of Understanding on Diplomatic and Consular Travel, nicknamed "Open Lands," together with Foreign Minister Saidkasymov, which ruled out closing areas to diplomatic travel that were otherwise accessible to the public and precluded requirements for travel permission or for advance notice of travel, in both Uzbekistan and the United States. I could quit worrying about the possible return of a Cold War relic.

Broadcasting Was a Step Too Far

When I arrived in September 1992, the U.S. Embassy already had a huge satellite dish looking at the sky from the side yard—not, unfortunately, for our own diplomatic communications, which were rather modest. Instead, the big dish had been built with the hope of receiving Voice of America (VOA) and Radio Liberty programs, including television, for rebroadcast by Uzbekistan's own stations. The idea that this was under serious discussion amazed me, and I welcomed it. Top officials of those two organizations who tried again to reach agreement with government officials visited with me on November 16, 1992. In the end, the rebroadcasting was never agreed to, the dish was never used, but in the meantime Uzbek officials were clearly reluctant to give us a simple "no."

President Karimov would have known that his government's abuse of human rights would provide ample fodder for Radio Liberty and VOA (and perhaps TV), and therefore rebroadcasting could be embarrassing and might encourage domestic opposition. Yet at the same time, I believe he genuinely wanted a closer relationship with the United States.

Hope for U.S.-Uzbekistan Relations

Why would President Karimov want close relations with the United States? There was never a clear-cut answer, but there were several factors that I thought contributed to his government's openness toward the United States and toward what we wanted to do.

First, and in my view most important, Karimov had to consider the possibility that Russia would try to reassert the former Soviet authority over Central Asia, including Uzbekistan. Although Karimov and his officials may have been somewhat surprised by the collapse of the Soviet Union, they were irreversibly committed to independence. The United States was far away geographically, but in the early 1990s Uzbekistan really had no other comparable counterweight to Russian influence, economically or politically.

Second, I think Karimov recognized that there were things to be learned from the United States. We had clearly prevailed over the Soviet Union economically as well as in the Cold War. The Newmont Mining project was an example: Newmont could extract gold from lower-grade ore and tailings that Soviet technology could not. Unfortunately, Karimov underestimated the changes in economic structure and policy necessary to build a growing economy and attract international business investment outside of mining.

Third, Karimov could see that the United States had not used the end of the Cold War or the collapse of the Soviet Union to subject Russia or any other former Soviet republic to its own rule. He never complained to me about the rush of Warsaw Pact or Baltic countries to join NATO. He supported Uzbekistan's participation in NATO's Partnership for Peace and seemed not to place any restrictions on our various exchange programs. Even without real reform, there were just more opportunities for beneficial cooperation in almost all fields than before the collapse of the Soviet Union.

Finally, Karimov could see that most of his countrymen were genuinely interested in the United States and friendly toward those of us who came to Uzbekistan.[52] As we met more people, they liked us better. The government of Uzbekistan at all levels, from the president on down, helped us launch the U.S. Embassy in Tashkent. It was not just a permissive environment; it was a *friendly* environment.

The overriding impression that I received during my first few months in Uzbekistan was that there were no clear limits to our bilateral relations. We could not assume that a project or program or policy would not work until we tried it out. If one idea didn't work, another might.

Prospects for Reform versus Washington's Pessimism

My basic instruction from President George H. W. Bush (see Appendix A), called upon me to promote American ideals.[53] Subsequent policies the State Department approved called for political and economic reforms. There seemed no more appropriate time to do so than while Uzbekistan was still getting organized as an independent country. So I was eager to get on with it and was ready to try any approach that made sense.

I could not rule out that President Karimov might tacitly, or even openly, agree to some political or economic measures that could lead eventually to reform. Sometimes he would hint about that possibility, as he did with Special Representative Strobe Talbott (chapter 5). When he returned to Tashkent after a summit meeting of the Organization for Security and Cooperation in Europe (OSCE), he said in a brief speech to ambassadors from OSCE member countries, including me, that he had great respect for the way in which Western countries recognized the dignity of their individual citizens. Uzbekistan's citizens might not be ready yet, he suggested, without ruling out the idea of moving the country in that direction.

In a private meeting on another occasion, Karimov challenged me to go out into Uzbek villages and talk with villagers, saying I would see that they were really not educated enough to participate in a democracy. In yet another, one-on-one meeting I had requested to discuss human rights (and perhaps other issues), President Karimov told me near the end that he was tired of hearing about human rights.

While no one faulted me for trying to carry out my instructions, and no one changed the instructions, after some months it became clear to me that Washington did not really believe reform would happen in Uzbekistan. A caricature of the differences among the five Central Asian countries developed into conventional wisdom in Washington: Kyrgyzstan, with President Akayev then sounding like a true democrat, was the star Westernizer; Kazakhstan, with its huge petroleum reserves, had the greatest potential for international business and was more important anyway due to nuclear and space issues; Tajikistan was lost to internal conflict; and Turkmenistan and Uzbekistan were mired in dictatorship. While I was not in an objective position to judge the other countries, I thought Uzbekistan's central location, its large population, and positive attitude did make it attractive for U.S. private investment and other forms of bilateral cooperation.

The obstacles to a rational reform policy toward Uzbekistan were not just pessimism but also the natural tendency of resources to flow toward those places that Washington feels are most likely to succeed. In principle, money was available to support reform in the former Soviet Union but apparently not for investing in long shots. Washington also did not think of Central Asia as key or a high priority for that strategy—Russia was crucial, and we in the "stans" were in the periphery.

My personal style as ambassador may not have reduced Washington's pessimism, because I did not evade or minimize problems. Contrary to traditional Central Asian dialogues with powerful people, I would not flatter President Karimov and his senior officials by telling them what they wanted to hear, because I did not want them to be misled about American views. I knew from experience in Romania that their subordinates might not always be candid with them. I believe my counterparts at various levels respected me. Some seemed to trust my honesty and knew I would not be shining their shoes. Likewise, my style with Washington was direct: we reported all the bad news, as well as the good, usually with a comment or recommendation. I would insist, from time to time, that there were still ways in which U.S. efforts could make a difference—but by then our reporting of bad news had probably confirmed Washington's pessimism and reduced the value of our advice in their eyes. But I did not lose the optimism that we needed to keep trying.

How could we make a difference?

I thought we needed to look beyond the responses of the Government of Uzbekistan. The country had some 22 million people, among whom were the largest number of highly educated people in Central Asia. Agency for International Development (USAID) colleagues resident in Kazakhstan told me that whenever they had a program involving training or education for Central Asians, the largest number of well-qualified candidates came from Uzbekistan. Tashkent had been the Soviet Union's de facto regional capital, with the most extensive higher education and academic research facilities. Unlike the Soviet Union, the newly independent regime did not prevent us from sending experts or educated, bright young people to the United States, or interfere with their contacts and learning when they returned.

When we began sending high school students to the United States on exchanges, we were flooded with academically and linguistically qualified applicants. The problem was not getting permission for them to leave; our challenge (met by young Americans working with ACCELS[54]) was choosing the best students, rather than sending less-qualified students who had more powerful parents. We could not escape the fact that the regime's supporters were eager to expose their own children to American education. I met with many of the selected students before they left, and again after they came back from a year in an American high school, and I was deeply impressed with how much they managed to learn from crossing what was really a huge cultural gap. Several students found themselves disappointed that their exchange program required them to return after only one year and prevented them from obtaining a visa immediately to enter an American college (some had received personal invitations to do so). Given the hard times suffered by higher education in Tashkent, I sympathized with them. I was not happy defending the terms of the exchange, even though I knew we could not run a program designed to help Uzbekistan if it offered an easier path to immigration for Uzbekistan's brightest youth.

The International Republican Institute (IRI) ran a program for high school students in Uzbekistan, teaching basic democratic organizing and attitudes. They developed a small cadre of local instructors to expand the program to more schools, which astonished me. With my Cold War background I could not believe that the regime was unaware of this American-managed program and yet raised no hand against it. If there was any specific threat against the program, I did not hear of it. Though IRI did not teach anything subversive—they gave no advice on what to be for or against—they provided lessons that empowered the students to choose goals for themselves. Yet due to Uzbekistan's bad reputation, and not the failure of the program, IRI soon ended all its programs in Uzbekistan. I concluded with disappointment that IRI was leaving the country that needed it most.

The Democratic Party's equivalent organization, the National Democratic Institute (NDI), operated at a higher level, organizing conferences among academics and officials, a welcome activity among the invited professionals. For example, in February 1993 NDI ran a well-attended seminar in the new University of World Economy and Diplomacy. Although the seminar seemed to achieve NDI's objectives, NDI decided to end its programs in Uzbekistan due to the Uzbekistan government's reputation in Washington as a dictatorship. I was told later that the NDI representative in Uzbekistan had been "hassled" in his apartment and told to leave, which surely did not help.

The Alternative: Disengagement

I have long disagreed with the "clean hands" principle, advocated most frequently by American liberals in foreign affairs. This principle holds that you can't "deal with" or "do business as usual with" countries that have governments with bad reputations, so you should cut off relationships and programs with their people, even if continuing the effort might help improve the situation in the future. The benefits of concentrating your efforts on places that have good reputations and are easier to work with: you are more likely to be able to claim a quicker "success," and more people will believe you are doing something useful. The places you ignore are the ones that need reform the most and are the least likely to begin the process themselves.

The old Russian fatalistic expression for a hopeless situation, with multiple reinforcing negatives, goes roughly, "You cannot never do nothing nohow." I've always liked the answer, "You can always do something," as being a more appropriate attitude for Americans. Having spent most of my Foreign Service career dealing with communist or post-communist dictatorships, I don't understand the "clean hands" principle of refusing to deal with unsavory counterparts. I don't think leaving dictatorships unengaged is a policy to accomplish anything. It is a nonpolicy, which may feel righteous but doesn't weaken those who oppose us and provides fewer points of contact and influence in their society. I joined the Foreign Service with the expectation that I would have to roll up my sleeves and work on what needed to be done. If working with an unpleasant system could be helpful to American goals, then neither the United States nor I would become "dirty" by association. In the early 1990s, I certainly did not see Uzbekistan as a hopeless case, just a very challenging one.

Politics in most democratic countries seems to require at least occasional high-minded rhetoric that either praises our own goals or criticizes others. Too often in the United States, however, writing the talking points or drafting the speech becomes the extent of the policy—a position is taken, but there is no substance behind it because we are not doing anything to make it happen. American diplomacy would be more effective if there were always something going on to support the rhetoric. This may not be obvious to politicians and voters, but when an American diplomat tries to explain a purely rhetorical policy to a well-informed person in another country, it doesn't go well, whether they represent a government or not.

There may be places where American influence or presence is so slight that there is nothing we can do to back up our rhetoric, or where trying to do so would be unproductive. Those places are few, I believe, and Uzbekistan in the early 1990s was not one of them.

Who Would Carry the Reform Ball?

The range of practical programs to promote long-run political re-form in Uzbekistan was indeed narrow. There was no real party system. The Parliament was a collection of Karimov admirers with no independent voice. The regime punished and scattered those who had openly opposed Karimov in the 1991 election, and no one was anticipating an election that would be open to effective oppo-nents any time soon. So there was not much to work with in the po-litical structure. Yet there remained the youth and the intelligentsia of Central Asia's most populous country.

Russia began the post-communist reform period with a huge advantage over Central Asia, including Uzbekistan. Although the Soviet Union isolated nearly all of its population from the rest of the world, it always had institutions that studied Western countries professionally. These institutions included the Foreign Ministry, the Foreign Trade Ministry, the KGB, the USA and Canada Institute, and a variety of other specialized research institutes—comparable to American think tanks and university research—where highly educated people were expected to understand Western countries. During my assignment to Moscow in the early 1980s I knew of very few institutions outside Moscow—one in Novosibirsk, for exam-ple—in which professors would write papers, mostly secret, but some leaked, promoting their ideas about economic reform in the USSR.

Although higher education in Tashkent was the best in Cen-tral Asia, and doubtless included individuals knowledgeable about various aspects of the outside world, as far as I could tell it inherited practically none of the Soviet Union's research infrastructure deal-ing with the West. There was thus no obvious cadre of intellectu-als who would fully understand, let alone promote, economic and political reform along the lines of Western models. If Tashkent had an international role within the Soviet Union, it was claimed as a "gateway to the East," meaning mainly India, Pakistan, and smaller

Asian countries. As best I could tell, that role was diplomatic and cultural, with some shared ancient history but not a strong role in political or economic relations, which were driven by Moscow.

Independent Uzbekistan took advantage of the proximity of Tashkent's international airport to the subcontinent to develop regular flights to India, Pakistan, and Thailand, in addition to major destinations in Western Europe and New York. It even competed for revenue with India and the United Kingdom on its London-Tashkent-Delhi route. But this expansion of air travel to both East and West could have little immediate effect on education and research in the early 1990s, other than to make travel easier.

Perhaps recognizing an academic gap in teaching international relations, by late 1992 the Government of Uzbekistan began organizing a new University of World Economy and Diplomacy in Tashkent. Although the new "university" was very small at the beginning, it acquired useful conference rooms and served as a way of holding academic events with foreign visitors of importance. One of NDI's conferences was held there in February 1993, and it may have been NDI's last one in Uzbekistan. Later, a different event was held there for Shimon Peres, whom I had met in Israel, and it gave me a brief opportunity to chat with him. Yet this institution, however useful in offering young people additional opportunities in education for international relations, and however useful in facilitating more international contacts, was not an instrument for changing Uzbekistan in the near term. The head of the university, Saidmukhtar Saidkasymov, highly educated in the Soviet academic system and a polished, articulate speaker, later became foreign minister and in that role seemed to me not especially open-minded toward foreign economics or diplomacy. At least Saidkasymov founded an institution intended to be outward looking, and perhaps it had the potential to become that.

In short, within Uzbekistan I saw no nucleus of people who would advocate or know how to implement reforms, despite the public's openness to Western ideas.[55] Nor did I see any evidence that waiting for Uzbekistan to become more observant of human rights would reduce the violations or lead to more basic reforms. Yet, I felt strongly that we needed to do what we could—in education, exchanges, and contacts—while Uzbekistan was still evolving into a new country.

An Advisor with No Audience

Imagine my astonishment when President Karimov told Craig Buck, USAID director for Central Asia, and me, that he would like us to find him an economic advisor. USAID found a candidate, Robert Campbell, a well-regarded retired professor of economics. In early July 1993 I telephoned him at his cabin in Colorado to persuade him to come to Tashkent to advise the president. He soon agreed and arrived with his wife in early August. We had an introductory meeting for him with President Karimov on August 9. After some delays, I signed a bilateral Memorandum of Understanding for a Senior Policy Advisor on March 1, 1994.

Professor Campbell was assigned to an economic organization that supposedly supported the president, but after the introductory meeting he practically never saw Karimov. Either the president changed his mind about wanting his advice, or the president's staff torpedoed Campbell's access. Campbell was sidelined and understandably frustrated. After some months he left, with no reforms to show for his efforts. I can just imagine how much he and his wife missed the Rocky Mountains while he was stuck in Uzbekistan's bureaucracy. The best I could say was that we really tried: USAID had worked quickly and found a well-qualified advisor. With regular access, Campbell could have offered the president ways to improve or manage the economy that his cabinet and other advisors would never be likely to think of. They didn't want that, so it just didn't work.

Status for Foreign Nongovernmental Organizations (NGOs)

After the departure of IRI and NDI, other NGOs remained based in Tashkent—and more with offices in Almaty, Kazakhstan— in Uzbekistan implementing humanitarian and technical assistance, mainly under USAID contracts. USAID Director Craig Buck once told me, "I don't do retail assistance," by which I understood that he was just the "wholesaler," who chose and financed NGOs and other contractors to deliver specific assistance programs.

NGOs working in medical and public health fields often succeeded, because they worked with a cadre of Uzbekistan's professionals eager to learn about American medical technology and procedures, and not afraid to apply them. The American International Hospital Alliance sent in a team of architects and technicians to inspect Tashkent's largest hospital and discovered that the hospital's infection rates were "way too high" in large part due to the way the ventilation system worked. A World Vision ophthalmological team came with an aircraft containing a functioning laboratory and trained some Uzbek doctors on the aircraft, using cow eyes. The Uzbek doctors who talked to Sylvia Babus were excited about the hands-on training.

USAID was anxious to get official recognition and privileges for its NGOs and their staffs, as its programs depended upon them. USAID wanted the Government of Uzbekistan to sign an overall bilateral assistance agreement to this end and to regulate other issues regarding taxes, customs, and property. I finally had the opportunity to sign the agreement with Foreign Minister Saidkasymov, also on March 1, 1994.[56] Some nine NGO representatives, plus the Peace Corps director and U.S. embassy officers attended the signing. By the end of 1994 a dozen U.S. grantees and contractors were working from Tashkent, some with several employees.

About a year after we signed the agreement, the Foreign Ministry notified NGOs that the Cabinet of Ministers had adopted a decree to coordinate humanitarian aid programs. The decree gave staff of accredited organizations providing humanitarian and technical assistance a status equivalent to administrative and technical staff of diplomatic missions. It provided a stronger status than was provided in our bilateral agreement (which gave that status only to U.S. government personnel engaged in assistance programs), and it applied not only to American NGOs but also to all accredited foreign NGOs. The ministry's letter also affirmed that the bilateral Peace Corps Agreement of November 1992 would not be changed.

Of course there is nothing infallible about agreements—they may or may not be fully implemented, accreditation for individual NGOs can be withdrawn, agreements can be terminated. The assistance programs under the agreement could succeed or fail. Yet a framework for cooperation was in place by 1995. The Government of Uzbekistan had (1) recognized the need for foreign assistance, (2) offered protected status for those delivering it, and (3) perhaps unintended, allowed foreign examples of civil activity for domestic nonpolitical, nongovernmental organizations. These were important changes for Uzbekistan, even if they did not ensure deeper reforms.

Foreign Minister Saidmukhtar Saidkasymov and I answering questions from the press, following our signing of three agreements between the United States and Uzbekistan, on bilateral assistance, on diplomatic travel, and on a senior policy advisor, March 1, 1994.
Source: U.S. Embassy photo.

7

LOST ECONOMIC OPPORTUNITIES

A Nonmarket Economy Adrift

Uzbekistan in 1992 looked a lot like the Soviet Union without economic direction from Moscow. Huge factories for aircraft, tractors, and other goods struggled to produce products that someone would buy, without the guaranteed buyers given them by central planning. These factories had helped bring Central Asia into the industrial age and had helped win World War II, but they had never faced the discipline of realistic cost accounting. Shells of uncompleted buildings, intended for hotels or industrial projects, littered the countryside; it was said that the builders ran out of money, having claimed a large part of the funds in advance. Possible domestic funds for investment went to other purposes. Nor were there new business plans likely to attract foreign investors. Outside Tashkent, hundreds of once-refrigerated rail cars rusted in rail yards—a fleet that once supplied colder parts of the Soviet Union with tomatoes, melons, and other fresh produce. The capacity to grow them was still there, but the trade had become disorganized.

Small factories for modest consumer goods and service shops continued to meet at least some of the needs of ordinary people. A corner bakery next to our embassy, with a traditional dome-shaped oven, produced world-class traditional Uzbek bread (baked while stuck to the inside of the dome), available hot all day long. I thought it was delicious with American crunchy peanut butter, cheese, or almost any other snack or meal. Some families had smaller ovens in their courtyards and sold the bread to neighbors and passers-by.

Across the street from our embassy, a soup kitchen made *laghman*, a steaming hot and greaseless beef, vegetable, and noodle soup—another traditional Central Asian dish that made a delicious fast-food lunch for us. All too soon the shop was shut down for no apparent reason—maybe someone more powerful thought the tiny enterprise should serve a more important bureaucracy than our embassy. Or perhaps they just quit due to extortion, as discussed below.

Retail trade was just beginning a substantial transformation. Before independence, thanks to its climate and farmers, Uzbekistan's local food supplies were often more ample than in European parts of the USSR, even though this was not necessarily reflected in estimates of the standard of living. In 1992 large Soviet-style department stores in downtown Tashkent were still functioning, with many of the goods they had always carried, but the large traditional markets (and some new ones), which had always been—and remained—the best sources for fresh produce, began also selling imported goods.

As soon as I arrived, I learned to buy good Turkish beer by the case in the outdoor markets. Drinking the first can told me my assignment to Tashkent would be very different from my assignments to Moscow or Bucharest. Communism could not produce decent beer; only the Czechs, and to a lesser extent the East Germans and Poles, managed to hold on to precommunist standards and produce a good beer, which they exported for hard currency; so it was not available in other communist countries except in diplomatic and Communist Party stores. In post-Soviet Tashkent the variety of imports expanded until we could get many Chinese, Turkish, Iranian, and some European goods in the open markets as we needed them. (For some American foods the U.S. embassy had support flights from Germany.)

Consumers of manufactured goods were so poorly served in the Soviet Union, it is no wonder that with its collapse, existing small businesses—and unemployed individuals—tried to sell something in the markets, or simply by standing on the side of the road with a handful of goods. They weren't necessarily better products: I brought a bottle of fake Uzbek cognac that way—the bottle and label were authentic, but the dark liquid inside was neither alcohol nor drinkable. On close inspection, the metal cap appeared to be from Siberia, although similar to the caps used for real Uzbek cognac.

Killing Infant Businesses in their Cribs

What should have happened but generally didn't would have been the opening of many new types of small business to develop better consumer goods and services. We soon understood why: governmental controls and taxes could not have been better designed to discourage new businesses. The officials carrying out these tasks, not well paid themselves, saw each applicant for a new business as a target for extortion.

We got a detailed view of the near impossibility of sustaining a new business from the experience of a Peace Corps volunteer in Tashkent. His idea sounded both modest and certain to succeed: making, selling, and delivering pizzas to university students in their dormitories. He struggled for a long time before conceding defeat by the bleeding from the multitude of official leeches that latched on to him for bribes. But he did write up his experiences and shared a draft with us, so we could see just how a good business idea could become impossible, no matter how hard you tried.

Approaching taxes from a different direction, in July 1993 USAID brought in a team of tax experts to study the situation and advise USAID and the government on tax reform, headed by a former Turkish finance minister. The team traveled to several cities in Uzbekistan and conferred with numerous tax officials at various levels. Their leader conveyed his conclusion to me: tax reform in Uzbekistan was hopeless, because local officials could not accept that their job was to encourage business, rather than squeeze it to death. Most unacceptable to Uzbek tax officials, as I recall his briefing, was the increase in transparency and accountability that would come with any reform worthy of the name, because that would have threatened the officials' ability to skim off personal gains from taxes collected.

One of the first Peace Corps volunteers to be assigned to Bukhara lived with a local family near the old part of the city. He proposed that families with large homes be encouraged to open "bed and breakfast" lodging for tourists. Considering that Bukhara's state-owned hotels were shabby and located outside the attractive part of town, and considering that there were indeed homes near important tourist sites that had once belonged to merchants before the Russian Revolution, Bukhara was the perfect place for such an idea. Not much came of the idea during his two-year assignment, perhaps in part due to the local assumption that he was a spy. In Bukhara, this was a natural assumption, dating not just from the paranoia of the Soviet era, but even earlier, when Bukhara was a target for spies during the "Great Game" between the Russian and British Empires, a game sometimes won by the emir when he caught them.[57] Instead of encouraging small business to support the tourist business, to improve services as well as strengthen private ownership, during the early 1990s the Uzbekistan assets of the huge Soviet enterprise Intourist were reconstituted into a similar state firm, Uzbekturism.

What Goals for Uzbekistan's Economy?

Uzbekistan's leadership, with its Soviet education and experience, did not see the vast potential for economic growth and employment that could have come from the removal of official obstacles and vigorous encouragement of the formation of new small businesses. Year after year, this cumulative neglect of the economic potential of private small and medium business development probably represents Uzbekistan's greatest single forgone economic opportunity—not creating jobs nor a middle class with entrepreneurial know-how.

President Karimov's low opinion of the capacity of his countrymen to make economic or political judgments did not help. On the occasion when he suggested that I talk to villagers to see how ignorant they were, he went on to say that perhaps someday, when there were competent and successful private businessmen in Uzbekistan, it might be worthwhile for him to discuss the economy with them. Clearly he did not think Uzbekistan had reached that level, and as far as I could see there was little effort to move in that direction. If Uzbekistan's leadership neglected private economic development, perhaps it was in part because they did not really know how to do it.

The United States offered an institution to promote such a policy: the Central Asian–American Enterprise Fund, an idea that had already been introduced in the newly independent Baltic republics. Former U.S. representative Stephen Solarz, as chairman, led the initial visits to meet with President Karimov and obtain his support. The fund was launched with its headquarters in Tashkent. (My remarks at the opening are Appendix D.) Offices were opened in each Central Asian country, with Uzbekistan providing the largest number of clients. The Fund served them all, with direct investments, joint ventures, and loans for small and medium private businesses. Although the launch was successful, financing was not the only instrument needed to develop a vigorous private sector.

Whether from President Karimov or from other senior officials, I did not get the impression that they considered that the wealth of their country might best be measured by the wealth of its ordinary citizens, although they would agree that a standard of living like that of Western countries would be a good thing. Instead I sensed an assumption that a country's wealth depended more upon what its rulers could amass for public purposes. So the economic greatness of Uzbekistan would be somewhat like the glory of ancient Samarkand, reflected in the ruler's monuments or other public sector activities, not the standard of living of the people.

What counted for the former Soviet leaders was production—in Uzbekistan's case, especially cotton, gold, oil, gas, and grain. Producing more of those commodities either increased exports or reduced imports. Production reportedly rose in these commodities in 1994 without noticeable benefit to ordinary people, who paid higher prices for the goods they needed, as subsidies and price controls over food were removed. Removing those subsidies and price controls did, however, introduce more realistic markets, eventually providing more incentives to owners of private plots and even farms to produce the foods in greatest demand. It should have removed a burden from the public budget, but I had no insight into whether that reduced a deficit or merely freed funds for other purposes.

Control from the top continued to be a major goal for the economy, which meant that reform measures could only proceed slowly and cautiously. Uzbekistan did discuss economic reform measures with the World Bank and the International Monetary Fund, not so much with me. From time to time the IMF representative would brief interested ambassadors, including me. Yet despite my lack of details, it appeared to me that control over production and sales of cotton—a source of Uzbek complaints against the Soviet economic system—remained almost as controlled under Karimov as under Soviet central planning, to the disadvantage of farmers.

A paper prepared by the government of Uzbekistan for the World Bank Consultative Group Meeting in Paris on March 1, 1995, asserted that the use of state orders to control production and sale of cotton and other products was being reduced.[58] We did hear of occasional exceptions, such as a cotton mill in Karakalpakstan purchasing cotton from local farms in exchange for mill products. But it was not clear that a real market in cotton was functioning outside of the state orders. It seemed that decisions about other major crops, such as wheat, and mining and manufacturing production continued to be directed administratively, and not by market signals. Except in the open retail markets for food, the great Soviet economic inefficiencies in arbitrary pricing continued. With those handicaps, the economy remained inefficient and unresponsive to market-influenced changes and opportunities in the world economy.

In Search of a Sound Currency

Uzbekistan still used the Russian ruble in 1992, but its value dwindled fast with Russia's hyperinflation. Using cash in U.S. dollars became the best means to avoid losing money while you held it. Normally the State Department requires its embassies to pay foreign employee wages, rent, and other local bills in local currency, and the Soviet Union and many other countries also required it. Our embassy appealed to Washington for an exception, and got it, so our employees became among the few in Uzbekistan whose salaries and purchasing power could remain stable. Salaries in dollars made us a favorite place to work. For the rest of the population, the inflation was disastrous: pensions became worthless, salaries nearly so.

Uzbekistan had established a Central Bank and inherited a state banking system from the Soviet Union, but these institutions were helpless to control the ruble, which depended upon Russian banks and printing presses. In Russia the banking system was out of control. Uzbekistan and any other former Soviet republic that wanted to be economically independent, or even maintain economic stability, would have to establish its own currency. It was unclear to me whether Uzbekistan deliberately preferred to do that, or whether it just could not agree to Russia's terms for remaining in the ruble zone, or both. Yet within two years of independence Uzbekistan introduced its own currency, the som, in two stages: first, som coupons in November 1993, then the actual som in July 1994. Intentional or not, breaking away from the ruble zone gave Uzbekistan a major increase in economic independence.

The first step had to be a currency exchange, in which the Uzbek banks would provide som coupons in exchange for bank deposits or cash rubles. The Uzbekistan government, following the recent example of their Russian counterparts, could not resist the opportunity to steal from its citizens, as a way to help absorb a big overhang of useless rubles. So they refused to exchange the first 200 rubles that each citizen had on deposit. Given ruinous inflation in the ruble, people did not keep a lot of ruble deposits. But most people had a bank account. Those under 200 rubles were simply wiped out. People whose tiny salaries or pensions couldn't really support them were the hardest hit.

I called on the chairman of the Central Bank to confirm the terms of the exchange, which he did. I told him this was confiscation—conducting the country's monetary policy at the expense of the poorest people. The chairman denied it, looking very uncomfortable, but he couldn't explain how an ordinary citizen could make up for the loss of his 200 rubles. The amount was not huge—the wealthy were untouched—but too many people in Uzbekistan had no more than that in cash at any one time. Here was another small modern example of what Karl Marx would have called "oriental despotism." It showed me that the formerly communist leadership of Uzbekistan had no more respect for ordinary people under Karimov's system than they did under Soviet rule.

In 1994 and 1995 Uzbekistan allowed limited but effective convertibility of the som. From my perspective, it worked: by being willing to sell dollars and other foreign currencies for som, the banking system provided an alternative to the black market (though not at the same rate) and psychological support for the value of the som.

It was a huge boon to everyone in Uzbekistan to have reason to believe that their money would actually buy what they needed, not just today, but next week or next month. It also meant that larger companies could plan their foreign trade. Newmont Mining expected to be paid in gold, but practically any other international company, or any Uzbek enterprise engaged in foreign trade, needed a basis for anticipating the value of their currency.

Foreign Investment

Three of the main attractions for foreign companies to come to Uzbekistan in 1992–95 were (a) Tashkent's central location in former Soviet Central Asia with ease of transportation to the other four states; (b) specific resources, including underemployed literate populations, especially in Tashkent and the Fergana Valley; and (c) the hope of stable, investment-friendly policies, including the right to repatriate capital. The last was problematic, given Uzbekistan's relatively limited experience with the capitalist world and its tendency to reject outside advice. But I thought that even without genuine reforms, Uzbekistan could—as less-developed countries had done in other parts of the world—have a leading, mainly foreign-owned export sector. Examples of profitability in the foreign sector could perhaps eventually lead to greater receptivity to reforms in the rest of the economy. Local purchases by foreign firms would strengthen local producers.

Uzbekistan's officials did welcome international investment. First Deputy Minister of Foreign Economic Relations Sadyk Safaev and I signed the first formal agreement between the United States and Uzbekistan on October 28, 1992, which permitted the Overseas Private Investment Corporation (OPIC) to insure direct American investments.[59] The Uzbek side accepted the standard American draft, so there was practically no negotiation. The OPIC agreement could not guarantee a successful investment, but it could help protect an American investor from downside risks of political instability, and such agreements had given U.S. businesses confidence to proceed with investments in many developing countries.

At the signing of the Investment Incentive Agreement on October 28, 1992, the first formal agreement between the United States and Uzbekistan. Left to right: Political Officer Daria Fane, Ambassador Henry Clarke, Public Affairs Officer Jerry Verner, Deputy Chief of Mission Michael Matera, and First Deputy Minister of Foreign Economic Relations Sadyk Safaev. Source: Author's collection.

The United States continued to build up its full range of instruments to promote trade and investment. Deputy Prime Minister Utkur Sultanov and I signed an Agreement on Trade Relations on November 5, 1993,[60] chiefly to permit U.S. Export-Import Bank, Commodity Credit Corporation, and other official export financing to operate in Uzbekistan, which was important to match European or Japanese export financing for major equipment and aircraft.

Director General for Civil Aviation Gani Rafikov, who was also head of Uzbekistan Airways, alerted me early in my assignment to Tashkent that Uzbekistan Airways wanted to fly directly from Tashkent to New York and was interested in buying long-range aircraft. The long-range Soviet aircraft Uzbekistan inherited from Aeroflot were too fuel-inefficient to operate competitively. Boeing was interested, too. For the new route we needed a bilateral civil aviation agreement, and Uzbekistan Airways in Tashkent would need clearance from the Federal Aviation Administration (FAA) certifying that it was technically qualified to support the route. Sadyk Safaev had been promoted to foreign minister, and he and I exchanged notes on March 31, 1993, agreeing that the terms of the U.S.-Soviet Civil Air Transport Agreement would "continue to remain in force" between Uzbekistan and the United States.[61]

In December 1994 an FAA team visited Tashkent and briefed me on their results. Unlike maintenance facilities that had belonged to Aeroflot in some other cities, Uzbekistan Airways' main maintenance facility at the Tashkent airport was fully qualified to support flights to the United States. Not long thereafter, Uzbekistan Airways began scheduled service to New York using Boeing aircraft. The airline also set up routes to Europe, the Middle East, and South Asia. In addition to the Boeings, they bought aircraft from Airbus, using their Soviet-built aircraft on shorter routes.

In 1994 and 1995 an increasing flow of foreign companies visited Uzbekistan, looking for trade and investment opportunities. Though many of the visits were just exploratory, I was optimistic that more U.S. companies would decide to come back and stay.

The earliest investments were showing the way. Newmont Mining's operation was producing gold around the clock. A large gas-injection project was underway in Kokdumalak, for which the U.S. company M.W. Kellogg was building huge compressors, supported by J.P. Morgan financing and Eximbank guarantees. In addition to the substantial U.S. (and Japanese) exports, this was a promising step toward greater energy independence for Uzbekistan, as I noted in my remarks at the signing ceremony (see Appendix E).

Other countries were investing, too. I visited a new Turkish-owned factory producing American-style blue jeans in a cotton-growing part of Karakalpakstan, which seemed to prove that manufacturing consumer goods could be a worthy goal for foreign investment. A South Korean automobile manufacturer, Daewoo, constructed a factory and began producing cars and vans in Andijan, in the Fergana Valley. Although the Valley was intensely developed for agriculture, it also had a high birth rate and high unemployment. When I left Uzbekistan at the end of September 1995,

I felt confident that this was only the beginning of economic growth led by foreign investment.

The year 1996, unfortunately, changed that. Faced with declining world prices for gold and cotton, the Government of Uzbekistan lost its nerve and ended convertibility of the som. What had been a growing flow of international companies visiting Tashkent soon slowed to a trickle, according to comments to me by my successor in Tashkent, Ambassador Stan Escudero. In meetings of the Uzbekistan-American Chamber of Commerce in Washington, which I attended for several years, Uzbek officials would try to explain that their currency controls should not deter new investments, but skepticism prevailed among businessmen.

As Uzbekistan's reputation for corruption has grown, so has this obstacle to business relationships, especially long-term investments. The U.S. Foreign Corrupt Practices Act makes demands for bribes a tangible obstacle for American companies, which can also cause foreign-based multinational corporations with important operations in the United States to become cautious. It became especially hard for a company that was new to Uzbekistan to calculate its risks, when for example President Karimov's daughter was widely believed to be a major source of corrupt demands.

Ownership and Privatization

From an American perspective, the obvious cure for inefficient, unprofitable state-owned enterprises would be privatization—except that it must be *successful* privatization. Privatization can also fail, due to mistakes by the seller or the buyer. Knowledgeable people with a sound plan must be the ones to buy the enterprise, and their market-oriented, decentralized decisions must be more efficient and profitable than decisions made under government ownership. In most cases, the buyers must also have substantial capital resources, beyond the purchase price, to invest in new equipment or facilities and for working capital. I did not sense that senior Uzbek officials, none of whom had studied or experienced how market economies work, had confidence that privatization would work. Their natural assumption would be that the most knowledgeable potential buyers would be the people already running the plant, so how could an outsider make better decisions? Yet some officials also expected that there would be some kind of windfall financial benefits at the time of sale.

The example being set by privatization in Russia was not inspiring, although I had not had the opportunity to follow it closely. Huge enterprises were being sold right and left without much planning or discrimination, under the concept of "shock therapy," and new private oligopolies were replacing state-owned monopolies. Vast personal wealth was created for some buyers. Slogans were passed around that even then sounded absurd, but some Americans accepted them, such as, "It is better to sell an enterprise to criminals than to leave it in state hands." It seemed to me that some of the most basic concepts of economic analysis—such as competition, due diligence, and transparent information—were being ignored. When President Karimov said, "No shock therapy," I remained silent, because on this point he was preaching to the converted. But would there be *any* therapy to create a market economy for Uzbekistan?

Craig Buck, the USAID director for Central Asia, resident in Almaty but a frequent visitor to Tashkent, had the unenviable task of introducing privatization to Uzbekistan. Our designated senior counterpart for the subject was Deputy Prime Minister Chzhen, a citizen of Uzbekistan from the Korean minority.[62] Craig and I met with Chzhen for a lengthy meeting, and Craig may have seen him more often. Rarely have I ever met such a high official who managed to convince me so quickly that we could not work with him. As I saw it, privatization was a very complicated process, both technically and economically, and without trust or common goals it would be a disaster. Craig was more patient than I was, but it did not take him much longer to conclude that we did not have an effective counterpart to work with. Perhaps Chzhen's instructions were just that—make sure it didn't happen.

Nevertheless, some small-scale privatization did take place during the mid-1990s. USAID-financed Price Waterhouse experts organized the first auction of about a dozen miscellaneous enterprises and buildings, including some restaurants and cafes, in the town of Namangan in the Fergana Valley on March 4, 1994, and I was glad to attend. To get buyers in the right spirit, traditional

Uzbek outdoor instruments—*karnai* and *surnai* horns and a big drum—welcomed all of us to the auditorium. A few of the bidders were indeed managers of the enterprises, including one poor fellow who bid far more than he could afford, so his purchase was not finalized. Except for one or two unfinished buildings, most of the enterprises were sold. The auction process was not complex and was as transparent as one could expect for Central Asia. The USAID contract called for similar auctions in some fourteen Uzbekistan towns in the following months and years. I did not have occasion to find out whether the privatized firms were successful, but the bidders believed they would be, even though they faced the same sort of obstacles as other new enterprises.

Another hopeful policy change occurred while I worked in Tashkent: privatization of apartments to their occupants. Like other major Soviet cities, housing was in short supply. So there was some official hesitation when it became obvious that prices would rise sharply. Nevertheless, privatization went forward. Many ordinary families benefited, and a real estate market developed. For families that were emigrating to Russia or elsewhere it was a boon, and for young families that stayed it was an opportunity to obtain their own housing.

During my assignment to Tashkent the large state enterprises remained in state hands, and Uzbekistan paid a price for that. Some state enterprises died, others limped along for years. Some could have been revitalized or given completely new functions, had there been a serious international privatization process, with favorable terms for qualified investors, supported by the national leadership.

The former bank of the Aral Sea and the desert it left behind, near Muynak, Karakalpakstan, November 1992. Source: Author's photo.

8

WATER, AIR, AND KARAKALPAKSTAN

If the most awesome manmade sight in Uzbekistan is its ancient Muslim architecture, the second-most awesome manmade sight is the desert left behind by the drastic shrinking of the Aral Sea, with its original banks and scattered windswept hulks of former fishing boats. After there were no more fish to process from the Aral Sea, the cannery near its southern bank near Muynak processed ocean fish for a time before being abandoned. The drying up of the Aral Sea may not be the greatest environmental disaster caused by Soviet planning and engineering—it would be a candidate—but it may be the most irreversible disaster caused by Soviet agriculture.

The climate and geography of Uzbekistan reminded me of California's Central Valley. Melting snow in the mountains of Kyrgyzstan and Tajikistan flows into two major rivers, the Syr Darya and the Amu Darya, which cross Uzbekistan, Turkmenistan, and Kazakhstan to the Aral Sea, once a large inland sea. Most of the wide varieties of crops that make California's Central Valley prosperous also grow in Uzbekistan. Both agricultural areas are former deserts, completely dependent upon irrigation.

The analogy stops there. California's farms are privately owned, free to grow whatever crops are most profitable for the owner, and the owner is free to use agricultural and irrigation practices that will best preserve his land and future profitability. Uzbekistan's state and collective farms were overwhelmingly required to grow cotton, a crop that uses large amounts of water even when managed well. Central planning also obliged farms to maximize each year's production, thus severely discouraging fallow or rotating crops and requiring excessive amounts of fertilizer and other chemicals. When the soil became too salty or chemical-laden, more water was used to flush it out—back into the river, or in some cases into special canals for polluted runoff into the desert.

The Russian Empire began developing irrigated cotton in Uzbekistan during the American Civil War, when obtaining cotton became difficult due to the blockade of Confederate ports. Development took on a vast scale after the Russian Revolution, as the Central Planning Committee pressed forward with the concept of Soviet economic self-sufficiency. New canals were dug, new villages established, and new farmland claimed from the deserts. As decades passed, the water of the two rivers declined severely in both quantity and quality: little reached the Aral Sea, which became heavily polluted. Over the years, the water table under the cotton fields rose from extreme depths—I seem to recall as much as 40 meters below the surface—to the surface itself, where it evaporated and left salts. The water that used to form the Aral Sea became groundwater in the irrigated areas of Uzbekistan, Kazakhstan, and Turkmenistan. The sea itself dried up, until there were only remnants left, no longer a sea.[63]

The biplane we used to fly from Nukus to Muynak and to overfly the desert where the Aral Sea used to be, November 1992.
Source: Author's photo.

Experts in Uzbekistan understood all this well in the early 1990s—if there were ever a point I didn't know or understand, I could always ask Professor Viktor Dukhovny, an expert in Tashkent who helped introduce me to the subject and was always ready to explain it. USAID and the World Bank studied Central Asian water management and organized conferences, but the costs of reversing the problems arising from irrigated cotton were considered astronomical. We saw no sign that the Government of Uzbekistan wanted to reduce cotton production—the crop that had always been the mainstay of the republic's total output, exports, and income. For a brief period in the early 1990s the government promoted growing wheat—but not at the expense of cotton (much of Uzbekistan's modest wheat production comes from hilly land that is not irrigated). It is hard to justify using a scarce and valuable resource like fresh water to refill a dry seabed in the desert, and no attempt was made to do that in Uzbekistan in the 1990s.

Instead, USAID and other donors began to examine the health of the Karakalpaks, who live along the final portions of the Amu Darya River, south of what was once the Aral Sea. (Karakalpakstan had been an Autonomous Soviet Socialist Republic and retained a similar autonomous status within independent Uzbekistan.) Among other maladies, surveys of public health and sanitation found dangerously high levels of anemia, high infant mortality from intestinal infections (including typhoid and diarrhea), and cancer of the esophagus. As the sea receded, dust storms increased, and there were even salt storms from the seabed. Although Nukus, the capital, had a plant for treating water from the river, in other parts of Karakalpakstan bacteria and pesticides contaminated the water. Villagers could boil drinking water to kill bacteria, but the pesticides even turned up in mothers' milk. Questions arose about whether villages and their agriculture could be sustained in some areas. For rural Karakalpaks, it wasn't just a shortage of clean water—salt and chemicals contaminated the air they breathed and the food they ate.

My first trip to Karakalpakstan, in November 1992, was mainly to Nukus, and from there via biplane to Muynak and to the edge of the Aral Sea. As everywhere else in Uzbekistan, the official hospitality was great, especially at dinner, with traditional music and dancers. As guest of honor, I was given the roasted sheep's head. Fortunately, an official coached me on how to deal with it—where the good parts were (notably the back of the neck), and how to share pieces with others at the head table before indulging myself. It was fun—and tasted good too.

In Nukus in 1992 you could sense how remote Karakalpakstan was: not remote from Uzbekistan, but from the rest of the former Soviet Union and the world. This remoteness enabled Nukus to preserve an impressive quantity of some of the best Soviet art of the 1920s and 1930s from Stalin's efforts to stamp it out—in Nukus the paintings were literally out of sight. Aware of this patrimony, our Karakalpak hosts made sure we (and other visitors) visited the Karakalpak Museum of the Arts. I was astonished by the story, and by the Savitsky Collection of Russian impressionists and avant-garde art. Over the following months and years the museum director visited collections in Russia and western countries and engaged in exchanges of exhibits, including one to the United States arranged by USIS in Tashkent.

USAID financed two projects in Karakalpakstan in 1993 and 1994: a study of the causes of anemia, carried out in Muynak District, and an assessment of the need for a water and sanitation education program for Karakalpakstan and Khorezm Oblast (the major jurisdiction in Uzbekistan just south of Karakalpakstan). Both studies were concluded rather quickly with recommendations for next steps. The anemia was found to be caused by poor nutrition, and thus not difficult to correct through education, dietary changes, and supplemental vitamins and iron.[64]

USAID then launched a dual project, one to improve water quality and the other an environmental education program, for Karakalpakstan and the Khorezm Oblast. A memorandum of understanding on this project had five signatures: one each for Uzbekistan, Karakalpakstan, Khorezm, the USAID director, and Michael Matera as chargé d'affaires of the U.S. embassy (in my absence).[65] USAID wanted a lot of details to ensure the cooperation and active support of all of these levels of government.

Under this project, USAID provided laboratory equipment to water treatment plants in Nukus and in Urgench, the capital of

Khorezm Oblast, to enable the plants to analyze water quality in real time. For the first time they could catch pollution problems as they came into the treatment plant, and not after they were already distributed into the water supply. I joined some American water experts in March 1995 traveling to Nukus and Urgench, where we found the laboratories were putting the equipment to good use.

The phenomenon of the disappearing Aral Sea, highlighted in Al Gore's 1992 book on the environment, *Earth in the Balance,* became increasingly well known. The first congressional delegation after my arrival, including Senators Paul Simon, Harry Reid, Hank Brown, and their wives, came to Uzbekistan in June 1993 to visit the Aral Sea, or at least where it had been. A group of us flew up to Nukus the day before to meet them there: U.S. ambassador to Kazakhstan William Courtney and his wife, USAID executive Paula Feeney; Central Asian expert Nancy Lubin; Embassy Tashkent's general services officer George Kent, and several local staff from our embassy to help with arrangements and interpretation.

Four young women in traditional dress brought out the traditional bread and salt to honor the senators on their arrival in Nukus. We flew in AN-2 biplanes to Muynak and over some of the expanse of the dry bottom of the former Aral Sea. The senators could have found less arduous destinations for their overseas travel, yet they were interested in and knowledgeable about water management issues in the American West. Water was Central Asia's most critical natural resource, and the Aral Sea illustrated its biggest environmental problem, so I found their effort encouraging.

The Soviet Union had used Vozrozhdeniya Island—which had been in the middle of the Aral Sea—for biological warfare research and experiments. As the sea dried up, the "island" became just another part of the desert, and no one I spoke to knew what had happened to the animals, insects and microbes that had been subject to research there. Although the desert was forbidding, it no longer provided the former island the same kind of isolation that the Aral Sea had. Lacking expert opinions on the potential risks, I made no attempt to visit there—the only part of Uzbekistan I avoided and did not encourage my staff to visit. After the end of my assignment, the United States did provide an expert assessment and assisted Uzbekistan with cleanup.

Sadly, environmental issues elsewhere in Uzbekistan were generally not addressed at all in the early 1990s. Tashkent's own water supply was contaminated, not from the source, but from polluted groundwater being drawn into the water distribution pipes, which were cracked and broken from age and earthquakes. There was also a shortage of chlorine. Bottled water generally came from the same pipes as tap water, so we had to boil water for drinking and preparing food.

My favorite Sunday escape in the winter was to drive my Neva to Chimgan and Baldersai, in the mountains not far from Tashkent, for skiing. From up high on the slopes of Baldersai, where there was often deep snow and bright sunshine, I could look down on the brownish smoggy clouds covering the plain from Chirchik to Tashkent and beyond. It reminded me of the ski slopes above Brasov, Romania, which overlooked the same brownish smog of Brasov city. I could see what more than 2 million people in Tashkent and surrounding towns were breathing, and what I too would be breathing for the rest of the week.

For sheer horror, nothing topped the story an environmental scientist told me. In a town near Tashkent there was a Soviet Defense Ministry plant producing rocket fuel, surrounded by Uzbek homes. The families living there invariably became sick and died from breathing the poisonous smoke from the plant. It was not a matter of contracting a long-term disease like cancer—they died directly from exposure to the poison in their air. For a period of years the scientist would document the mortality and try to close the plant, but the Defense Ministry in Moscow was impervious—they needed the output of rocket fuel from the plant, regardless of what happened to the local people, including the plant's own workers. Finally the plant did close, and the scientist considered it his greatest achievement. But he was not in a position to know whether the ministry even needed the fuel, and if they did, how they replaced it.

My last trip as ambassador to Uzbekistan was again to Nukus, Karakalpakstan, for an International Conference on Sustainable Development of the Aral Sea Basin, sponsored by the United Nations Development Program and by Central Asia's own Interstate Council for the Aral Sea, September 19–21, 1995, only a few days before my departure from Uzbekistan.

If international attention alone could solve such problems, then the problem of the Aral Sea would have been solved. We had a letter of best wishes from Vice President Al Gore, who had visited the area some years before becoming vice president. Washington sent Ambassador-designate (for Pakistan) Tom Simons, a career officer whom I had known in previous assignments, as chief of the American delegation to the conference.

Four Central Asian presidents were on hand—Karimov, Nazarbayev from Kazakhstan, Rakhmonov from Tajikistan, and Akayev from Kyrgyzstan—who all signed a Nukus Declaration on the Aral Sea Basin. The absence of Turkmenistan's President Niyazov was notable, because the Amu Darya and the Kara Kum Canal provide large amounts of water for irrigation, and the Amu Darya collects pollutants in its long journey across Turkmenistan before reaching Uzbekistan.

For me the most colorful and memorable event did not take place at the meetings. It was watching the horseracing of the Central Asia Horse Festival, held in Nukus at the same time.

After the signing, the presidents went home, and Tom Simons and I returned to Tashkent on President Karimov's aircraft. Then Deputy Chief of Mission Sharon White took over the job of looking after Simons and his schedule, so I could turn my attention to packing out.

9

MILITARY CONTACTS OPEN UP

Access

In 1992 the U.S. military had few contacts with the new Uzbekistan military. An assistant defense attaché at the U.S. Embassy in Moscow became accredited as a defense attaché in Tashkent and visited from time to time. But he had difficulty meeting with counterparts beyond the protocol level at the Defense Ministry. Normally, a defense attaché discusses defense issues with officers in the host country's military and visits military sites or exercises that are not secret, such as training facilities.

Visiting U.S. military officers and embassy officers sometimes had better luck than the accredited defense attaché. Sylvia Babus accompanied a U.S. Air Force colonel on a visit to the Combined Arms Academy in Tashkent, where they met with the faculty. At the brand new Uzbekistan Air Force Academy, the commandant told Sylvia that during his efforts to get ideas for the academy from former Soviet Air Force colleagues, he was told, "But you know, Uzbek boys can't fly." He assured her that they can and said the academy was receiving ten applicants for every student position. One National War College group was able to visit a military driving school in Samarkand and met with Defense Minister Akhmedov in Tashkent while I was not in Uzbekistan. Yet acceptance and access remained difficult for the accredited attaché.

The U.S. Defense Intelligence Agency (DIA), headquarters for American defense attachés worldwide, was eager to assign a defense attaché and staff to our embassy, to be resident in Tashkent. I welcomed military-to-military contacts, and I welcomed having an officer on my staff who would have frequent meetings with defense counterparts. But neither seemed possible without better access. I tried to meet with the defense minister, as a way to explore what might be possible, and was turned down—one of the very few appointments that I was denied in Uzbekistan.

I knew establishing relations with Uzbekistan's defense establishment might be important to the United States someday, but I initially thought this could not be my highest priority. From a strategic perspective, the most unstable countries in the region that could affect Uzbekistan were Afghanistan and Tajikistan. Yet Washington did not consider the situation in either country to be a matter of U.S. national security concern, as I have described in chapter 3. That, in turn, suggested to me that the U.S. would not have any operational military need to work with Uzbekistan, except perhaps to evacuate our embassy, or, as already happened in October 1992, to help evacuate U.S. Embassy Dushanbe in a crisis.

The Turkish Embassy in Tashkent had a resident Turkish Army colonel as defense attaché. As the first NATO defense attaché resident in Tashkent, he had been appointed (apparently by NATO headquarters) to take the lead among NATO defense attachés for Uzbekistan. Yet even he had difficulty meeting with counterparts or visiting installations. At the end of his assignment in 1994, he called on me and said bluntly that Tashkent had been the worst two years of his military career, because there had been nothing to do.

My skepticism toward establishing a resident U.S. defense attaché became opposition, so long as we had so little he could do. The last thing I needed was an energetic American officer with no legitimate official contacts other than the Defense Ministry's Protocol Office.

During 1992–93, when Uzbekistan was genuinely concerned about spillover from the war in Tajikistan, and when Russia and Uzbekistan provided some military support to the government of Tajikistan, I would really have welcomed the advice of a U.S. military officer. Yet if he had no authorized contacts with the Uzbekistan military other than the Protocol Office, I could not imagine him sitting on his hands in Tashkent. I was not moved by the fact that we had defense attachés in Kazakhstan and Tajikistan, because I believed that they had been given more access and had more clearly defined and important goals in those countries.

Overcoming the Obstacle

Then we got our breakthrough, straight from the top. I called on President Karimov on September 16, 1994, to introduce our new deputy chief of mission, Sharon White, who would soon take charge of our embassy while I traveled to Washington for consultations and some leave with my family. To my surprise, Karimov complained that the U.S. should do more to show support for Uzbekistan's independence—the U.S. didn't even have a defense attaché in Tashkent! I quickly pointed out that in presenting my credentials to the president two years earlier, I had emphasized American support for Uzbekistan's independence, and we still supported that. But our military had no access at all to ranking Uzbekistan officers. I could meet with the president himself, but I was not allowed to meet his defense minister. Karimov usually showed little emotion, but he was clearly shocked to hear this, and that gave me hope that our access would change.

Not long afterward I found some excuse to invite Defense Minister Rustam Akhmedov along with others to a lunch at my residence. While the two of us were talking, away from the tables, he said that denying access to him was not his idea; the meetings had been blocked by the president's own staff. I do not know who did what or how, but I can guess. Our requests for a meeting, or a visit, or a social invitation, went to the Protocol Office of the Ministry—staffed mainly, perhaps exclusively, by secret police wearing army uniforms. They would check with their secret police superiors, very likely represented in the president's staff, and the event would be turned down routinely without anyone informing the busy president.

I was eager to see whether we could make a turnaround in access, or if, after a few courtesies, we would go back to being frozen out. I made an office call on the minister, and we began discussing a closer military-to-military relationship. During the following months, the idea of a visit by Secretary of Defense William J. Perry began to take shape, linked to his planned visit to Kazakhstan.

In late January 1995, the U.S. Army sent us Brigadier General Dale R. Nelson, a first-class diplomat, and the Defense Ministry made it a good visit. The best parts were, of course, not the obligatory formal meetings, but outside them.

The highlight of that visit for me was the Tank Training School in Chirchik, not far from Tashkent. I had served as a tank platoon leader in the 3rd Armored Cavalry in Germany and wanted to see how the Soviets trained their tank crews. We always imagined the Soviets must have harsh training—but in Chirchik the tank firing positions were covered with a roof! Although the targets were outside, barely visible in the falling snow, the crews weren't! I don't think the U.S. Army ever covered our tanks on a firing range, certainly not against rain or snow (wet or cold soldiers and equipment were considered part of "good training"). In winter we had to worry about the tanks being stuck, if the mud froze around their tracks where they (and we) were standing, yet under the roof during the snowfall the Chirchik crews had dry earth and no mud to freeze.

The Chirchik barracks were simple, but they were barracks. At Grafenwoehr, our best tank gunnery range in Germany, thirty years before, we had slept in tents with coal heaters that in cold weather emitted thick, foul smoke while we slept and coughed. Despite electric lights, the smoke was so thick we could barely see the crews going in and out for night gunnery. Surely the Soviet tank crews experienced more real conditions when they went for field training. American tank crews would never trade their tanks for Soviet models, neither for performance in combat nor for comfort during training. But despite my nostalgia as a former tanker, as a diplomat I said nothing about these comparisons.

Dinner at the Tank Training School started out a bit stiff—the senior Uzbekistan Army officers, mostly of European origin, with their blazing red and gold (formerly Soviet) uniforms on one side of the table, our officers in their dark green class A uniforms on the other, and all sorts of *zakuski* between them. Then, with a little help from the vodka, the magic of military-to-military contacts began. The generals discovered that not many years before, they were stationed on opposite sides of the East German border, preparing for World War III against each other. They talked about the Fulda Gap, their efforts to learn about each other's capabilities and personnel. They even recognized opposing commanders' names. The conversation became more than courtesy; there was humor, and respect, and goodwill. The hospitality that I saw so often in Uzbekistan now extended to our military, and it came from theirs.

The SecDef Visit

By the end of March 1995, we were in the final stages of planning for Secretary of Defense Perry's visit. An issue for the embassy was the size of the entourage—he was coming in a Boeing 747. There would be more passengers on board than we could possibly accommodate at either my residence or the U.S. embassy chancery for a welcome briefing. The biggest room we had was the embassy atrium, where we could clear out some of the office furniture and partitions, and use folding chairs. So I made a decision that was to prove very unpopular with most of our visitors—we could have two or three dozen key visitors in the embassy, and the rest would go to the hotel to settle in, since it would already be early evening. Somehow, however, the busloads of people who did not attend the briefing wound up waiting outside the Embassy, in their buses, adding insult to injury. The secretary and his immediate staff were too nice to complain; I learned about it later from others.

The next day, April 6, was devoted to the secretary's program. In the car, Secretary Perry asked me whether I could agree to a defense attaché. I said yes—now that we were getting good access. As far as I could see the Government of Uzbekistan was doing all it could to make the visit work well. Offering to send a defense attaché to Tashkent, and to receive one in Washington, gave Secretary Perry something to propose, and when the Uzbeks agreed to it, something specific to announce.

In his first meeting, with Foreign Minister Kamilov and Defense Minister Akhmedov, Secretary Perry outlined an agenda for bilateral cooperation between his Defense Department and the Ministry of Defense (MOD). This included modest amounts of training for Uzbek officers in the United States, the possibility of an American military consultant on restructuring the MOD, and creating a bilateral working group from specific members of each side. Assistant SecRetary Ashton Carter or one of his deputies would lead the U.S. side. Perry suggested the group could discuss conversion of defense industries to civilian use, the process for Uzbekistan's participation in NATO's Partnership for Peace, and bilateral exchanges. Akhmedov suggested that the first meeting be held in Tashkent on May 8, to coincide with the celebration of Victory in Europe (an attractive idea, but the meeting took place a month later). Perry invited Akhmedov to the U.S. in the fall.

The positive bilateral atmosphere continued during Secretary Perry's meeting with President Karimov. Karimov painted a lengthy and sometimes colorful picture of the many differences between Uzbekistan's policies and those of other former Soviet republics, especially in Central Asia—emphasizing Uzbekistan's stability and its insistence upon independence, and contrasting that with what he saw as most other leaders' acceptance of Russian hegemony, including Russian control of their borders. Karimov also expressed his concerns about Iran, and about Turkmenistan as a "launching pad" for Iran in Central Asia. He expressed appreciation for the potential value of domestic economic and political reforms in Uzbekistan, and said Uzbekistan would pursue them, but also stressed the need to be cautious, using his familiar line, "Don't destroy the old house before you build the new one." He said he was jealous of Akhmedov's trip to the United States. Uzbekistan would place a part of its gold reserves in New York, and part in Europe.

Secretary Perry emphasized that three countries would be the most critical for maintaining independence (from Russia): Uzbekistan, Ukraine, and Kazakhstan, because loss of independence of any one of the three could make it more difficult to retain for the others. Karimov replied that Perry's words about independence "have given me an infusion of new strength." Those words impressed me too: it was the first time I heard a top American official rank Uzbekistan's independence along with Ukraine's and Kazakhstan's in importance.

At the end of the meetings, Secretary Perry held a press conference, a transcript of which is Appendix C below.

We then flew to Samarkand for the lighter part of the trip—Secretary Perry visiting Registan Square and drinking green tea at the front of the central madrasa, wearing his Samarkand robe and black and silver Uzbek hat that the local authorities had just given him. Then we flew back to Tashkent, and the secretary left in his 747.

The U.S.-Uzbekistan relationship on defense and military matters had come a long way from near zero. It had become a positive influence on the overall relationship. Even though the substance behind the goodwill was still modest, there were now practical steps to discuss and implement.

U.S. Secretary of Defense William Perry and I, drinking green tea in front of the Tilla-Kari Madrasa, built 1646-47, in Registan Square, Samarkand, April 6, 1995. Secretary Perry added a note when he sent me this picture: "Ambassador Henry Clarke, where is your robe?" Source: U.S. Department of Defense photo.

Escorts to Termez and Dushanbe

Secretary Perry's visit did not end our defense diplomacy. In May, when I asked about visiting Termez, on the border with Afghanistan, on my way to Dushanbe, Tajikistan, Defense Minister Akhmedov offered to take me to Termez in his aircraft. After we landed, we had a rather ceremonial meeting at the Termez State University in the city. We visited the bridge over the Amu Darya to Afghanistan, and then watched Uzbekistan fighter aircraft practice landings at a nearby airbase. After lunch at the base, I said goodbye to Minister Akhmedov and journeyed onward, up the valley of the Surkhandarya River in my official car.

The minister, uncomfortable that I was traveling alone with my Uzbek driver, provided a guide to make sure I reached the U.S. Embassy in Dushanbe safely. The guide pointed out some interesting sightseeing features along our route. But when we reached the U.S. Embassy and he saw the metal detector, he suddenly declined to go in, and said goodbye to me outdoors. I had traveled with him for several hours, and I had not realized that he was armed. Surprised, the most I could think to say was thanks for his assistance.

Multilateral and Bilateral Contacts Increase

By the early nineties, NATO, a Cold War institution that had suddenly succeeded beyond its most optimistic hopes, found a line of applicants for membership forming among the former member states of the Warsaw Pact. Some former republics of the Soviet Union were interested in contacts with NATO too, ranging from hopes for membership among the Baltic States, to deep skepticism among some others. The Russian military was particularly alarmed by the prospect of NATO's enlargement. NATO wanted to establish a positive relationship with Russia without closing out its growing cooperation with the rest of Eurasia. So it established the Partnership for Peace, a way NATO members could conduct multilateral military relationships, including exercises and maneuvers, with nonmember countries.

Uzbekistan signed up for Partnership for Peace (P4P). It had earlier set up a diplomatic mission in Brussels to deal with Belgium, NATO, and the European Union, so it had its own means to coordinate participation in P4P with NATO staff, and did not rely on embassies in Tashkent. Uzbekistan chose an appropriately modest exercise as one of its first efforts to take part in P4P—sending an army platoon to small-unit exercises in Fort Polk, Louisiana. I had never been there, but my father had trained at Camp Polk on the eve of World War II and had declared it "a miserable place," even though it was less than fifty miles from the small town where he grew up. He wasn't specific, but I imagined humidity, mud or dust, swamps and mosquitoes, even alligators and rattlesnakes. I cautioned Defense Minister Akhmedov that although Louisiana would not have higher summer temperatures than Uzbekistan, it would have humidity approaching 100 percent. He had already heard about that. He said he was sending a very tough platoon. Since there was practically no humidity in Uzbekistan in the summer, he required the platoon to do their pushups and other calisthenics on asphalt, while it was sprayed with water to create lots of vapor. It sounded logical to me, and I am sure they did fine. Tashkent's Russian-language newspaper *Narodnoe Slova* proudly but briefly reported on September 7, 1995, that the Uzbekistan platoon was "in America with dignity."

Predictably, the Pentagon did not drop the ball either. Assistant Secretary of Defense Ashton Carter came to Tashkent in June 1995 to inaugurate the bilateral defense working group. Deputy Assistant Secretary of Defense Elizabeth Sherwood visited in August 1995 for further talks. President Karimov invited all the resident ambassadors in Uzbekistan on a trip to his new country house outside Tashkent, and included her in the group. The newly arrived British ambassador and I were seated at the head table, and unlike most of the ambassadors present, I had several opportunities to speak with the president.

In short, the United States got the access we needed for a dialogue with Uzbekistan on defense issues—not just for a full-time resident defense attaché, but also for our Defense Department and our embassy. The breakthrough came at a time of minimal tension, at no cost to other issues, and the Uzbeks began learning how to deal with our defense establishment.

10

STAFFING UP

Creating—and Filling—State Department Positions

While still working in Tel Aviv, but starting to prepare to become ambassador in Tashkent, I had a telephone conversation with the executive director of the Bureau of European Affairs, Douglas Langan, about plans for Embassy Tashkent's American staffing. The executive director controlled the State Department budgets and personnel positions for all the bureau's embassies, consulates, and other posts, which literally stretched all around the northern hemisphere—from Canada across the Atlantic, across Europe, and across the former Soviet Union to the Pacific Ocean.

"Since we don't know exactly how many Americans you will need, with which skills, we decided to give each of the newest posts five Americans, with the understanding that after gaining some experience on the ground, you ambassadors will make recommendations to us about what you need. Obviously, Uzbekistan is a big country, five Americans will not be enough, but we just don't know what the additional positions will be," I was told. This decision sounded reasonable to me on the telephone, and I liked the chance to make my own recommendations for staffing.

Reasonable, that is, until I realized what five—actually we got six—permanent State personnel meant (not counting other agencies): an administrative officer, a communications officer, two political/economic reporting officers, a deputy chief of mission (DCM), and me. WHAT? NO AMERICAN SECRETARY? Not a traditional secretary to take dictation or retype drafts, as all of us would be writing directly into computers. No, I needed an executive secretary to help manage the embassy.

I expected that most of the American staff and I would be outside the embassy most of the time, doing our representation and reporting jobs, and when we came back to the embassy, we would need to be writing on a computer, often in a room with no telephone permitted. I just couldn't imagine who would control the classified paper flow, the telephone calls and scheduling questions, and solve countless other problems while most of the staff was scattered around the city or out of town. Our communicator would be with his equipment (with no local telephone). Our administrative officer would have more than enough serious administrative issues to establish a new embassy—often issues that had to be solved outside the embassy—and while in the embassy she would work mainly with locally hired employees on unclassified papers, on a different floor of the building. DCMs have a critical role in managing the embassy, but with our small, young staff, I also wanted him, with his experience, out of the office as much as possible, dealing with people.

I asked for an American secretarial position to be established and started recruiting for it before I left for Tashkent. Mary Jorgenson arrived just a few months later, in early February 1993, fulfilling every wish I had for her job. I had met her in Tel Aviv and knew I was lucky to recruit her, but I didn't fully appreciate how able she was at handling a lot of people simultaneously until she came to Tashkent, and we all relied on her. Probably I benefited most, but all of the Americans' productivity went up as she took charge of day-to-day office coordination. With her desk placed directly at the top of the stairs to the second floor (where all classified materials were kept and handled), she was also the key person overseeing our internal security procedures every day. Some other American ambassadors at the newest embassies were less interested in obtaining a position for an American secretary, but I concluded that they had a different concept about where they and their staffs would be during working days. Getting Mary was one of the best staffing decisions I ever made.

Assistant Secretary of State for European Affairs Tom Niles and Executive Director Langan were justifiably proud of their efforts to establish so many new embassies simultaneously. Moscow had been around for a long time, Kiev had been converted from a consulate general to an embassy, and the three Baltic capitals had only recently received U.S. Embassies. Yet Secretary Baker's decision to establish an embassy in every former Soviet republic meant setting up ten more at once. Moreover, it was a time of zero growth in the State Department budget. The money, and the positions, had to come from other posts or the State Department, and certainly Moscow could not spare more than a few positions, now that Russia was changing so rapidly. Normally that would be the cause of much agony and delay as the different posts fought over resources. It was a huge shift in resources to the former USSR; and, as far as I could tell from Tashkent, it went amazingly smoothly.

Finding positions wasn't enough; we needed qualified people to fill them. So in addition to Foreign Service officers, Washington found volunteers from the State Department Civil Service. Many were Russian speakers. We had employees on a temporary basis to get the new embassies started but then needed people for a normal tour of two years. Tashkent received two well-qualified civil servants, Sylvia Babus and Jennifer Scotti, among the initial permanent staff.

An early addition to our staff in February 1993 was Chris Paul, our regional security officer, based in Tashkent and assigned to cover several other embassies in Central Asia. I valued his advice even if I did not always take it (see chapter 12). Chris deserves great credit for the morale and effectiveness of our local guard force, and for guiding us through the security aspects of preparing for an IG inspection (chapter 15).

Starting up a new, full-fledged embassy requires a disproportionate administrative effort, with a lot of training time for locally hired employees. As we acquired housing, we had a lot of new housing issues, as explained in the next chapter, and for that we needed at least one general services officer to supervise the locally hired employees. Real embassies are expected to issue visas and passports, so before we could start continuous consular service, we needed a consular officer and a trained backup consular officer (except for immigrant visas, which were still being issued in Moscow).

Staffing support from the European Bureau was a gift that just kept giving, as Langan had promised me in that first telephone call. We received three junior officers to cover the general services and consular jobs: Jennifer Scotti, George Kent, and Chuck Zapinski. George and Chuck opened the Consular Section on June 7, 1993, and let me cut the ribbon. We thought we were ready to serve the public with continuous service. But in those days processing depended upon microfiche films, and we had only one reader. When it broke down, Chuck borrowed a microscope from an Uzbek organization to read the microfiche films.

In time we received additional junior officers for the administrative work and for the political/economic reporting section. We even got two summer interns, Kerem Bilge and Larry Hanauer, who later went on to careers in the Foreign Service and Defense Department.

U.S. Agencies Other Than State

The European Bureau's executive director and his office worked miracles, but they did not control the budgets or staffing positions of other agencies. Each ambassador has a veto over the assignment of all U.S. Government employees to his embassy, but I could not create other-agency positions or pay for them. In the early 1990s, with heavy pressure on the budgets of many agencies, I found that agencies fell rather neatly into two camps: those eager to participate in the adventure of dealing with the newly independent countries, and those who did not think it worth the budgetary sacrifice elsewhere. The Defense Department was the most eager, and I've described my contentious but ultimately successful effort to obtain access for a defense attaché.

Also interested were intelligence agencies, which proposed stationing personnel inside the embassy in Tashkent. Knowing something of the importance of intelligence throughout the Cold War and especially in dealing with the Soviet Union, I considered the question seriously.

We couldn't discuss the objectives of this proposal through telegrams, since we were not allowed to have telegrams classified so highly. So I had to make my own assumptions. I judged that Uzbekistan, a non-nuclear country, posed no predictable threat to the United States, so the agencies' objectives in Tashkent would not rank high among their worldwide objectives. Of the neighboring countries, Afghanistan had become low priority. Russia, China, and Iran were important and nearby, but Uzbekistan did not border directly on any of them. Thus Tashkent's importance as a source of intelligence had to be judged largely in terms of Central Asia. Of course, it is always helpful to have intelligence assets in place before you need them; but if you are making such an investment for future, unknown contingencies, the need could not be urgent.

Where would we put the additional people without endangering their mission or that of the rest of the embassy? The agencies must have known our building in Chilanzar District was not at all secure and could not easily be made secure. To work there, they would have to build a workspace that was electronically isolated from the rest of the building, or construct a new building just outside the existing building on our property. Both alternatives would be very obvious to our locally hired employees as well as anyone in the neighborhood who might be watching us, as would the comings and goings of the American employees of these workspaces. Both our building and our existing American staff were just too small. The inevitable attention would be awkward for the new people, and the secrecy about their functions would call into question the overall peaceful intentions of the U.S. presence in Tashkent. I began to suspect that I had been given the job of turning down an idea that perhaps the agencies themselves knew would not work. I conveyed my reservations, and that was the end of the discussion.

Public Affairs and Commercial Relations

Uzbekistan's size and historical lack of contact with the United States led me to the conclusion that the embassy needed to give priority to engaging Uzbeks throughout the country and to generating a more knowledgeable, positive attitude toward the United States and its values. I did not see a lot of short-term potential for introducing reform through official institutions. So if we wished to sell our ideas, we needed to take a long view and deal with the public on various levels, but especially among well-educated Uzbeks. That was preeminently the job of the U.S. Information Agency. We had only one officer on a one-year assignment, Jerry Verner, yet he had more experience dealing with communist countries than I did.

He chose a very able local journalist, Anna Terterian, to take charge of press relations, and Shukur Askarov, another well-educated and experienced local employee, and an artist himself, to manage cultural programs.

With another American officer, even a junior one, they could do a lot more travel within Uzbekistan and reach a lot more people. Having an American doing it would make the message more effective. I knew USIA had large staffs in some other countries. I hoped the agency would appreciate the greater opportunities to advance their goals in Uzbekistan, since Uzbekistan had been cut off from most of the world for so long. I made my pitch to anyone who would listen, but was turned down at a high level in USIA. I expected to work with only one Foreign Service information officer in a country of 22 million people, whose numbers were growing rapidly.

Somehow, USIA found our second officer, Teresa Conboy, and she arrived before Jerry's departure in May 1993, for one year before going on to a new consulate in Vladivostok. Jerry's replacement as Public Affairs Officer, Richard Hoagland, arrived in August 1993 for a normal tour. In due course, Teresa was also replaced. I had won my battle, but neither I nor anyone else admitted it, and I never found out who in USIA made it happen.

The Peace Corps operated independently, and I had no influence whatsoever on their staffing. Representing the American people, not the U.S. Government, the volunteers made up a major part of the whole American presence in Uzbekistan. Nearly all of the volunteers were initially scattered in cities and towns outside Tashkent, beginning early in 1993. In my contacts with individual volunteers I am convinced they served us, and Uzbekistan, unusually well.

I expected that U.S. trade and investment relations with Uzbekistan would and should grow in the coming years, as discussed in chapter 7. I assumed that if the early ventures succeeded, there would be many more. Not because Uzbekistan was rich—it wasn't—but because the Soviet economic system had left so many gaps in its development, gaps that Western companies knew best how to fill. Many industries that did develop under the Soviet system were hopelessly inefficient and could not compete with the capitalist world—and we had companies that could fix or replace them. While Uzbekistan's agriculture was relatively successful within the Soviet Union, the technology and productivity were poor by American standards, and that opened other trade opportunities for agricultural equipment. During my tour, 1992–95, the Government of Uzbekistan was quite open to both trade and investment; and I saw some indications that they would permit the financial prerequisites for economic growth—including a relatively stable and convertible currency. Or so I thought then.

Our first step to increase commercial staffing was to hire Bela Babus, Sylvia's husband, to supplement others in the embassy, including me, in helping U.S. businessmen find their way in a very, very new market. In May 1993 the Commerce Department sent us Tim Smith to replace Bela for one year. I strongly supported the idea of stationing a permanent commercial attaché in Tashkent, even if he had to spend part of his time in a neighboring country or two. My old colleagues and friends in the Commerce Department were on the same wavelength, and sent a very able commercial attaché, John Breidenstine, who arrived in June 1994. He brought his large Kuwaiti tent from his previous assignment, which was ideal for outdoor entertaining in his courtyard in Tashkent.

Technical and Humanitarian Assistance

To promote reforms effectively in Uzbekistan, we needed programs financed by the U.S. Agency for International Development (USAID). In 1992 their headquarters for Central Asia was being established in Almaty, Kazakhstan, at the same time as the U.S. embassies in the region. They came up with a number of initiatives that included Uzbekistan, often more humanitarian than reform-related. I supported those and asked for more.

Most of USAID's programs in Uzbekistan could not be launched or carried out from a desk in Almaty, so USAID executives and program people traveled to Tashkent, which required us to have an ongoing liaison with them, and with their counterparts in Uzbekistan. At first we assigned one of our political/economic reporting officers, Sylvia Babus, to be the principal USAID contact. It soon became obvious that USAID needed a full-time local employee in

Tashkent to do the coordination with local institutions and visiting USAID officials, and Sylvia hired Delia Barnohodjaeva, who did an exceptional job and gave Sylvia more time for her reporting. Eventually USAID recognized the need for an experienced development officer of their own in Tashkent, and in 1994 an American USAID officer, Herb Miller, joined us and began work. A permanent US-AID officer, David Mandel, followed him in 1995.

Although I was never an advocate for a big embassy in Tashkent, over three years I was able to get *all* of the American positions I wanted, with the right skills, for the long-term American presence I then expected we would need. The additional positions and people came one or two at a time, but this gradual process ensured that there was a real need for their full-time services, and that we could support them better. By the time I left, U.S. Embassy Tashkent was still the smallest American embassy I had ever served in, but it had most of the range of skills and capabilities found in larger embassies.

Equally important, our administrative staff hired highly qualified local people in Uzbekistan, and with solid support from Washington and from the New Post Support Unit in Bonn, trained them to support the Americans and to carry out many functions that did not require security clearances or diplomatic rank. I claim no credit for choosing these employees, and I still admire the loyalty and dedication that nearly all of the locally hired staff demonstrated every day while working with us. Together with the Americans, it was a good team.

11

"CLUB MED" AND
THE "BEST LITTLE EMBASSY"
IN CENTRAL ASIA

You might think that a story about establishing a new embassy in a new part of the world would start off with a description of how we found places to live and how we chose an embassy building. My story does not, for two reasons: (a) these had been taken care of, for the time being, by the officers on temporary duty who ran the embassy before I arrived in early September 1992, and (b) I gave my personal priority to bilateral relations, reporting, and staffing.

Yet there can be no doubt that housing and working conditions matter enormously in the long run to the morale and efficiency of any embassy, and I was glad to have a role in our decision-making about them. The process was challenging, but we also had opportunities.

The Short Life of "Club Med"

In September 1992 some of the American staff were staying in a curved row of small dachas (houses surrounded by gardens) on the edge of town, in a compound that had been used for visiting Communist Party delegations. They had more space and comfort than in the cramped and often dirty hotel rooms of Tashkent and other new capitals. One of the administrative staff in Washington called our dacha arrangements "Club Med." We did not envy the staff at any of the other new posts. Most of them were living and working in hotels, and pictures circulated of American embassy staff washing their dishes in hotel bathtubs.

Autumn in Tashkent was warm and dry well into October, our trees and grounds invited us outdoors, and an early snow in

November was beautiful. We were looking for more permanent quarters, of course, but I felt no need to hurry. The dacha made it possible for my family to stay with me during the children's Christmas vacation, though space in our dacha became quite snug for the four of us.

It was too good to last, and it didn't. Some time in late December the central heating for the American-occupied dachas began to die out, and my dacha was near the end of the hot-water pipe, so my radiators soon died completely. The walls, bedding, and everything else became not only stone cold, but also very damp. I had an electric space heater that helped only if you sat close to it—the rest of the room and dacha remained cold. We had winter visitors that I offered to accommodate, and afterward I thought they would have been better off in a hotel room, if they could stand the roaches, than in my cramped extra bedroom. Subconsciously, perhaps, I wanted them to see that "Club Med" was strictly seasonal, that we were not pampered. I've never been quite sure that the heating problem was technical—perhaps the management had other plans for the dachas, and wanted to move us out. My suspicions were fed by the knowledge that some other foreigners' dachas in the same compound had heat all winter.

A Better Housing Solution

Tashkent had more private housing than any other large Soviet city I had seen—and not just in the whitewashed, clay-walled old part of the city, with its medieval winding streets. Large parts of the city consisted of one-story, private residential compounds, and looked almost suburban, although the concept of a compound was similar to traditional Central Asian homes for extended families. The usual Soviet four-story walkup and high-rise elevator apartments existed, but were not as ubiquitous as elsewhere in the USSR. With the collapse of the Soviet Union, lots of better-off Tashkent homeowners put their money into building or improving the private homes. Some were ready to rent or sell to foreigners—at prices that seemed reasonable to us, and fabulous to them.

I thought this was the most ideal housing situation we could hope for in the former Soviet Union. Having lived in a high-rise in

Moscow occupied solely by diplomats and other foreigners, with our own KGB guard, I wanted no part of a foreign ghetto. Having our language-trained Americans living in various parts of town, among ordinary Tashkent citizens, with indoor and outdoor space for entertaining local friends and counterparts—that would be great. People in Tashkent were not afraid to be seen with us informally. There was no easier way to develop a feel for what it was like to be a citizen of Uzbekistan. Other posts were considering building their own townhouses, or combining small Soviet apartments into larger apartments (as we had done in Moscow), and I did not blame them, given their physical circumstances, but we had a chance to beat that.

Our embassy's support for the housing would be more complex without having it all in one place, and we needed to think about commuting distance before accepting each house, but embassies do that around the world. Asked about the vulnerability of scattered families to security threats, I tended to discount that: I felt that (a) there was no apparent opposition to our presence; (b) if any political opposition might develop, they would be likely to attack large targets (such as the embassy building) rather than individual family homes; and (c) ordinary crime did not appear to be a major problem. The typical Tashkent houses often had a place to park a car inside the walled compound, behind high steel or wooden doors, so the typical houses deterred theft, burglary, and vandalism.

First we had to find houses that met our minimum needs for sound construction, utilities, and space—a time-consuming process. A retired general services officer came out to Tashkent temporarily to screen about forty houses, of which he accepted only two or three. By then we had also found a few ourselves. To me it was reassuring that we were starting to solve our housing needs immediately, house by house. Most of us were not camping indefinitely in hotel rooms. We were not waiting for a list of construction projects that Washington might take years to consider, plan, and execute.

Once we found "suitable" houses, we usually had to invest in upgrading them. They did not have adequate electric wiring to support a minimum of appliances that Americans expect to use. One of the first families to move from their dacha into a rented home, Bela and Sylvia Babus, found that if they were using the vacuum cleaner when the refrigerator motor started, it would blow the nine-amp fuse, shutting down both appliances. Some places badly needed kitchen or bathroom upgrades. Naturally, the owners did not mind our paying for improvements, since they could then expect higher rents in the future. Sound construction was not guaranteed—the DCM had to get a new residence when a corner of the house we had chosen began sinking into the ground.

It took a lot of work to find suitable houses, determine what they needed, negotiate for them, and upgrade them. Our administrative officer, Barbara Martin, gave high priority to the effort. She said she would not move out of her hotel until she had found houses for everyone else who needed them. This she managed in about nine months. In the summer of 1993 she had a big dancing, housewarming party in her own (rented) house for all of us to celebrate.

Using the dispersed, Tashkent-style homes with courtyards had just the effect we had hoped for: Americans getting to know and interacting with their neighbors in ways that were practically impossible during Soviet times. American staff members would be invited to Uzbek wedding celebrations just by being there. The Babus family met Uzbek families just by walking their dog. Meeting other dog owners led to going to competitions; their schnauzer won "best schnauzer." Bela Babus bought some local pigeons and got to know pigeon fanciers. He then brought four pairs of homing pigeons into Uzbekistan on his return from leave, telling the customs officer they were "biological material." At the end of their assignment, Bela distributed his flock among his pigeon-loving friends.

A Workable Residence for a Working Ambassador

Barbara was especially keen to find a great ambassadorial residence. The colder I got in my dacha, the more I appreciated her urgency. We had both been in the Foreign Service long enough to know what we needed—the question was whether we could find that combination of assets in an available house in Tashkent. The one-story residential compounds were generally too small to have important guests spend the night or lacked extra bathrooms for guests. And the entertaining space was often not large enough for a reception or a large dinner indoors. I was not especially fond of entertaining for its own sake, but to do my job effectively I had to do all the entertaining that ambassadors did in other capitals. I welcomed that—conversations at a social event in a home are usually more candid than in an office, so people come to understand each other better. Or, to look at it another way, since the Uzbeks cared so much about their hospitality, shouldn't we Americans be able to show our own?

Visiting high-ranking Americans not only needed a decent place to stay (and a real home was the best in those days), it was also great when they could meet the people they needed to meet socially in the same place. I could talk with the visitors privately in a relaxed environment and help make their schedules work. I expected that Tashkent's airport and central location among the Central Asian countries would ensure there would be a steady flow of visitors, and there was.

Barbara found the best house at 66 Intizor Street. A Soviet-style "businessman"—one who traded outside the State planning and State supply systems, and who later also distributed imports—had built a two-story house in a residential neighborhood, designed for entertaining and for a family or frequent guests. It was not completely finished—interior doors still lacked latches and handles, and it needed some light fixtures, but it was usable. The German wiring and circuit breakers and the plumbing were not just great; they were exceptional for Tashkent. Tiles were laid straight and smooth, proof of privately financed construction. Guests could retire upstairs and have their own bathroom, separate from mine—unheard of in Tashkent in those days, and really handy when you have a tight schedule. There was a big reception room that could also be used for large dinners, a more intimate dining room, a two-story living room, a den, and a big kitchen to serve them all. I mention these details to illustrate how fortunate I was to be able to begin operating a normal embassy residence so soon, compared to colleagues at the other new posts.

We did make some compromises in choosing this house. I am no big fan of sitting in a sauna, and the electric sauna in the house took two hours to reach a proper temperature. The little indoor pool to cool you off after the sauna was nice, but so small you could

Decorating the U.S. Embassy in Tashkent for the Fourth of July 1994 was an excuse for our interns and my son Dobby to rappel from the roof. For more about the U.S. Embassy building, see page 130.
Source: Author's photo.

not swim more than one stroke; and I doubt that the pool was ever used for as many hours as it took to maintain it. The house did have a small, walled garden compound, with space for a car, but no attractive space for outdoor entertaining. The herd of sheep and their manure pile next door were out of sight from the first floor, but not from upstairs, and the smell was not pleasant in hot weather, until we received window air conditioners. Fortunately we had lots of swallows, some with nests on the side of my house, helping to keep the flies under control.

The house was not a security officer's dream: there was no setback from the streets on two sides. Probably that is why later ambassadors decided to replace it. But in the absence of a security threat, the house was close to perfect for my purposes. Moreover, it was available and the alternatives at that time were so much less practical.

It took quite a while before I could choose and receive some fine contemporary American Indian artwork from the State

Department's "Art in Embassies" program. The pieces came by airfreight in perfect condition. Whatever my visitors may have thought of these works, I found them appealing. They made me feel as if I were representing a small sample of the quality of uniquely American culture. Diplomats live in a world full of impressive art and cultural artifacts, most of which are beyond the means of professional diplomats. These works were American originals.

Some draperies and additional lighting were not installed until December 1994, nearly two years after finding the house. The last draperies were finally hung in February 1995, and I enjoyed them for less than a year. These delays were small prices to pay for the privilege of being the first American ambassador in Tashkent, and I was pleased with what my staff and I achieved.

To Rent or to Buy?

Over time we confirmed that several of the houses, including mine, worked quite well. After we upgraded and furnished them, we were most likely to keep them for as long as we could. Rents continued to go up, with increasing demand for good housing from other diplomats and businessmen. Since World War II the U.S. Government had lost vast amounts of money in many capitals worldwide as the costs of our rental housing multiplied. Eventually the State Department got congressional authorization to purchase selected housing and office buildings. We asked the State Department to consider buying the better houses we had in Tashkent, as a hedge against further price increases. We even had a purchase option in our rental agreement for the ambassador's residence, and the owner was interested in selling.

The Foreign Buildings Office (FBO) had a program for identifying property for purchase, and in 1995 sent us a team of real estate appraisers to assess our houses. As expected, the team didn't like everything, but they did like my residence. It had security shortcomings, especially the absence of setback, but its excellent construction, wiring, and other utilities suggested that it would be a good investment, even if some day we might sell it. Several smaller houses also made the list of buyable properties. In 1995 this process was only beginning, but I was glad we had launched it.

When I invited the appraisal team to a reception at the residence, to show them how practical the house was, as well as to thank them for coming, a real estate expert from Florida complained that the beer was not cold. Worse, he was right. I had planned to pick up ice from the Hotel Uzbekistan on the day of the event, since I had nowhere to store it. I did not know that their one ice-making machine was broken until I got there. So my driver and I spent part of the afternoon driving around Tashkent trying to discover an alternative source, and came up with nothing. My freezer had enough cubes for mixed drinks, but I did not have space in my refrigerator or any way to make sufficient ice for soft drinks and beer. Unfortunately, the real estate people were mostly beer drinkers, at least until they found out that the beer had been cooled but was not cold. I was already exasperated, and I realized that making excuses would not help. American ambassadors do not serve warm beer, no matter what. A Floridian would never believe that I could find only one (broken) ice-making machine in a city of 2 million people anyway. So I just apologized. We sent in an order the next working day to get our own ice-making machine.

A Clubhouse Becomes the "Best Little Embassy"

We were lucky with our embassy building, too. It was originally intended to become a young communists' club, then a young businessmen's club when nobody wanted to be a communist anymore. It had a large central two-story atrium, a few offices on three sides on both floors, and a basement with a decent bar and a big room intended to become a kitchen. It had relatively large grounds, including a setback from the street and a parking lot for official and employees' cars inside the fence. Ambassador Nicholas Salgo, a real estate professional who had served as U.S. ambassador to Hungary, had visited Tashkent, among other new capitals, as a special envoy to look for and negotiate for property. President Karimov had given him the building, still under construction, for rent from the local Chilanzar District. Thus Embassy Tashkent had opened for business in March 1992 in its own building, and not in a hotel. At first the big atrium was hardly used, except for occasional meetings of our entire staff, or for press conferences. As we increased our staff, or received working visitors, we added desks and cubicles in the space.

For a time we may have had the best little embassy building in Central Asia, but it had shortcomings. Within a few months my office on the second floor was invaded by yellow jackets. We had window screens by then, so it was not obvious where the well-armed invaders came from. Not one or two, but lots of them, almost a swarm. We had a clue: my office began to stink, to the point where meetings there became impossible even for people who didn't mind the yellow jackets. True, the women's rest room on the first floor was just underneath my office, but it did not smell nearly as bad as my office.

Fortunately, at that time we had several American Seabees, sent to help us upgrade the building's electrical capacity and replace our very hazardous aluminum wiring, and they found the problem. Perhaps in haste to complete construction of the building—or maybe as a joke—the builders had simply cut off the sewer vent pipe from the women's toilets so that the open end was inside the floor of my office. The Seabees reinstalled the pipe to vent outdoors, and both the smell and the yellow jackets soon disappeared, with a little help from some insect spray.

It was great to use my office for meetings again, and better yet, thanks to the new wiring, the building did not burn down. The amount of electrical and electronic equipment we were using was modest for an American office, but far exceeded the capacity of the building's original spark-prone aluminum wiring. Had the State Department denied us the Seabees and their electrical upgrade, our little building could have become a scandalous fire.

Other Bugs

Since Tashkent had been a major city of the Soviet Union, and since the embassy had been built in its last stages by Uzbekistan's authorities for the use of the United States, it was inconceivable that the local successors to the KGB would not take the necessary measures to listen to what we Americans said to each other. Every time we opened the walls, we hauled out lots of seemingly unconnected wiring. As the first tenants, we didn't really believe the builders would waste so much wire, which had value even as scrap. We had to assume that at least some of it was intended to collect or retransmit the transmissions of audio bugs throughout the building.

We had no shielded room in which to discuss classified matters. Even our tiny communications room, which we hoped was swept clean and in which we kept and used our secure satellite phone, had no soundproof booth. So if I spoke with someone senior in the State Department, what he said to me probably remained secure, but whatever I told him might or might not be picked up by a bug in our walls or floors. If I were asked a direct question, I did not want to give an evasive answer for the sake of confidentiality. This insecurity, together with the nine- or ten-time-zone difference to Washington, discouraged me from placing such calls.

Thus I encouraged the staff to put all classified reporting or inquiries into telegrams that could be encrypted without any audio. This reduced the opportunities for a real give-and-take with Washington officials, but had the merit that our desk officer in Washington could stay in the loop of practically all of our communications, including informal messages as well as official reporting.

Someone kindly decided that my office, where I would receive other ambassadors or hold small staff meetings, would be better off with some music to partially mask our conversations and got me a good stereo boom box. I brought in some of my classical CDs and appreciated Mozart's concertos for various instruments more than ever.

If we needed to discuss something seriously classified, the best solution was the adjoining park. With lots of trees and a variety of paths, we could have a quiet one-on-one while walking around unpredictably in the park. We didn't do it often, and to be private we could not have done it regularly; but depending upon the weather, it was a pleasant option.

Early Entertaining

The basement bar, something that we never would have built for ourselves, was most useful during the early months, while most of Tashkent's diplomats were in temporary housing or hotels. With a lot of people coming and going, we held casual gatherings there to greet or say goodbye to them, and with a relatively young staff, the dance parties were fun and nice breaks for our morale. We could invite people from other embassies and foreign organizations, and include members of our locally hired staff whenever that seemed appropriate. Such entertaining shifted to our homes as they became available, but the bar was still there for an office gathering. An adjoining would-be kitchen (without appliances) gave us space to prepare food for our Fourth of July receptions or other events at the embassy.

On the whole, our location in the residential Chilanzar neighborhood worked well. We had city bus service and a subway stop near the park for employees without a car. Although not walking distance, the drive to Uzbekistan's government buildings for meetings was not far, and traffic was light.

Preparing for a Post-Clubhouse Embassy

Recognizing that we would eventually outgrow our modified club and that the United States would need a more secure embassy building, Ambassador Salgo had started a dialog with the Uzbekistan government about a more centrally located space where we could build to our own requirements. I followed up early in my assignment, knowing that any such construction project would take years to complete, which meant it was not too soon to identify and acquire the grounds. My designated counterpart for these discussions was the mayor of Tashkent, Mr. Fazylbekov, known as a faithful servant of President Karimov. The undeveloped plot that looked most attractive was near the road circling around the statue of Tamerlane in the very center of the modern part of Tashkent. I met Fazylbekov at the site to discuss it. He said it wouldn't work because it was too close to the subway tunnel. When I proposed another nearby space, to my amazement he claimed the subway was actually there too. I didn't see these conflicts on my map, but nevertheless every proposal we made in the center of town allegedly threatened the subway. It became obvious that moving subway tunnels were not the problem. He just had no plausible excuses for saying no.

Clearly the problem was more serious. Someone, probably President Karimov, no longer liked the idea of a U.S. Embassy in the center of town, and it was Fazylbekov's job to withdraw the offer without embarrassing his boss. Perhaps there was a concern that we might be able to spy on communications lines or other facilities in the middle of town. Another possible objection: the place originally suggested by Ambassador Salgo was very close to Tamerlane's statue. Karimov wanted to promote Tamerlane as an Uzbek national hero, and a relatively large foreign embassy nearby might detract from that image.

I was annoyed with Fazylbekov's disingenuous stonewalling and vented about it in our bugged embassy, but I had to admit to myself that it was not the first time I had experienced such a tactic. Someone suggested an alternative spot downtown, but it adjoined a potentially noxious bus station, and the space was just too small. The State Department had no budget for a new embassy project in Tashkent, so when I ran out of attractive ideas for the location and grounds I did not pursue it further. With all its shortcomings, for the time being we still had the best little embassy in Central Asia.[66]

Opportunities to increase the American presence in Tashkent pushed us beyond the space in our embassy building anyway. The Department of Commerce was eager to establish a commercial office in the center of town that did not have a guard force and would be easier for businessmen to access. Having a commercial attaché to work there made this proposal more realistic. Similarly, USIA wanted a cultural/information center with more space and easier access than our embassy, to provide more information about the United States. We managed to find some appropriate space: two suites on the second and third floors of the Sharq building in the very center of town, above the stores on the street level. They opened after my departure, in 1996.

While these two new locations were not likely to attract hostile attention, they did represent commitments by the Department of Commerce and the U.S. Information Agency, with greater openness to the public and even less physical security than we had at the embassy. Why were we so relaxed about our safety?

12

HOW MUCH PHYSICAL SECURITY?

One of the blessings of serving in Tashkent from 1992 to 1995 was our minimal concern about physical security, thanks to the absence of threats against us. Everyone had to participate in maintaining security for the embassy and for each other, one way or another, but we were not hemmed in by too much of our own protection. Even so, we still had security choices to make that mattered. Some of our choices—and those we failed to make—may be instructive for future new posts.

A few months before I arrived, in broad daylight, an intruder climbed the embassy fence, ran into the atrium waving a gun, and scattered the employees. He then left, having injured no one, but having delivered a very effective lesson: hiring embassy guards could not be postponed any longer. Wisely, the decision was made to hire guards directly, as embassy employees, and not to contract for them with a security company. This meant that the temporary security officer did not delegate the all-important tasks of vetting, interviewing, and selecting candidates to an outsider, and that the embassy paid each guard directly. There were lots of young men in Tashkent who had completed military service and were unemployed. By the time I arrived, the guard force was functioning around the clock, and soon we were able to pay them in dollars.

Procedures to Protect the Embassy

Starting in early 1993, our first permanent regional security officer (RSO), Chris Paul, lived in Tashkent but covered several embassies in Central Asia. This meant that we got more of his attention and advice than the other new embassies. Naturally, the Bureau of Diplomatic Security in Washington wanted the RSO to install the measures and procedures that were in place in established embassies. We did not, however, have a construction budget. At the time, that was reasonable—probably none of the new embassies could predict when they might have to move to completely different premises.

Given our limited resources and a low threat level, I reserved the right to limit our security measures to those we really needed. For example, after an incident and investigation involving some Marine security guards in Moscow in the mid-1980s, the State Department decided that U.S. embassy employees everywhere would wear identification cards. Having served in Moscow, I did not see how ID cards solved Moscow's problem, much less Tashkent's access problem. Tashkent had no Marines, nor anyone else designated to check the cards.[67] In the early 1990s only a handful of Americans in Tashkent had security clearances and were permitted in the classified, upstairs embassy offices without escort. Knowing each other personally was far more effective in controlling access to that area than wearing cards. Should we really accept someone we did not know just because he had a card hanging around his neck? Who was going to detect a forged card? Our locally hired receptionist at the entrance to the embassy building, and at the foot of the stairs leading to the classified area, had no security clearance. The only way to secure the classified offices was to have all the cleared Americans working there, including me, challenge anyone they did not know. Visitors with security clearances were simply introduced to us by the officer responsible for them. I did not agree to issuing and wearing ID cards until mid-1994, when we were preparing for a post inspection, and I expected that the inspectors would insist on the general instruction to wear cards, whether logical or not.

Without a cleared American present in the building around the clock, we could not store any materials, incoming or outgoing, classified higher than Confidential. We could receive items with higher classifications if we destroyed them after reading. In practice, however, our instructions and our reporting were not classified above Confidential, the lowest level for national security purposes.

Most U.S. embassies and large U.S. consulates solve the need for overnight protection of classified storage and other physical security problems with a Marine Security Guard detachment, which we did not have and did not expect to receive. To man a single Marine post around the clock, and to cover leave, training, and other vacancies, would have required a detachment of six men, a number roughly equal to the rest of our American staff in 1992. Even though our American staff was gradually growing, to me that would have been seriously unbalanced. To have one or more Marines standing guard would have required a "hardline" around all classified areas, including a protective enclosure for the Marine, built to Washington standards, a long-term project. There was also no place for a detachment to live at the embassy. A Marine house outside Embassy grounds creates another vulnerability: if the embassy were attacked without warning, the off-duty Marines would not be there and could be ambushed when they tried to get there. So I concluded that first we would need a new embassy building with adjoining Marine quarters. With no sign of that on the horizon, I did not ask for Marines.

We informally designated a cleared American to close the embassy each night. He or she was to check to make sure no one got locked inside, and then pass the key to the person who would open the next day. That was not sufficient, however, if we received classified equipment—somebody would have to sleep with it. After the decision was made to reopen U.S. Embassy Dushanbe, Embassy Tashkent received a big pile of their new communications equipment. Our general services officer, George Kent, informed Dushanbe, and they sent a first-tour junior officer in a pickup truck to collect it. Until she arrived, a cleared American had to spend each night inside the embassy with the gear. When she arrived, she told George she would check into a hotel. He rejected that idea; it was Dushanbe's equipment. He would lend her a sleeping bag, it was her turn to sleep in the embassy with the gear, and she did. In fairness, Embassy Dushanbe's entire staff slept and worked in the same floor of a hotel with their communications equipment, so probably she didn't foresee the requirement.

In short, we relied on our local guard force to control the embassy's perimeter around the clock and, during the workday, to help control the flow of visitors, especially to the Consular Section, which had a separate entrance. But for controlling access into the building at night, and access to the second floor during the day, we civilian Americans had to be our own guards.

Our Cash Courier

In the fall of 1992 Embassy Tashkent had a huge vulnerability, and it grew every week that it went unresolved. The U.S. Treasury transferred funds for U.S. embassy operations through their usual bank in Moscow to the cashier in the U.S. Embassy in Moscow. Although the Tashkent branch of the Soviet Foreign Trade Bank was one of the biggest in the Soviet Union, with Uzbekistan's independence it became independent too. The U.S. Treasury didn't know them and was in no hurry to set up a normal banking relationship with them.

Thus our little embassy had to send an American officer by air to Moscow to pick up a diplomatic pouch full of cash dollars to pay our employees and our rents and all other local expenses. As we hired more people and rented more houses, the pouch became bigger—and a richer prize to steal, in thousands of cash dollars—so we sent a local employee along to help. The most dangerous part of this transfer was Moscow's Domodedovo Airport, which served flights to the Caucasus and Central Asian destinations, and usually had dozens, sometimes hundreds of people camping on the floor, waiting for flights. From time to time there were criminal incidents at the airport, and we had an increasingly difficult time finding a locally hired employee to volunteer to accompany the unlucky officer whose turn it was to be the courier. Our pleas through our usual administrative and finance channels to set up electronic transfers to Tashkent elicited no positive action.

Then we received a short, routine telegram: an Inspector General (IG) team was about to inspect the State Department's Administrative Support Unit in Germany, and did we have any issues we would like the IG to look into? I saw my chance. In a first-person message to the IG team, I laid it out as tersely as I could. My letter of instructions from the president said that I was personally responsible for the safety of my employees.[68] The failure to set up electronic transfers meant that I could not do my job. It was not just a risk; it was a near certainty that carrying the cash from Moscow would, sooner or later, result in a robbery. We would certainly lose the money, and the accompanying American and Uzbek employees could be killed or injured.

It worked. Test transfers to our bank in Tashkent began right away, and our local bank account quickly became our routine source of funding. I had to admit, gratefully, that sometimes inspectors do help.

Chief of Mission Authority and Security at Overseas Posts

While asserting my personal responsibility for safety was useful in resolving the issue of how to transfer U.S. Government funds to Embassy Tashkent, the authority of U.S. ambassadors and other chiefs of mission to make decisions affecting the safety and security of all their mission's U.S. government personnel is a bedrock principle. It ensures that (1) security measures taken are based upon the best available judgments in the specific threat environment of each post, and (2) there can be no question about who is accountable for those decisions. President Clinton's letter to me, replacing President Bush's, which referred to my personal responsibility, continued my responsibility for all U.S. government personnel in Uzbekistan but left out the word "personal," saying instead, "I expect you to take direct responsibility for the security of your Mission."[69]

My authority to make a final decision did not mean I was free to act alone or by impulse—actually, to me it meant the opposite. It meant that before making a final decision I should consult with anyone on my team who could provide useful input—especially the regional security officer (RSO) and the deputy chief of mission (DCM). It meant that if there were a threat arising outside Uzbekistan, I was entitled to the best available intelligence and analysis from Washington to evaluate how that threat affected my post. If I concluded that I needed additional assistance—in personnel, equipment, or in the worst case, evacuation—then Washington would be obliged to provide it or convince me otherwise. By "convince me otherwise" I do not mean some knee-jerk bureaucratic response, such as "no funds available." The U.S. government can always find funds and personnel to save lives, from the Defense Department if not from the State Department, if the threat warrants it. To overrule a chief of mission's decision on security should require a higher-level intervention, perhaps sending a senior official to the post to discuss the situation. Fortunately, with no discernable threats to our embassy, I had no disputes with Washington over security.

Unfortunately, our benign security environment in the early 1990s was an anomaly, a pause between earlier, mostly local attacks against U.S. embassies, such as Tehran, Beirut, and Islamabad, and the later al-Qaeda attacks against our embassies in Nairobi and Dar es Salaam. The latter attacks made clear that lightly defended U.S. embassies were now targets worldwide, certainly including Central Asia. That has created a particularly serious challenge to setting up any new posts, which can hardly begin with all the physical protections and security measures available at established posts. My views on the security principles that should apply to new posts go somewhat beyond the scope of this memoir, in that I believe they apply to more dangerous environments than we had in Tashkent in the early 1990s, so I have included them in Appendix B.

A Guard for the Residence?

After I moved into the two-story residence on Intizor Street, our RSO asked me whether we should ask the host government to post a guard outside. Knowing from my Moscow experience that this would probably inhibit unofficial Uzbekistan citizens from visiting me, I said no. I said I would reconsider the question if we ever got a credible threat against me, the house, or the Embassy. As I walked around the city I found people universally friendly toward me and toward Americans in general. We didn't even hear rumors of anyone who objected to us. Frictions between the authorities and practicing Muslims in the Fergana Valley seemed distant from the largely secular and open city of Tashkent.

In the 1980s in Bucharest, my DCM residence was only guarded when there were specific terrorist threats. At those times I found the guard helpful in deterring strangers from parking vehicles next to our house. So I did not feel that I was taking an unreasonable or irreversible risk in Tashkent by declining to have a permanent guard. On more than one occasion a policeman appeared on the corner, across from my house, but not for more than a few days. Had there been a credible threat, I would have again been glad to have a guard to prevent cars with a possible bomb from parking next to the house.

Instead of a guard, I suggested that we install video cameras outside to cover the front door and the high vehicle gate to the back-yard—entrances on different streets—so that my domestic staff or I could see who was there before opening either door and possibly being overwhelmed. That camera request took more than my three-year tour to fulfill, but my successor received the cameras.

Protecting the Car

In order to start up our embassy quickly, the State Department bought an unarmored Ford Scorpio in Germany and shipped it to Tashkent. It arrived just before I did. My driver had driven officials around Tashkent and other cities in Uzbekistan for his entire career, so we never got lost. In three years I never felt threatened in that car or any other.

My son Dobby had a different experience. While my family was visiting Uzbekistan in the summer of 1993, the embassy and my driver had a day off on July 5, and I took the Ford to drive my wife and my mother-in-law to the Museum of Applied Art. My son, then 14, came along for the ride. He stayed in the back seat of the car, while the ladies shopped at the museum store, and I accompanied them to interpret. The car had a broken window, which meant we could not lock the car. A man suddenly opened the front passenger door and tried to remove the car's radio. Dobby tried to stop him, took a few bruises and a burn on his face from the man's cigarette, and finally climbed into the front seat and literally kicked the man out. The man left, and my son then feared the criminal would get a weapon and come back to finish the job. He yelled, but we didn't hear him. About that time I decided to take some of the purchases to the car. I found a brave but very upset youngster in the front seat. He could have run to the museum across the street and found us, but he chose to stay to protect the car.

We reported the incident to the police, and as word spread around the embassy, Dobby became a sort of embassy folk hero for "saving the car" (or at least the radio). As the only witness to the crimes of battery and attempted theft, Dobby had to help identify the perpetrator from the photo album of usual police suspects. He did, and soon the police arrested the perpetrator, whom they knew. Dobby then had to come to the police station and identify him in person. Dobby sat next to the accused, who was without handcuffs, and Dobby pointed his finger at him while the police took a photograph. Dobby was quite sure that the police got the right man, and he found it frightening to face him again so closely—just as other crime victims have experienced.

I stayed away from the proceedings, as I did with all other court cases of interest to the embassy, and our RSO represented the embassy with an interpreter. At the trial the accused was kept in a Soviet-style cage. He confessed to the attack and attempted theft. As a repeat offender, he was sentenced to jail. Afterward, the judge expressed some surprise to the RSO that I wasn't there. On reflection, I should have been. I was entitled—as father more than as ambassador—to support my son, and by all reports, the case was handled fairly. At the time I was anxious not to give the appearance of influencing the trial, and now I think my presence as ambassador would not have affected that, at least not at the sentencing, and not in this case.

Recovering a Stolen Car, Uzbek Style

Uzbek citizens relied on each other and on their neighborhood networks for security, and it worked for one of our American families too. Sylvia and Bela Babus, animal lovers and horse people, spent an evening with an Uzbek horse trader and his family. The Babuses parked their pea-green, Soviet-built Neva just outside the gate, and the host assigned his son to keep an eye on it. During dinner the teenager burst in to say that the car had just been stolen. While the mother punched her son in the kitchen for his negligence and for bringing shame to the family, the menfolk quickly organized themselves into teams and went rushing off into the neighborhood. They had some ideas about who the hooligans might be. Sure enough, after about forty-five minutes, one of the teams returned, pushing the green Neva. Everyone cheered, and a bottle of champagne was opened and sprayed on the recovered vehicle.

An Ambassador Who Was Not a Target

With few exceptions, I considered Tashkent and Uzbekistan generally a safe place during my time there. I felt free to wander around Tashkent whenever I wanted. After some months I bought a used Neva, so I would be free to drive to the mountains whenever I had the time, and it enabled me to give my driver more time off, especially Sundays. Although I was entitled to the Ford and my driver for personal as well as official use, I liked the idea of giving him Sunday and other occasions off, except when I had something official to do. I loved hiking and skiing and never accepted the idea that my driver should sit with an official car at the bottom of the mountains all day long. (It would not have been safe for us to leave a nice official car unattended for long periods of time in an isolated area.) The Neva had its occasional mechanical problems, but with four-wheel drive and high clearance, it did make unpaved mountain roads passable that would be risky for a sedan like the Ford Scorpio. The Neva had a diplomatic license plate, but unlike the sedan it did not advertise that it belonged to a chief of mission, and there were plenty of Nevas, so it blended in. I relished my Sunday freedom, all the more because I knew it was a privilege many American ambassadors elsewhere did not have.

I did adopt one rule for my personal safety: when going somewhere alone and off duty, my departure times and destinations were not easy to predict. I avoided discussing them in advance, even on the telephone. This would be a disadvantage in the event I had a random accident or criminal attack, in that it might take longer to find me, but it made it difficult for anyone to plan an attack on me. With no schedule, I was free to spend the time alone as I chose. If I spent my spare time with others, I might discuss the schedule on the telephone, but those occasions too were often spontaneous. There was no fixed routine. Years later, in Bosnia and then in Iraq, where I could not go anywhere without a team of armed bodyguards in three SUVs, I remembered just how privileged I had been in Tashkent.

Not everyone approved of my behavior, however. Barbara Martin, our chief administrative officer, was not afraid to run around Tashkent by herself. She did not think I should, but she never convinced me. Similarly, ordinary Uzbeks would sometimes express alarm when they learned who I was and that I was alone. Toward the end of my assignment, I had been on television often enough that more and more Uzbeks could recognize me.

One of my favorite longish walks was to Tashkent's Botanical Gardens, really an overgrown arboretum in need of serious catch-up gardening. For the price of walking quite a few blocks from my house, I would then be in the closest thing to nature within the city. The Gardens themselves covered a large area. On my last visit, I spoke with the gatekeeper, who recognized me. He said he couldn't allow me to go alone in the Gardens—there had been some assaults there (none very recent). I tried to insist that actually I knew the Gardens pretty well and felt safe, but he came along anyway. The conversation was pleasant enough, but I lost some of the relaxation and feeling of freedom that were my reasons for coming there.

I visited a polling place about a block from my house in the evening of an election day, as an informal observer. I identified myself, and conversed with the election workers when they were not busy. After dark, when it became time for me to go, the chief of the polling place tried to insist on walking me home. I refused: not only did he belong in the polling place, but also I felt silly being accompanied for one block when often I walked or hiked alone for hours. I like walking in the dark, and there were occasional streetlights.

A Bomb in My Neighborhood

As a city of 2 million people, Tashkent could not be entirely without violence. One Saturday morning our RSO called to say that there had been an explosion at a house belonging to Pepsi Cola, two or three blocks from my house. I agreed to meet him there, and walked over.

At the scene, it was apparent that a small bomb had been placed at the front of the small house, just under the floor level, above a lattice-covered crawl space, and it had blown away most of the front wall and what might have been a bay window of that room. A Turkish engineer working for Pepsi had arrived the evening before, and had gone to bed in that room, to be awakened by the blast and a shower of glass in early morning. No one was hurt, but he was frightened and already planning to catch the next flight back to Turkey. I had a big portable radio telephone, and used it to call the State Department's Operations Center to confirm that the bomb was at Pepsi's house, and that no one was hurt, American or otherwise. I walked home.

We never got the real story about the bomb. The police said they were not sure that Pepsi was the target; they suggested that the bomber might have gotten the wrong address. All I knew was that Pepsi had been the exclusive American cola partner for the Soviet Union, and one of their many bottling plants had been producing and bottling Pepsi in Tashkent for years. After independence, one of President Karimov's sons-in-law, Farid Maqsudi, had gone to work with Coca-Cola. He became Chairman of the company bottling Coke in a newly rehabilitated bottling plant in Tashkent. The Pepsi plant was losing its market to the new competition. Could it be that someone wanted to prevent Pepsi from trying to improve its bottling operation in Tashkent? Maybe, but why bomb Pepsi's house, when they could bomb the plant? The house was probably more accessible.

The bombing didn't happen again, so we had no pattern. Maybe it was indeed something personal, or a mistake. The most obvious motive, to intimidate Pepsi, was the one the police would have been reluctant to pursue.

Women Who Were Targets

In my neighborhood was a small, open-air bazaar, mainly for fresh produce, and on a summer day my wife, Kathy, walked over to it. She was wearing a thin gold chain as a necklace—not at all showy, the kind that husbands like me hardly even notice. But a man did notice, ran up to her, grabbed the chain, broke it from her neck, and disappeared among the many other pedestrians. She was shocked and upset, but unhurt. We reported the theft, but the chain was never found. It was a reminder, sadly, that we needed to be very careful about what we wore or carried in public places.

From the outset, the Peace Corps arranged for most of its volunteers to live with Uzbek families. Since the volunteers had only a very limited introduction to the Uzbek and Russian languages, this gave them an opportunity to improve one or the other language rapidly—and to learn about local culture. However, one young woman volunteer had her own apartment in one of the towns in the Fergana Valley, and on her way home, probably after dark, she was ambushed and raped.

Peace Corps volunteers are independent-minded, self-reliant, and prepared for more risks than most people—or they wouldn't volunteer. No wonder some volunteers might prefer the independence of a separate apartment. Yet sexual assaults against female volunteers have occurred in many countries where the Peace Corps has served, and I felt the Peace Corps staff misjudged the situation in Uzbekistan. I knew from the 1980s that the shortage of apartments was so acute in the Soviet Union that single women were not entitled to them. People assumed—and the attacker in this case probably assumed—that any exceptions for single women were apartments for prostitutes supported by the KGB.

Conversely, an Uzbek man would also assume that a woman staying as a guest (paying or otherwise) in an Uzbek household would be under the protection of the men in that household, who might take an attack on their guest more seriously than would the police. The Peace Corps typically does its best to remain as independent as possible from the U.S. embassy in each country where it serves, which may explain why the staff did not seek our advice. Only the rapist can be blamed for the crime, but I felt that if the volunteer had been living with a family, that might have prevented this one.

I did not learn until 1995, from a GAO report, that there was a more general problem of physical and verbal harassment and attacks, especially on women volunteers in rural and small-town sites in Uzbekistan. Half of the first group of volunteers left early, and others had to be relocated.[70] I feel sure that our embassy community could have helped support these volunteers if we had been informed in time.

On another occasion we were again reminded of a gap in perception when it came to the safety of foreign women. Two young American women flew from Tashkent to Samarkand on business. On arrival they were not met, and there may have been some confusion about their ground transportation. So they got into what they thought was an informal taxi, with a male driver and a second man. The men drove the women to a secluded spot and raped them. While there can be no absolute safety against criminals, and this type of attack is possible anywhere, it seemed to me that this attack might also have been avoided with a clear, responsible plan for the airport pickup.

For Americans, traditional Uzbek restrictions on women in public seem onerous, such as requiring a male relative's escort under some circumstances, while Uzbek men tend to believe they are necessary for the women's protection. As the more violent attacks on women showed, the Americans either were unaware of local customs or presumed there was no practical basis for them, while the attackers considered these women to be available and easy targets.

A Ransomed Schnauzer

The Babus family kept a horse, some sheep, and a goat in stables at the Hippodrome, a horseracing stadium on the southwestern edge of the city. During one of their visits there, the Babuses' dog, Toto, wandered off, and could not be found even when they mobilized the entire Hippodrome staff. The dog was wearing a tag with the U.S. Embassy telephone number on it, but the Babuses wanted to do more. With the help of the USIS press office, they got a lost-dog announcement and a picture of Toto on TV, just before the news. The TV station had not done this before, so it took a while to calculate how much to charge. Presumably using the number from the tag, or from the TV ad, someone called the embassy and demanded a ransom for the return of the little schnauzer. Although instructed to come alone, Sylvia went to the meeting with another American and two embassy security guards. The meeting went smoothly and a happy little Toto went home with a happy Sylvia.

Travel Hazards by Road, Rail, and Air

One of the few times I worried about safety, and not security, was while traveling between the cities of Karshi and Shakhrisabz in late January 1993, with a police escort—sirens blaring and driving incredibly fast. My driver (and the Scorpio) did fine in keeping up with the police, but I wasn't sure that was a good thing, because we didn't slow them down. All I could think of was of an incident long before in Bulgaria, where a person was killed by a speeding motorcade escorting a busload of members of the U.S. House of Representatives. On my trip to Shakhrisabz there were police road-blocks at crossroads, so we were not likely to smash into another vehicle, as long as we made all the turns. I was the first American ambassador the provincial officials had ever seen, and no doubt they wanted to impress me. They did. But a non-driving pedestrian, or a child, might not have understood the risk to his life. After that, whenever there was a polite opportunity beforehand, I suggested that we travel quietly (*spokoina*) along with the rest of the traffic. Uzbek courtesy toward me was always more than sufficient, and with or without escorts, I did not have to be part of any more Hollywood-style car chases.

Although the Soviet Union had a well-developed railroad system, unfortunately in Central Asia in the early 1990s the railroad did not offer a reasonable alternative to automobile or airplane travel. Stories abounded about Wild West train robberies, where passengers were shaken down at gunpoint. The longer the ride, the less likely you were to arrive at your destination with your money and possessions intact. Thus taking the train to Moscow or Almaty, which was certainly reasonable ten years before, was no longer an option. Our embassy did not use trains for travel within Uzbekistan either. Freight trains were not much better: containers unloaded from vessels in St. Petersburg for shipment to Central Asia would be looted. Companies like Newmont Mining learned to weld their containers shut, with better results.

My son Dobby, with a couple of friends, did try a short trip by rail, to go to the mountains. I had agreed to the trip in principle, in part because one of the friends, an embassy security guard, was a native Russian speaker, spoke English, and could resolve any language problem. Only much later did I find out how the trip really went. They started out by catching the wrong train, and before long found themselves in nearby Kazakhstan. Getting off the train, they found that it would be twelve hours before there would be a returning train, and Dobby had forgotten to take his passport with him! So they flagged down a car, and convinced the driver to take them back across the border. Dobby lay down on the floor in the back of the car and they covered him with blankets. There was a border control where they crossed back into Uzbekistan, but the guards did not look into the car. (At the time it would not have been surprising that Uzbekistan had begun establishing border controls on some routes from Kazakhstan, while Kazakhstan had not yet done so. If the guards had found a hidden foreigner with no identification coming into Uzbekistan, it could have been embarrassing, at the least.)

Dobby and his friends then caught an unofficial taxi to an Uzbekistan military base. There they met another Uzbek friend, a soldier, who brought along his service AK-47, ammunition, and some Soviet rations. Another car ride and they were off hiking. While consuming the rations, which Dobby described as "horrible," they instructed him on the AK-47. Apparently he had earlier talked about guns and the military, so the Uzbeks correctly thought he would enjoy shooting. So they practiced shooting, even though Dobby had only expected to go hiking. The military ammunition had tracers, which caught some dry vegetation on part of the hillside on fire, and they spent some time putting out the fire. No wonder Dobby was not in a hurry to share the details of this trip with me. Even though no serious harm had been done, a parent can easily imagine how it might have ended differently.

Uzbekistan Airways inherited Aeroflot's fleet of commercial aircraft based in the republic. With a country the size of California to cover, flying was for me sometimes the only realistic travel option. I tried not to look too closely at the tires or condition of the Antonov-24s, sturdy Soviet-built propeller aircraft with twin engines and a high wing, designed in the late 1950s and much like the Fokker/Fairchild Friendship. The Fokker Friendship was not a new model when I had flown in them in Nigeria in the early 1970s. Uzbekistan's AN-24 fleet in the 1990s probably included the same individual aircraft that my family and I had used during our visit to Uzbekistan in 1983. The AN-24s usually operated in the early morning or in the cool evening, because during the hottest parts of the day in Uzbekistan the air did not give them enough lift for a safe takeoff and landing. One advantage of the AN-24: since you had to carry your own bags and load them yourself in the rear of the aircraft and unload them at your destination, you didn't worry about losing your baggage.

Returning from the western city of Urgench to Tashkent, I was pleased to learn that we would be on a YAK-40, a quite small commercial jet, thinking that it was probably a lot newer and faster than the AN-24s. It also had an autopilot, so during the flight I had a chance to talk briefly with the pilots. They cheerfully pointed out that we were flying in an aircraft that was built before either of them was born. OK, I thought, it's not new. But the pilots do this every day, and they have faith in this aircraft. Maybe I should too.

13

CREATING A CLINIC

The main lobby of the State Department building on C Street in Washington has long had a series of plaques with the names of American diplomatic and consular personnel who died while serving overseas. Most were victims of violence or disease that they would not have faced, or would have survived, if they had been in the United States. Eventually the U.S. government concluded that these losses were unacceptable and established a State Department medical program to support American employees' health needs overseas. Small embassies and consulates general typically have a very small clinic staffed by a nurse practitioner. Like the rest of the State Department in the early 1990s, the medical program was underfunded, and this could affect medical decisions overseas.

In 1992 I had no idea how hard it would be to set up such a clinic in the middle of Central Asia, or that doing so would be one of our most successful accomplishments. What I did know, from six years' diplomatic service in Romania and three in Moscow, was that the medical services of communist countries, while satisfactory in some situations, in other situations were completely inadequate and did not approach the American standards that employees had a right to expect.

The nurse practitioner is the critical element of the program at small posts. She has to know what local medical resources are available in her host country and what kinds of treatments they could safely perform by American standards. She has to make the diagnosis for a serious injury or illness, by herself or in a telephone consultation with a doctor, and recommend whether the patient should be evacuated or go to a local hospital. The embassy would approve the evacuation administratively, but without a competent medical diagnosis and recommendation the post would be in deep trouble making such a decision.

On my first weekend as chargé d'affaires in Bucharest, a Marine fell from the second story of the Marine House onto a steel fence and from there hit his head on the driveway, causing multiple injuries. Within a few hours we had him on a commercial flight to Germany, accompanied by the nurse practitioner, because she could not fully diagnose the head injury in Bucharest and needed to be able to assist him on the flight if necessary. Apart from this dramatic example, I had no doubts about the value of having quick access to such a person in countries like Uzbekistan, with limited local medical care, whether because of insufficient training of doctors or the absence of medicines or equipment.

The Peace Corps had a similar program to support its volunteers and staff overseas, and when its first volunteers came to Uzbekistan in early 1993, along with them came a nurse practitioner, Judy Sutton, and a modest amount of equipment for her use in Tashkent. She was happy to give the embassy Americans her advice and administer immunizations. Since both the volunteers and the diplomats were mostly young and healthy, she had ample time for us. It was a great solution.

The first warning flag about our support from the State Department came during my meeting with the newly arrived British ambassador, Paul Bergne. He had been immunized against hepatitis A in London before coming to post. We did not have this new vaccine. We were getting periodic shots of gamma globulin, which was supposed to strengthen our immune systems against hepatitis, but it is not a vaccine. For those of you who have been spared gamma globulin: a large dose is injected into your largest muscle, your butt, and it feels like a golf ball under your skin until it gradually dissipates. Every few months you need another one.

Our Health Was Not Worth the Cost of a New Vaccine

We soon found out why we were not getting hepatitis shots: the State Department had purchased the vaccine only in large quantities, and could not break out small numbers of doses without somehow spoiling it. Tashkent didn't have enough Americans to justify immunizing us. REALLY? The State Department did not actually know how many small posts there were worldwide, many in areas like Central Asia where hepatitis was endemic, or could not order immunizations to be packaged accordingly?

Not long afterward, our energetic DCM, Michael Matera, contracted hepatitis A, a very disabling disease, and was evacuated to the United States and then on to his home city, San Francisco. It took him a good two months to recover. When he returned to Tashkent, he initially had to conserve his energy carefully—we did not want him to risk a relapse. I don't know how much of his evacuation and treatment was paid by the State Department Medical Program—in any case the State Department picked up airfare halfway around the world and back. Denying us the vaccine was a gross example of "penny wise, pound foolish." Not just foolish for the medical program, and for Michael: the State Department continued to pay Michael's salary while he couldn't work, and Michael's absence was a serious loss to our embassy and the amount of work it could do.

Not everyone thought Michael was a random victim. Our embassy drivers were sure that Michael caught hepatitis because he was a vegetarian. He was obviously physically fit, so in their view, if he had just eaten enough meat he would have been okay. It was true that Michael went to some lengths to find real vegetarian food. One place he liked was a little cafe near the embassy that served visiting sports teams, because the cafe claimed they had soup dishes that had been prepared without any meat stock. I tried the place a few times and decided I would rather fast than eat there. Everything was greasy. (I had never encountered vegetarian grease before, but since I was not a vegetarian, what did I know?) It appeared the cafe didn't wash dishes, tables, the floor, or anything else with really hot water and soap. Since water supplies are suspect for spreading hepatitis, I could see a connection: Michael's vegetarian preferences led him to a dirty cafe where he could have caught it! Americans in Tashkent boiled drinking water and took precautions with fresh vegetables at home; but of course eating out was more of a gamble, and Michael could have picked up hepatitis anywhere.

Tashkent in the early 1990s also had a few good restaurants. I was invited to join a group of American and Uzbek doctors, who were participating in a conference, for dinner at the Teon, one of Tashkent's best restaurants, in a classic Russian building down-town. At some point I noticed the bottle of vodka being used to serve us—Bowman's, from Virginia USA, complete with the Sur-geon General's warning to pregnant women. I made light of it—the Soviet Union must really have collapsed if the successor states had to import vodka from the USA! I also joked about doctors toasting to each other's health with alcohol. This was a bad idea: at least two doctors pointed out to me later that moderate use of alcohol was good for reducing cholesterol and various other benefits. Reflecting on this later, I had to admit that vodka was surely safer than drink-ing tap water without boiling it. What's more, maybe vodka was the best medicine we could get for hepatitis.

More Bureaucratic Rigidity

Then the Peace Corps decided it was not appropriate for their clinic to support embassy staff. There was no mechanism to enable the State Department to reimburse the Peace Corps for supporting us, so we were forced to duplicate their services. We had to find our own nurse practitioner or doctor. The State Department Medical Program decreed we could pay for one of them, but not for more than half a day. Moreover, we could not hire just anyone; we had to have someone medically trained in the United States or equiva-lent. I argued that the Soviet Union did not train doctors or nurses to American standards, and there were no such medical person-nel immigrating to Uzbekistan. I was given the ignorant response that all over the developing world American embassies had found doctors and nurses who had been trained in the United States, so we could, too. Or have no medical support. The State Department Medical Program, which had supported an American doctor and clinic in Moscow for many years, had apparently not managed to learn anything about medicine in the former Soviet Union.

Judy Sutton offered to leave the Peace Corps and serve the em-bassy, but of course she could not work for half a day, she needed fulltime work and pay. Another appeal to the State Department failed: no, they would not pay more than half a day. So Judy and Michael came up with a solution that was ultimately acceptable to all concerned: the embassy would find other international partners to pay the other half of her salary, and the partners' employees would also use the clinic.

Michael undertook to do much of the work himself, canvassing other embassies and foreign companies to come up with enough money to pay Judy and equip a clinic. He had the moral support of all of us. Some medical furniture and equipment that was surplus to the U.S. Air Force became available in Germany, and our administrative support unit in Bonn shipped it to us. Other equipment had to be purchased. The United Nations Mission in Tashkent found extra rooms on the ground floor of their building for the clinic. The Tashkent International Health Clinic was born, with a full-time American-trained nurse practitioner that we all knew and liked. It was a welcome solution for us and for our partners in the clinic.

After I went on to my next assignment, at the National War College in Washington, I was surprised to receive an invitation to a ceremony at a national convention of nurse practitioners. Judy Sutton was named "Nurse Practitioner of the Year" for her work in Tashkent. She certainly deserved it, and I was happy to go and say so at the ceremony. The convention introduced Judy along the following lines: "Some of you may not know where Uzbekistan is. It is south of Kazakhstan, west of Kyrgyzstan, and north of Turkmenistan and Tajikistan. So now you know!" The cheerful audience of nurses loved it.

14

LANGUAGE HAZARDS

As I prepared to take up my assignment to Tashkent in 1992, it wasn't obvious to me which of Uzbekistan's two main languages I should be studying, Uzbek or Russian. I had learned Russian and used it while assigned to Moscow, 1982–85. But my Russian had become rusty, and I had interference from Romanian, which I had spoken more fluently in Bucharest for four years after Moscow. I had learned some Turkish as a student in Istanbul in 1961 but had forgotten a lot, and I did not expect that to help me much in learning Uzbek after thirty years, even though Uzbek is a Turkic language.

It would be great to make polite conversation in Uzbek, because it was, after all, the Uzbeks' national language. They would be pleased, even if there were no prospect that I could make enough progress quickly to use Uzbek in official discussions. But starting from scratch in Uzbek would mean that for most or perhaps all of my assignment I would be dependent upon an interpreter, and I did not like that prospect.

Uzbekistan had two parallel school systems, one teaching in Russian, the other in Uzbek. In the 1980s those Uzbeks educated in rural Uzbek schools often did not speak Russian well. Uzbek families who hoped their children would receive higher education, or get higher-level jobs and become Communist Party members, as well as most minority ethnic groups, sent their children through the Russian-language school system. Thus members of the educated elite in Tashkent in 1992 were likely to speak Russian better than Uzbek, regardless of their ethnic origins.

What I was not willing to do was study two languages at once. No matter how valuable speaking a local language might be, language was not the most important part of my job as ambassador, and I could not afford to spend lots of time studying. The choice was really personal: how would I feel most comfortable using one language or the other? Within forty-eight hours after arriving in Tashkent I had my answer: Russian was my only reasonable choice, because it was the actual working language of my most important counterparts. One top official had reportedly grown up in an Uzbek family that used Russian in the home, and it was said that he didn't speak Uzbek at all. President Karimov was an Uzbek but married to a Russian, and in 1992 ordinary Uzbeks told us his Uzbek was poor. He was studying Uzbek, however, and by 1995 he was using it successfully in public speeches.

The first Russian tutor suggested to me turned out to be perfect. She worked with me on problems in my Russian that either she noticed or I identified from my work. She was a professor of English at the university, and with the collapse of the Russian ruble, she earned more purchasing power in a few hours each week from my few dollars (though I paid her poorly) than from her full-time ruble salary. Surrounded by spoken and written Russian, the measure of competence I had reached in Moscow came back. If I used an interpreter in Russian, I could tell whether the interpretation was accurate or not, which was very reassuring to me.

Unlike well-established embassies in other countries, we still had substantial language challenges in dealing with newly independent Uzbekistan, despite the ability of most of our Americans to speak Russian.

Searching for a Professional Interpreter

The president's interpreter was, as far as I could tell, always right. But for most other meetings we Americans had to bring our own interpreter if we needed one, and during the early days I also wanted an interpreter for all public events. The U.S. embassy already had one: Tomila Lankina, daughter of a former Soviet diplomat, who had been in high school in India and had studied in Tashkent. Her interpretation was also always correct, and her English was fluent and colloquial. Unfortunately for us, she was overqualified. Within a few months she won a scholarship for study in the United States and left us for a new career.

Most of the staff, both American and locally hired, spoke both Russian and English, and most of our Uzbek employees spoke Uzbek; but their skills as interpreters varied, and all of them had other work to do. While I personally needed an interpreter less and less often as time went by, others in the Embassy and I needed an interpreter when accompanying visitors from the United States. Despite our advantages as a paymaster, for months we couldn't find anyone really qualified. We looked, and looked some more. People said that Tashkent had ample interpreters for Russian and English when the city was the Soviet Union's "gateway to the East" and to the English-speaking countries of South Asia. But with the influx of Western companies to Moscow, which started before the collapse of the USSR and was continuing, most of the English interpreters had gone to Moscow for better pay.

Finally, we found a young woman who seemed fully qualified interpreting to and from Russian. Our security officer made a routine background check—and then came back with a hard veto. I don't believe there was any justification offered, but I assume it had something to do with her employment before the collapse of the Soviet Union, or perhaps even where she did her language training, such as with an intelligence agency. I had met her and welcomed her, so the veto had come as a surprise; and now it was my job to fire her. Not only had she done nothing wrong for us, we didn't even have a fallback candidate. So I told her plainly that the only problem was her background, and the embassy could do nothing to overcome it. Her first question was, did this mean we would blacklist her from working with other embassies? I said we had no desire to do so, but I was not sure what rules other NATO embassies might have. She soon found a job with the United Nations Mission in Tashkent. I learned another lesson: many rules that applied to the American embassy in Moscow during Soviet times had been washed away in the newly independent countries, but obviously not all of those relating to personnel security.

Our recruiting took on a different strategy: instead of looking for an experienced, fully qualified interpreter, we considered hiring someone with the obvious potential, if not the experience. So we hired Guliya, or Guli, the top graduating student from Tashkent's Foreign Language School, and got a bonus: she was qualified to interpret not only between Russian and English, but also between those languages and Uzbek. She was from a Uighur family, a small minority in Uzbekistan but the largest Turkic-language population in western China. Uighur and Uzbek were said to be rather similar Turkic languages.

By the time we hired Guliya we knew Uzbek would become Uzbekistan's official language. As it was phased in, it would become more important to our work. By 1995 we began to see more official notices in Uzbek and more public speeches only in Uzbek. I particularly recall a speech by President Karimov in Uzbek, which Guliya interpreted fluently.

But first we needed her Russian interpretation, and her experience came a little too fast. Soon after we hired her, I had to take a senior American visitor to see the foreign minister, and we needed an interpreter. Although I could converse without an interpreter, I never considered myself qualified to interpret for other people, except perhaps socially. Moreover, I wanted to take notes, and when appropriate, to contribute to the conversation. After greetings, the minister and the visitor sat down for their conversation, and Guliya was struck dumb. She could not say a word, perhaps overwhelmed by having to deal with such high-ranking people. Then she suffered the further indignity of having to listen to me as the interpreter, with my inevitable minor grammatical mistakes going into Russian. Fortunately, she did catch on quickly after that meeting, and she was never again speechless. I must have showed her that she could interpret better than I could, and she recovered her confidence.

Conferences Without Communication

Though having our own interpreter was crucial, it proved insufficient for conveying American ideas into Russian for every audience. Our embassy helped arrange a visit by a special U.S. "Blue Ribbon" delegation on the subject of telecommunications policy, in May 1993. The counterpart organization in Uzbekistan provided interpreters. The main papers that the U.S. wanted to present were already written in English, so the interpreters could look them over in advance of the meetings, which should have guaranteed a professional translation. I was invited to attend the opening session. It was immediately apparent that the interpreters were having a hard time.

The first substantive paper, which told the history of the pricing of local and long-distance telephone calls in New York, was a linguistic disaster. The paper would have been dull for an American audience, and I can't imagine using it to start an international meeting without a careful explanation of why nineteenth century pricing in America mattered. For people educated in the Soviet Union, where pricing of goods and services was arbitrary and not thought to be economically significant, it was unlikely the local audience would understand the author's points or his logic. With a very rough translation, it was impossible—clearly the interpreters didn't understand the author either. The U.S. delegation may have noticed that the Uzbekistan participants were distracted, and some were dozing, but our American telecommunications experts did not realize that there was just no communication at all. As soon as there was a break, when I was scheduled to leave, I had to take one of the key Americans aside and tell them urgently to upgrade the interpretation or risk failure of their mission.

Worse was yet to come. In January 1994 USAID organized a high-level conference on reproductive health, together with the Uzbekistan Ministry of Health, and the latter promised to supply two interpreters. I expected that discussing birth control in an overwhelmingly Muslim country might be rather sensitive, but the ministry officials understood the danger of rapid population growth to their country and to the health of their people, and their top doctors and officials all turned out for the conference. I was invited to give brief opening remarks.

Since the very impressive American delegation spoke no Russian, I decided to give my remarks, on how the conference related to U.S. policy toward Uzbekistan, in English. As I paused for interpretation, I was amazed that the interpreter began discussing what a fine city Tashkent was, all about its climate and other attractions, not a word of which related to what I had just said. There was no diplomatic escape: if I ignored what she said, the Americans wouldn't even know that their counterparts had not heard any of my remarks. If she continued to invent her own speeches as the conference went on, the conference would be a complete failure for anyone who spoke only Russian, precisely the target audience. So I repeated in Russian what I had said in English, annoyed with myself that I had not prepared a Russian version in advance.

The next presentation was by the senior American on the delegation, who described what he hoped the conference would achieve. It was the turn of the other interpreter, a man, who stood up but then said nothing at all. So again I stood up and did my best with an impromptu interpretation into Russian. We then broke for coffee, and everyone understood the conference could not go on until they found real interpreters, which eventually they did. The initial so-called "interpreters" spoke English, and I still can't imagine how they thought they could manage their interpretations. Perhaps they just hoped that they would be the only persons in the conference who knew both languages.

An Unintelligible Diplomatic Note

Diplomats naturally assume that official documents translated into another language will be accurate, because they assume the translation was done carefully. Yet that does not guarantee that the translation will be easy. Both Russian and English have very rich vocabularies: an English word can have up to six or eight meanings, and for each, there is a different Russian word, each of which can also have up to six or eight different meanings. If you don't really understand what the original text was intended to convey, you are not likely to choose the right words in the other language.

In Tashkent, we tried to put everything formal, written or oral, into a Russian version, to make sure it would be understood. If we had a specific text, we could provide a diplomatic note in Russian. If we made an oral presentation of an American policy position, we would try to leave a "non-paper" or "talking points" in Russian. Our initial American diplomats were nearly all Russian speakers, and we were hiring our local staff in part based on their competence in English. But we were not hiring people primarily for their translation skills. So early on I insisted that every diplomatic note we issued must be translated and checked by *both* a language- qualified American and a qualified local employee. The native Russian speaker would try to choose the right Russian words and grammar, and the American Russian speaker would double check the draft translation against the English original to make sure the translation conveyed the original ideas.

Some rules never become real until they are violated, and then enforced. In this case, we received a routine requirement from Washington, a lengthy diplomatic note to be translated and delivered formally to the Government of Uzbekistan and every other U.N. member government in the world. It was about the U.S. position on the "economic zone" in coastal waters, beyond territorial waters, and was full of legal and technical language based on the Law of the Sea. Uzbekistan is landlocked, but it was already a member of the U.N., where votes are counted whether or not a country has a maritime border. I skimmed the incoming English text, and delegated the preparation of a Russian diplomatic note to our political/economic section.

A few days later I got a copy of our outgoing Russian note to the Foreign Ministry and was shocked to see that, after the standard introductory phraseology, the note became simply unintelligible. It was not a translation at all. Someone had paged through the English-Russian dictionary, picking out words without understanding what the English meant. The junior American officer assigned to the task had failed to check the "translation" against the original English, and his supervisor (who would have signed off for the U.S. embassy) did not check it either. The would-be translation was so bad that there was, at least, little danger of our position being misinterpreted, since no one could tell from the Russian version what the position was. But I was horrified that my embassy had actually put out such trash when we had the competence to get it right. I sent the responsible officer scurrying over to the Foreign Ministry to recover all of the copies of our note. He was obliged to redo the whole assignment and issue a new version.

"We Will All Become Illiterate!"

In Soviet times, Uzbek was written in the Cyrillic alphabet, like Russian. Yet after the collapse of the Soviet Union, the newly independent countries using Cyrillic had the opportunity to consider whether they really wanted to use that alphabet. Moldova, where Romanian was spoken but written in Cyrillic, easily adopted the Latin alphabet used for centuries by Romania. Of the Turkic languages, Azeri was the closest to modern Turkish, and Azerbaijan quickly adopted Latin letters, bringing those languages even closer to each other.

The idea of converting to a different alphabet was less obvious for Central Asia. Before Cyrillic there had been Arabic script. Turkish had been written with Arabic script before Ataturk introduced the Latin alphabet. So the example of Turkey as an independent country with a proud history and a Western, fully phonetic alphabet may have influenced Uzbekistan too. There was a huge difference, however: about 3 percent of the Turkish population was literate at the time Ataturk introduced the Latin alphabet, whereas Uzbekistan's 22 million people were almost all literate in either Uzbek or Russian or both.

It was one thing to make Uzbek the official language, which many Uzbeks seemed to accept as natural, but it was something else to insist on spelling it differently. Uzbeks who spoke both Russian and Uzbek were alarmed, and one complained to me, "We will all become illiterate!" I tried to be reassuring, pointing out that it would be the same language, and that they would read through the new letters to the language they knew very quickly. I gave examples from my own experience—reading Russian in Latin letters was exotic, but rather fun. I could read Romanian more quickly than the same Romanian words in Cyrillic, but my reading speed increased rapidly as I got used to it.

Non-Uzbeks who relied entirely on Russian and had not really learned Uzbek were even more alarmed by the language changes, as Uzbek began to replace Russian. It may have increased the attraction of emigrating, especially if they were also concerned about losing their jobs.

Pride and Independence

Why change languages at all? For Uzbekistan, it was a declaration of cultural independence, in my view. Not so much aimed at bringing Uzbekistan closer to the West, although for young children, having a similar alphabet might make European languages like English somewhat easier to learn. More important, I think, was the idea of separating Uzbekistan more clearly from Russia and the Soviet past, and the government was committed to that. Yet by the end of my tour in 1995 the authorities seemed not to be pushing hard to change the alphabet quickly. Instead there were just more and more examples of the new spelling in public. One of the first places I noticed it being used consistently was the new spelling of O'zbekiston with Latin letters (rather than Uzbekistan in Cyrillic) on officers' military uniforms. Many of those formerly Soviet officers were not Uzbeks but native Russian speakers who had used only Russian on the job.

We saw how heavily the language challenge fell on the Ministry of Foreign Affairs and the Ministry of Foreign Economic Relations. On top of the need to recruit, almost from scratch, people with the diplomatic skills and foreign languages to staff these ministries and their new embassies, their own language was changing.

When signing the first United States agreement with Uzbekistan, I was astonished that the Ministry of Foreign Economic Relations accepted the English text as definitive—and did not require, as is common worldwide, an equally definitive text to be signed in a language of their own at the same time. I thought they considered this first agreement, on the Overseas Private Investment Corporation, as basically technical and dependent upon U.S. law, which it was. But beginning with that agreement, each agreement we signed contained the same final sentence: "An Uzbek language text, when prepared, shall be considered equally authentic upon an exchange of diplomatic notes confirming its conformity with the English language text."[71] This approach enabled Uzbekistan to sign agreements much more quickly and without accepting Russian as an official language.

Later the Foreign Ministry told Sylvia Babus, our political/economic officer, that Russian was only to be considered an "acceptable copy," not binding, and that the ministry was not confident enough in its Uzbek expertise to make a definitive text. So, despite a shortage of English speakers, they were using English for the definitive text of treaties, at least with English-speaking countries. An officer of the ministry even sought out help from Sylvia and Delia

Barnohodjaeva, an Uzbek employee of USAID who had been an English professor, in finalizing the English in one document.

From 1992 to 1995, the U.S. embassy, including USIS and our guard force, increasingly needed employees who spoke Uzbek as well as English. For some jobs dealing with the public, such as those in the Consular Section, it was best if they could handle all three languages. I do not recall anyone making or suggesting a policy decision about this—Uzbek simply arose more often as a job requirement when we needed to hire someone.

Language Training for American Staff

American diplomatic posts worldwide, other than in English-speaking countries, have language-designated positions that can only be filled by Foreign Service officers who have been tested as competent in that language. Officers who do not have the language would have to bid on the job early enough to go to fulltime language training first. In the USSR it had been nearly impossible to work effectively outside the Embassy or Consulate General without Russian. So U.S. practice had been to designate almost all American diplomatic and consular positions there as Russian-speaking. When positions were drawn up for embassies in the newly independent countries, most were also designated for Russian. The Foreign Service Institute did not yet have teachers for many of the other national languages of the former Soviet Union, and certainly there was no cadre of Uzbek speakers among Foreign Service officers.

The State Department knew using only Russian might not be a permanent solution, and in late 1992 asked each new embassy for recommendations. Our embassies in Kazakhstan and Kyrgyzstan quickly replied that they needed only Russian speakers. At that time roughly half the population of Kazakhstan didn't speak Kazakh, and the government used only Russian. Although Kyrgyzstan had fewer ethnic Russians, the Russian role in the capital, Bishkek, was so pervasive that our ambassador there did not anticipate any need for a Kyrgyz speaker.

My answer was different. I wanted one position in the Political/Economic Section designated for Uzbek language, starting with the very next transfer cycle, so an officer could begin learning Uzbek at the Foreign Service Institute in time for his or her assignment to Tashkent. I argued that Russian would remain important in Tashkent among the elite, but outside Tashkent, Russian had never been as universal as in Kazakhstan and would be fading fast. Many families already wanted their children to learn English, rather than, or in addition to, Russian, and were not enrolling as many children in the Russian school system. Our embassy had begun to receive communications in Uzbek from citizens, some official invitations were already in Uzbek, and we imagined that eventually all official communications would be in Uzbek. We could not remain totally dependent upon local staff for Uzbek for the foreseeable future.

Once again, the State Department accepted my recommendation on staffing and did designate the Uzbek language position right away. I later heard that the leading candidate for the job, Jim Martin, was not happy about it—his wife already spoke Russian and he wanted to learn a language that would be useable in more than one post. Nevertheless, as time passed, and the role of Uzbek as the language of official communications increased, I became more convinced that my initial recommendation was correct. Traveling outside Tashkent I noticed that when I was in a car with Uzbek officials, they would generally talk to each other in Uzbek and then speak to me in Russian.

When Jim Martin arrived, he became a sensation among Uzbeks—an American diplomat who had learned Uzbek! Uzbek, like Turkish, was thought to be a hard language. He had apparently learned a lot and continued with Uzbek lessons in Tashkent. Jim and our interpreter Guli accompanied me on a trip to Zarafshan and Navoii at the end of November 1994, and we could talk to anyone in whatever language they preferred. Guli had to work hard—when she wasn't interpreting for me to and from Uzbek, she was interpreting for Jim to and from Russian. By that time, however, she showed no strain in doing it all fluently. We had built into the American embassy in Tashkent the language competence we needed.

I still appreciated my own early decision to improve my Russian. While my grammar was never perfect, I discussed political and economic issues fully with senior officials without an interpreter. I was glad to rely on the president's interpreter during formal meetings, but also glad to be able to converse freely with President Karimov or almost anyone else without interpretation at social events, or in chance encounters, such as at the airport or in a polling station.

That was the right decision then, though I could imagine that two decades later, a new ambassador might choose to study Uzbek to converse with a new generation.

15

INSPECTORS HAVE THEIR SAY

I was dismayed when the State Department announced that a team from the Inspector General's Office would inspect Embassy Tashkent in November 1994, barely two years after the first of the permanent staff and I had arrived. We had ample warning that they would come, but there were still aspects of our embassy operations that were more primitive than those at long-established embassies. It is no fun to have to explain why you can't, or haven't yet, implemented this or that regulation.

It is also extra work. The embassy spends months preparing paperwork that can help correct deficiencies. Then for a few weeks, hopefully without neglecting other responsibilities, it hosts the inspection team of auditors and senior Foreign Service officers, headed by a former ambassador. No matter how long or short my assignments were, I never served anywhere without an inspection. The inspectors give written critiques of each section of the embassy, plus a report on each Foreign Service officer. I never enjoyed this, and do not know anyone other than inspectors who did, even though in one or two cases an inspector's report may have helped with my next promotion.

We had worked hard, we had seized many different opportunities to develop our capacity to represent the United States, and I had no plans to apologize. Primitive or not, we were in many ways a full-fledged embassy. I felt we had done a conscientious job of installing essential internal controls—over funds, property, personnel, and so on. I also thought we were good at reporting about Uzbekistan and that our State Department colleagues would be fair judges of that when they talked with the inspectors.

The inspectors' final report came out very well for a new embassy with our limited resources. Inspectors *must* find areas of embassy operations that should be improved, and I expected a list of them. The two biggest faults: (1) there was no inventory of property, including equipment and medicines, that had been purchased or donated for the new international health clinic that we had founded only a few months before; and (2) the embassy should have more meetings to keep all the agencies represented in Tashkent coordinated and knowledgeable about what we were all doing. There was also a list of lesser recommendations, some of which were helpful to us as reminders or because they urged more support from the State Department.

Michael Matera, our first Deputy Chief of Mission, and Judy Sutton, the Peace Corps nurse practitioner we had recruited, had created an international medical clinic (chapter 13) to serve Americans and other foreigners in Tashkent. Putting all the elements together—support from other embassies, meeting medical requirements, donations of equipment from military bases that were closing in Germany—was imaginative, exhausting, and a major success story. The rest of us should have helped them with inventories and other U.S. government requirements. Thanks to the inspectors, we still could.

The lack of general meetings was my fault. I loved the informal way a very small embassy could accomplish a lot with brief coordination, much of that one-on-one. We knew each other well, and I didn't worry about misunderstanding. I had spent too much of my career at other posts in endless meetings that often had no obvious outcome, so I held few regular general meetings in Tashkent. I typically met with specific people on specific subjects.

But by the end of 1994 Embassy Tashkent was no longer tiny—several agencies had their own representatives who were essential parts of our team. USIA and Commerce were two of the agencies I considered most important, because of their contact with Uzbek citizens and businesses and their ability to draw American private organizations into our bilateral relationship. They were now preparing to operate offices in the Sharq building in the middle of town to deal more conveniently with their constituencies, and they would have less frequent contact with the rest of the mission. Moreover, most American officers on the original team had been replaced at the end of their two-year tours, and the newcomers were still settling in and getting to know each other. So I readily agreed with the inspectors that we needed more meetings to keep everyone informed.

The final report included very welcome general compliments on the way the embassy had grown and accomplished its mission. There was also specific praise: the final report said our guard force was likely "the best embassy guard force at any Commonwealth of Independent States post—well-trained and efficient."[72]

Looking back at the inspectors' report, I should have invited everyone in the mission (meaning the embassy and all related U.S. agencies) to my house for a real party, with toasts to ourselves and to the departed inspectors. The inspectors had looked us over, inside and out, and their concerns were easy to resolve. We were doing well, in a short time, what the United States had every right to expect from us as its representatives in Uzbekistan. Instead of cheering, I just felt relieved and went on with the job. No one else in Tashkent had read as many embassy inspection reports as I had—it was up to me to judge this one a winner and to invite the winning team to celebrate, and I missed the chance.

Somebody—not me—did insist that we have a reception in the embassy on the March 16 anniversary of our opening, which we did every year. It was for the whole staff, not just Americans, to entertain their official counterparts and their friends at other embassies, not just for our highest-level contacts. Like many diplomats, I usually focused on how specific entertaining events could help us serve a specific purpose. What I underestimated was how much a major event, like the anniversary reception or the Fourth of July reception, in which everyone on the staff worked hard to prepare and throw a big party, could strengthen morale and job satisfaction throughout our own embassy. Such occasions reminded us, as well as our contacts, that we felt at home in Tashkent, and we actually enjoyed representing the United States of America in independent Uzbekistan.

EPILOGUE

WILL INDEPENDENCE ENDURE?

The U.S. government's basic goals in establishing an embassy in Tashkent were to understand Uzbekistan, support its independence, and defend U.S. interests. Thirty years later, Uzbekistan and the other independent states of the former Soviet Union remain independent, although as of 2022 Ukraine's independence is under intensive assault by Russia. Uzbekistan's future independence will depend above all on its government and people, but it may also be affected by the actions of other governments. It is fair to ask whether that independence is an appropriate U.S. goal and whether it is likely to continue to succeed.

As the first U.S. ambassador to Uzbekistan, I understood that the goal of supporting the independence of all the new states was not just to ensure the permanent breakup of the Soviet Union, although I welcomed the idea that a new cold war might become less likely with the end of centralized Soviet power. American support for the new states' independence was also based on the assumption that it is legitimate for ethnic and linguistic groups to govern their own affairs and that, when they do, their political stability and economic opportunities flourish more than when under colonial or other external control. For decades the United States recognized the rights of the Baltic republics to regain their independence and with the collapse of the Soviet Union saw no reason to deny those rights to the other republics such as Ukraine and Uzbekistan. After thirty years, the legitimacy of Uzbekistan's independence and its membership in international organizations is beyond question. It would thus make no sense for the United States to withdraw its support for Uzbekistan's independence now or in the foreseeable future.

From a practical perspective, the Union Republics themselves acted to obtain their own self-government and to abolish the Soviet Union, and the United States had little choice other than to embrace the republics' independence. We established relations with each of them because we needed to know whether and how our national security and other interests would be affected throughout the huge former Soviet territory.

Since I left Tashkent, it has been argued that the Uzbeks do not constitute a real nation, and that their nationalism was artificially invented by Soviet and post-Soviet propaganda.[73] If that were true, then presumably ethnic Uzbeks would feel more loyalty to smaller groups, such as clans, or a larger, multilingual Turkestan, than to a nation of Uzbeks. But I did not see either tendency during my three years there. Clans do represent important local loyalties, but in my experience in Uzbekistan they did not compete with national priorities. I saw no identification with a larger Turkestan. The Uzbeks' closest neighbors, the Tajiks, do not even speak a Turkic language, and both groups are accustomed to living on both sides of their Soviet-drawn border. From others' research I am persuaded that Uzbek national identity, including ethnic and linguistic nationalism, has existed for a very long time.[74] As outlined in chapter 2, Uzbek nationalism strengthened in reaction to harsh Soviet purges in the 1980s, leading Uzbeks to warmly welcome independence.

Islam Karimov was a natural leader for independence. He had seen the way in which the Soviet Communist Party in Moscow had destroyed so many Uzbek leaders around and above him only a few years before. Perhaps the trauma of that period influenced his brutal treatment of potential opponents. In any case, his efforts to prevent a Russian takeover in Uzbekistan, most notably by rapidly eliminating the Communist Party, avoiding the vulnerabilities of dual nationality, and ensuring Uzbekistan's authority over border guards and other security forces, showed his keen determination to assure Uzbek — and his own — authority.

Misunderstanding Uzbekistan's Independence: Three Myths?

While in the 1990s I saw Uzbekistan moving toward a rather normal form of national independence by twentieth century standards, outside observers saw more dramatic changes. One concept was Uzbekistan as an imperialist power, dominating its smaller neighbors. A second concept was a new version of the "great game," in which outside powers would compete for influence in Central Asia. The third concept saw all of Central Asia as a sphere of Russian influence, like Latin America under the Monroe Doctrine, which the United States and other foreign governments should accept. While there were elements of truth behind each of these concepts, I considered them serious exaggerations, lacking in factual or logical support, and thus misleading as a basis for American policies in the region.

In the fall of 1995 I was assigned to the National War College to become its International Affairs Advisor, which enabled me to continue to follow developments in the former Soviet Union. It also brought me into more current contact with academic and intelligence community views on that part of the world. To my surprise, I found that all three exaggerations had evolved into accepted generalizations. I wrote an article for *Central Asian Survey*, one aim of which was to debunk all three concepts.[75] I have since revised my views somewhat as explained in the paragraphs that follow.

The idea behind Uzbekistan as the "instinctive imperialist"[76] arises from Uzbekistan's much larger population and potential power as compared with Kyrgyzstan, Tajikistan, and Turkmenistan. In all of the Central Asian states, including also Afghanistan and Kazakhstan, there were large and important Uzbek minorities, mainly living near the borders of Uzbekistan. The flimsy, then undefended borders among the Central Asian states, which were especially convoluted in the populous Fergana Valley (see map, with enclaves, in chapter 3), where Uzbeks live on both sides of the borders, suggested the potential for "imperial" expansion or interference in the smaller countries.

Yet the only reasonable measure of a country's imperialism has to be what the country actually does with its greater power, not what it might do. In the fall of 1992, as Tajikistan was sinking into civil war among regional groups, Uzbekistan's leaders did fear that, along with Tajik and Uzbek refugees, the war could spill over into Uzbekistan. Russian forces stationed in Tajikistan were drawn into the fighting, and Uzbekistan also provided limited air and ground forces, which the recognized government in Tajikistan at the time welcomed. Uzbekistan did not set up a continuous presence, nor did it encourage northern parts of Tajikistan to secede and join Uzbekistan, even when such sentiment arose in Tajikistan's Khojand (near the Fergana Valley, see the same map) and in Leninabad Oblast. An instinctive imperialist would have tried to do much more.

The element of truth in the "imperialist" label was apparent less in substance than in the Uzbekistan government's heavy-handed style in dealing with Kyrgyzstan and Tajikistan. Under the Soviet Union, Tashkent had been a regional administrative center for Central Asia (usually not including Kazakhstan), perhaps giving Uzbek officials a tendency to lean on its two smaller neighbors when disputes arose. Kyrgyz and Tajik officials could be quick to complain when they thought Tashkent was trying to dominate them on one issue or another. From my perspective, most of the disputes turned out to have two sides and were eventually resolved without significant imperial gains.

There were also unconfirmed rumors in the early 1990s that Uzbekistan and Russia provided covert assistance to ethnic Uzbek forces in Afghanistan, led by General Abdulrashid Dostum. Yet it was more remarkable to me that there was so little involvement by Uzbekistan in Afghanistan, considering the large ethnic Uzbek minority and the serious interethnic conflict there. It seemed to me that President Karimov wanted to avoid being drawn into a protracted conflict in which Uzbekistan's involvement would not be decisive. Watching active conflicts affecting Uzbek minorities in both Tajikistan and Afghanistan from 1992 to 1995, I concluded that Uzbekistan's foreign policy was cautious and conservative, seeking to preserve the status quo for Uzbekistan and its inherited borders and hoping that the Uzbek minorities across the borders would eventually find safe homes in their countries.

The "great game" comparison came from the idea, now that the Soviet Union no longer controlled Central Asia, that outside powers would compete with Russia and each other for influence there. Publication of Peter Hopkirk's marvelous history, *The Great Game: the Struggle for Empire in Central Asia,*[77] perhaps made this comparison inevitable and even romantic. Yet apart from Russia, which seemed to largely accept the independence of Central Asian states, what other power had an interest comparable to the British Imperial interest in protecting India? The Indians and Pakistanis opened embassies in Tashkent that did not seem especially competitive. The country working hardest to develop its relations with Central Asia was Turkey, and its interests were primarily commercial and cultural. I couldn't see any "game," let alone a great "struggle for empire."

What seemed so clear to me in the 1990s now deserves another look, because China's interest in formerly Soviet Central Asia has changed. Then, China's role seemed to be chiefly as a seller of cheap consumer goods wherever it could find a market. But in the twenty-first century China has a new strategy, the Belt and Road Initiative, under which it has invested in infrastructure in many Asian countries beyond its borders. That includes investments in Central Asia, such as electric power, roads, and rail lines in Tajikistan. There are reports of a Chinese military presence in southeastern Tajikistan, near a disputed part of Tajikistan's border with China, as well as near China's short border with Afghanistan and its longer border with Pakistan.[78]

It now seems reasonable to assume that China's interest in Tajikistan is not purely financial but rather more imperial: perhaps the protection of its territorial claims, but more likely control of its own non-Chinese ethnic groups. Most of China's population in Xinjiang Province is not Han Chinese. It is mainly Uighur, plus Kazakh, Kyrgyz, Hui, and other ethnic groups that are at least nominally Muslim. Fearing their disloyalty, and in response to some extremist violence, China has undertaken highly repressive measures against them, including surveillance and incarceration. Extremist groups and individuals have traveled to Afghanistan and made contact with extremists in other countries. Thus China has reason to seek closer relations with the independent Central Asian countries that border on Xinjiang Province and to track cross-border activities of its Muslim minorities.

Even if we call China's interests in Central Asia "imperial," I do not yet see a "great game" that directly challenges Russian influence or threatens the independence of the Central Asian states. Unlike the original "great game," Central Asia, including Uzbekistan, may have an opportunity to receive more economic investments from China than it is likely to receive from Russia. Even if a "struggle" between the two empires develops—not now obvious—strategic analysts should treat this as a new and different situation, not a reflection of an out-of-date model.

A weaker version of the "great game" idea, that the United States would somehow "contain" Russia in Central Asia, seemed bizarre to me in the 1990s. Our small American embassies in Central Asia were no more than diplomatic outposts, where we could talk, learn things, promote business, and perhaps assist the newly independent countries to develop themselves into more democratic and market-oriented societies. These potential American interests were significant but not vital. American military power was thousands of miles away, and in the early 1990s we Americans in Tashkent were comfortable with that.

The most seriously misguided myth I found in Washington in the mid-1990s would have labeled Central Asia, and most or all of the non-Russian republics of the former Soviet Union, as a Russian "zone of influence." This was definitely not U.S. policy.[79] Many Russians would have argued, then and now, that Russia had a dominant interest in the other former Soviet republics. Russia was the dominant trading partner, at least initially, and continued to have a wide range of other interests, including ethnic Russian minorities in the "near abroad." With the important exception of the Baltic republics, there was little impulse initially from any direction to reduce those ties. Russia would naturally have influence, as all large and many small countries have with each other. The real question was, why should we and other countries accept Russia's dominant influence and acknowledge a special zone for its influence?

The concept of a zone of influence is a slippery slope. It implies that Russia would have rights in the newly independent states that no other country could have, and that Russia could legitimately seek to exclude other countries. It could also mean that Russia's rights were superior to those of the supposedly independent countries themselves. It could support claims that conflicted with international law, even treaties. It invites ambiguity: there is no clear line between a zone of influence and outright hegemony, so demands for "influence" tend to increase. The concept of such a zone also obscures analysis: the nature of legitimate Russian influence will differ among the independent states. Russian influence may never be the same in Uzbekistan as in Kazakhstan, with its large Russian population, so how does that put them into the same zone? Certainly Russia has exercised more influence over Kyrgyzstan, or war-torn Tajikistan, than over Uzbekistan. That Russia might feel nostalgia or even pride for its past imperial role in Central Asia is reasonable, but nostalgia does not entitle it to an imperial role among now-independent states, and the United States and other Western countries have no basis for according Russia such a role.

The Monroe Doctrine is often seen as the model of an American zone of influence, in which we claimed to defend smaller countries from European imperial powers and then interfered in Latin American affairs. That is why the Monroe Doctrine was, and should be, abandoned both in its original form and as a model: it is inconsistent with modern concepts of sovereignty and independence. Independent countries do frequently enter into agreements that limit their independence or sovereignty in some way, according to specific terms. Those agreements may be desirable or even essential. But it is up to the countries themselves to make or accept such agreements.

Each of these concepts—Uzbek imperialism, a great game for empire or containment, and a Russian zone of influence—grew out of inappropriate analogies. They are unhelpful in judging whether each of the newly independent states is capable of sustaining long-term independence. Each concept makes wrong or misleading assumptions about Central Asia, especially Uzbekistan, and wrong assumptions tend to produce wrong policies.

The simplest interpretation, which we made in Tashkent and in the State Department in the early 1990s, was the right one: the newly independent states were just that. Each new state had differing degrees of influence, dependence, or competition from other countries, as do states all around the world. Yet the only appropriate U.S. policy was to treat them as fully independent states, as we did then and should do in the future.

What Future Will Russia—or China—Allow?

The first generalization, a safe one, is that every newly independent state of the former Soviet Union has a different relationship with Russia, with different kinds and degrees of vulnerability. The second judgment is that for the foreseeable future, the most serious threat to these countries' independence from a foreign power is from Russia under Vladimir Putin. The third, less safe judgment is that a rational Russian government will see that it can have varying degrees of influence in its neighboring countries without being obliged to conquer them, unlike its military occupation of Crimea and eastern Ukraine. We cannot assume that reason will always prevail, but at least it provides a starting point for estimating what might develop in the future.

Since those three judgments apply to Russian relations with Uzbekistan, most likely Uzbekistan will be able to continue its independence from Russia. The costs of a Russian takeover and control of a country as big as Uzbekistan would be serious, while the benefits to Russia—apart from nostalgia for the Russian Empire—would be modest. Uzbekistan's economic assets and potential may be sufficient to sustain itself, but hardly offer a bonanza to an imperial power. Finally, a secular government in Uzbekistan would not be able to seriously threaten Russian interests and thereby provoke Russian interference.

Uzbekistan is not without vulnerabilities. One of them is that its neighbors are, in different ways, all more dependent upon Russia than it is. Kazakhstan has its huge ethnic Russian population, Kyrgyzstan and Tajikistan are financially vulnerable to Russian pressure, and Turkmenistan's natural gas exports must cross Russian territory. Uzbekistan's independence would be stronger if these weaknesses were not so close geographically and potentially of use for indirect Russian pressure against Uzbekistan. Even so, I still doubt that a new Russian empire in Central Asia makes sense for Russia, while Russian cooperative relationships with all these states certainly do. Uzbekistan can best deal with its neighbors' vulnerabilities by strengthening its own cooperative relationships with them.

The worst future threat, to Uzbekistan and to Russia, would be an extreme Muslim takeover in Uzbekistan that also created a platform for subversion of parts of Russia in which Muslims are dominant, such as in the Caucasus. Yet a secular government in Tashkent would have every reason to try to prevent that, and might seek Russian or other foreign assistance. If Uzbekistan threatened to fall under jihadist control, even the United States would have to consider the implications of another failed state with a Muslim population that is about as large as Afghanistan's.

China might judge that a Muslim extremist takeover of any Central Asian country would threaten stability in its Xinjiang province, since it borders on all of them except Turkmenistan and Uzbekistan—and Uzbekistan is close. That prospect could cause China to tighten border controls as a precaution. China might seek even closer relations with the existing governments. Conceivably it might even wish to consult with Russia and the United States on measures to assist the maintenance of secular governments in Central Asia, although it is hard to imagine those three governments agreeing on what to do.

Domestic Peace and Independence

So Uzbekistan's future independence may depend more on its internal cohesion and domestic tranquility than upon the absence of threats from foreign governments. We Americans often believe we have the answers to domestic tranquility, and the answers are to be found in our two-centuries-old Constitution and the institutions created by it. We like to believe that people will not overthrow the rule of law and political institutions if they are widely perceived as just and able to protect individuals and their rights, even as these change over time. Overlooking the American Civil War and other failures of our own democracy, we Americans expect democracy, backed by an independent judiciary, to be the political system that will be most capable of assuring internal peace and stability. Our foreign policy often reflects these beliefs.

We Americans are not likely to give up our beliefs, but we do need to understand that the people and government of Uzbekistan do not share our experience. They have instead an unbroken history of dictatorship, with varying degrees of repression. Moreover, the legacy of the Karimov years has made democratic reforms more difficult, because these were years in which repression worsened and a growing share of the population became more alienated from government.

In the early 1990s, American human rights policies toward Uzbekistan were not unrealistic or utopian: we objected mainly to extreme forms of repression, especially by protesting extra-judicial beatings. We can conclude that we did not succeed, because the beatings and political imprisonments did not stop and eventually became worse.

We did not fail due to ignorance. From 1992 to 1995 I was the U.S. government's principal interlocutor with President Karimov, meeting with him more often than most other foreign ambassadors and attending most of Karimov's meetings with other Americans. His policy lines were clear enough. Although our small embassy could not know everything going on in Uzbekistan, we were able to confirm Karimov's policies by observing what his government actually did. Our small staff had more access to people and information throughout Uzbekistan than was possible in Soviet times, and we found a consistent pattern of policies and actions as outlined in the early chapters of this book.

Nor did we fail because the United States had the wrong policies. We maintained a full bilateral dialogue, especially on foreign relations, without hesitating to object to extreme violations of human rights. Those U.S. policies were correct, because in the early 1990s President Karimov *could* have improved Uzbekistan's human rights performance if he had wished to do so. He could have stopped the brutality. He could have stopped the planting of false evidence against prominent Muslims and against those he considered political opponents. He could have introduced more economic, legal, and political reforms, even gradually, without serious risk to his regime. He could have done more to strengthen the growth of small business and private farming, attracted more foreign investment, and given more Uzbeks and other citizens reasons to believe that their own lives were improving.

Had Karimov undertaken more of such reforms, I believe he would have strengthened public support for his regime and reduced the longer-run risks of violence against authority. Despite his expressions of sympathy for Western standards of governance,[80] over time it became clear that he and his advisors did not see introducing such changes as being in their interests.

You might say that U.S. human rights and reform policies did not succeed because we were not sufficiently persuasive, but then you should ask, why? Were we inarticulate? Or was it just impossible to convince leaders whose whole experience depended upon authoritarian control that they should decentralize ownership and control in the economy, insist on due process and fairness in administering laws (and thus permit judicial outcomes to be unpredictable), or allow uncontrolled, alternative voices in the political system?

Supporting the U.S. Military vs. Violent Repression in Andijan

When I left Uzbekistan in late September 1995, the relationship between Uzbekistan and the U.S. Defense Department was still improving. President Karimov's personal interest and that of Secretary Perry and his senior staff were evident. I do not intend to relate the history of Uzbekistan after 1995, but the crisis in Andijan in 2005 is a necessary exception, because it illustrates dramatically a basic conflict for U.S. policy, between defending American national security interests abroad and maintaining a close relationship with a repressive Uzbekistan. The crisis also dramatically illustrates how extreme Karimov's violence against a large number of people in the Fergana Valley became.

Following the al Qaeda attacks on the United States on September 11, 2001, the United States suddenly needed air bases to support its invasion of Afghanistan to attack al-Qaeda. Suddenly Afghanistan itself went from being America's lowest priority in South and Central Asia to its highest. Once American lives were committed to the war there, Afghanistan became a vital interest, and the former Soviet infrastructure that could support our forces became important too. The lesson to me from the news in 2001 was clear: no corner of the world is so unimportant that American diplomats do not need to develop and maintain good working relationships there, including a healthy relationship with the U.S. defense establishment.

Khanabad airbase, near Karshi, Uzbekistan, was well suited for supporting military forces in Afghanistan, for the Soviets in the 1980s and for the United States after 2001, when Uzbekistan allowed us to use it. I visited the Khanabad airbase in early 1993, with its huge runway, unobstructed approaches, and large empty spaces for additional construction, before U.S. policy cared (again) about Afghanistan, not imagining we would need those assets for a new war there. Khanabad became just what we needed.

In 2005, resentment against the Uzbekistan government's repression boiled over in Andijan, a major city in the Fergana Valley. Twenty-three respected local businessmen had been imprisoned and then sprung from prison. Large numbers of protesters gathered in a central square, surrounded by security forces, and the protesters called publicly for President Karimov to heed their appeals for help and justice.[81] By some reports Karimov did travel to Andijan, but not to meet with protesters.

Without warning, the security forces began killing unarmed protesters, including mothers and children who were watching and not expecting violence. Hundreds of Uzbeks, fearing for their lives, fled across the nearby border to Kyrgyzstan. Uzbekistan demanded the return of the refugees, but the United States and the international community, citing international law on refugees, pressured the Kyrgyz Republic to allow the resettlement of the refugees in third countries. The United States publicly criticized the slaughter in Andijan.

President Karimov retaliated against the American response to Andijan by withdrawing permission for the U.S. to use the Khanabad air base. He also reduced the number of diplomats with regional responsibilities at the U.S. Embassy in Tashkent. The U.S. did not back down on international principles, even though we lost access to valuable assets supporting our troops. The massacre and aftermath of Andijan sharply reduced but did not permanently end all defense cooperation with the United States.

The crisis demonstrated the extreme violence that the Karimov regime could use in response to a challenge to its security forces in the Fergana Valley, a response that seemed to rule out any attempt to reach a more peaceful solution. Control was reestablished at the price of great suffering and bitterness in and around Andijan.

Repression and internal controls generally increased as well. For example, Uzbekistan's government sharply restricted the legal status of nongovernmental organizations and their financing, compared with the bilateral assistance agreement that Foreign Minister Saidkasymov and I signed in March 1994.[82]

A Future Without Karimov

Islam Karimov's death in 2016 has given Uzbekistan's government the chance for new directions, especially because Karimov's regime was so personally identified with him. Uzbekistan's people deserve a new beginning. Uzbekistan must find a balance in domestic policies that enables it to maintain public safety and control over extremists, without alienating the rest of the population. More benign, conciliatory policies, ruling out physical brutality and reducing the numbers of political prisoners, will certainly help. Vigorous, more inclusive economic policies would help in the long run to give the population hope.

Yet Uzbekistan needs more than better specific policies. Somehow Uzbekistan's society must find greater tolerance and mutual respect between Muslim believers and secular citizens, something like a "social contract," a broad social understanding allowing both sides to live their lives without interference or intimidation. Perhaps this would require institutional change, but at a minimum the president could ask the Mufti to routinely alert him to points of friction between Muslim and secular citizens and advise him on steps to reduce the friction. The Mufti could in turn develop a network of advisors to assist him in this function.

For society as a whole, Uzbekistan needs a new system of laws, justice, and governance, without which domestic peace will be fragile. Installing such a system would depend upon a major transfer of knowledge and best practices, both by bringing experts, NGOs, and private companies to Uzbekistan and by deeper, firsthand exposure of educated Uzbeks to how foreign systems actually work in other countries.

There is a danger that members of the corrupt elite of Karimov's Uzbekistan will try to block reforms that would reduce their ability to exploit their countrymen. Our world has a certain amount of corruption everywhere, and in Tashkent I had an initial tendency to dismiss corruption in Central Asia as pervasive, endemic, and unavoidable. That much was true, but corruption was not just endemic and unavoidable—corruption was a major obstacle to Uzbekistan's future and should have had a higher priority on the U.S. reform agenda in the 1990s. I began to understand that as I learned about the hopelessness of creating a fair system of taxation, or indeed any economic system, without extortion. Now it may take something like a revolution, hopefully not violent, to overthrow and root out corruption in Uzbekistan.

Without a revolution, what can be done? In the April 6, 1995, meeting between President Karimov and Defense Secretary Perry, Karimov asserted that economic reform should come before political reform, while Perry argued that both types of reform could proceed in parallel (see Appendix C). It was a theoretical discussion, because little reform followed.

Based upon my later experience as supervisor of Brčko District, Bosnia and Herzegovina, where comprehensive legal reforms preceded successful privatization[83] and where business expanded under my supervision, I strongly recommend giving priority to legal reforms. Uzbekistan cannot greatly expand small business, privatize publicly owned businesses, or successfully encourage foreign investment, without shielding those businesses and processes from corruption. Moreover, a market economy cannot function efficiently without the laws, courts, and due process procedures appropriate for settling civil disputes and criminal prosecutions fairly. Creating new businesses successfully will only work if they are protected from extortion, and that includes overhaul of the tax system.

Effective legal reform will likely require a task force, including Uzbek lawyers and prosecutors and international advisors, which would (1) draft the new criminal, civil, and administrative laws necessary to support a market economy; (2) review the performance of officials, including judges, to replace those who have exploited their positions; and (3) establish a process of rehiring those who are not found guilty of corruption or malfeasance. Giving such top priority to establishing the legal preconditions for a successful, growing market economy and for a more just criminal law is not a radical proposal, or unique to Uzbekistan. It has universal validity and will be essential to replacing what is left of the Soviet command economy with a system that works efficiently and can earn the respect of businessmen and consumers.[84]

After a generation of lost time, and despite the events that have occurred since the early 1990s, Uzbekistan is now again faced with many of the same reform issues it faced then, and reform is arguably now more critical to its future. Uzbeks and Americans are, or should be, wiser now. We have seen what has worked and what has failed in other countries. So the way ahead is also clearer. If the people of Uzbekistan wish to keep their independent state, free from foreign interference, free from domestic violence, and free from jihadist control, its laws and institutions must be reformed as quickly and deliberately as possible.

While it is natural for the World Bank to take the lead in proposing and monitoring economic reforms, the United States and the European Union also have experience with legal and political reforms in many other countries, including other former Soviet republics. But it will be up to Uzbekistan to adopt the reforms and implement them.

Reporting by *The Economist* in late 2019 suggests that President Shavkat Mirziyoyev has chosen the path of gradual economic, legal, and political reforms. The magazine even awarded Uzbekistan with its "country of the year" award, based on its overall improvement since 2018. Given the repressive system created and left behind by Islam Karimov, the improvement started from a very low base. It remains to be seen whether it will be sustained. But even one year of progress is worth commending and gives reason for some optimism.

Whatever Uzbekistan may decide about its future, it remains the home of the most populous ethnic group in Central Asia, and the United States will need to have an embassy there.

Appendix A

LETTER OF INSTRUCTION FROM PRESIDENT GEORGE H. W. BUSH

THE WHITE HOUSE

WASHINGTON

August 11, 1992

Dear Mr. Ambassador:

I send you my very best wishes and appreciation for your efforts as Chief of the United States Mission in the Republic of Uzbekistan. We are entering a new, exciting time of change in international relations. The postwar era is drawing to a close. As leader of the democracies, our Nation faces an historic opportunity to help shape a freer, more secure, and more prosperous world, in which our ideals and our way of life can truly flourish. As President, I intend to advance these objectives and United States interests around the globe, and I look to you, as my personal representative in Uzbekistan, as my partner in this task.

As my representative, you, along with the Secretary of State, share with me my constitutional responsibility for the conduct of our relations with Uzbekistan. I charge you to exercise full responsibility for the direction, coordination, and supervision of all Executive branch U.S. offices and personnel in Uzbekistan, except for personnel under the command of a United States area military commander, personnel under the authority of the Chief of another U.S. Mission (for example, one accredited to an international organization), or personnel detailed to duty on the staff of an international organization.

The Secretary of State is my principal foreign policy advisor. You will receive policy guidance and instructions from him or from me. Except in the most unusual circumstances, as I shall determine, messages on policy proposals and policy implementation will be sent to you through official Department of State channels. You will normally report through the Secretary. I want to emphasize that the Secretary of State has the responsibility not only for the activities of the Department of State and the Foreign Service, but also, to the fullest extent provided by law, for the overall coordination and supervision of United States Government activities abroad.

-2-

You are to provide strong program direction and leadership to all Executive branch agency activities to carry
out United States foreign policy. It is also your responsibility to foster conditions in which our regional
or worldwide activities can achieve success. I have
notified all heads of departments and agencies accordingly and instructed them to inform their personnel in
the United States and abroad.

You should cooperate fully with personnel of the U.S.
Legislative and Judicial branches in Uzbekistan so
that United States foreign policy goals are advanced,
security is maintained, and Executive, Legislative,
and Judicial responsibilities are carried out.

You should instruct all Executive branch personnel
under your authority of their responsibility to keep
you fully informed at all times of their current and
planned activities, so that you can effectively carry
out your responsibility for United States Government
programs and operations. You have the right to see all
communications to or from Mission elements, except
those specifically exempted by law or Executive
decision.

As Commander in Chief, I retain authority over United
States Armed Forces. On my behalf you have responsibility for the direction, coordination, supervision,
and safety, including security from terrorism, of all
Department of Defense personnel on official duty in
Uzbekistan, except those personnel under the command
of a U.S. area military commander. You and such
commanders must keep each other currently informed
and cooperate on all matters of mutual interest. Any
differences that cannot be resolved in the field should
be reported by you to the Secretary of State; unified
commanders should report to the Secretary of Defense.

I expect you to report with directness and candor. If
there are policies or programs with which you or personnel under your authority disagree, the Secretary of
State and I will always welcome the opportunity to
consider alternative courses of action. Nevertheless,
there can be only one United States policy, which I
expect you and all members of your Mission to follow
and articulate.

-3-

I am committed to a lean personnel profile overseas
for reasons of foreign policy, security, and economy.
Thus, it is my policy that overseas staffing be tied
directly to the accomplishment of specific national
goals, and reduced whenever and wherever possible. I
therefore want you to assess regularly the staffing
levels and overall costs of every element of your
Mission to make certain they are consistent with our
overall efforts to reduce the official U.S. presence
abroad. You may initiate changes when you believe the
staffing of any agency is either inadequate or excessive to the performance of essential functions. Every
agency under your authority, including the Department
of State, must obtain your approval for any change in
the size, composition, or mandate of its staff. You
must make the hard choices, and I expect you to relate
Mission resources directly to priority policy and
program activities, genuine need, and safety. However,
you should be aware that overall staff reductions
notwithstanding, some diplomatic missions may, as the
need arises, be asked to accept augmentation to meet
new and pressing national security demands.

If an Agency head disagrees with you regarding staffing, he may inform the Secretary of State, to whom I
have delegated responsibility for resolving such
issues. In the event the Secretary of State is unable
to resolve a dispute, the Secretary of State and the
Agency head will present their respective views to me,
through my Assistant for National Security Affairs,
for decision. In such instances, both the Secretary
of State and I will uphold the party arguing for the
best use of increasingly scarce resources.

The protection of all United States Government personnel on official duty abroad and their accompanying
dependents is a crucial responsibility in this
dangerous time. You must always keep security in the
forefront of your concerns. The security of your
Mission is your direct, personal responsibility. I
also expect you to support strongly counterintelli-
gence and counterterrorism activities that enhance
security both locally and in the broader international
context.

I know you share my total commitment to fair and
equitable treatment for all, regardless of race,

-4-

color, creed, sex, or national origin. It is your
duty to demonstrate our shared commitment to equal
employment opportunity. I expect you to run your
Mission in an atmosphere free of discrimination. From
my own personal experience as an Ambassador, I know
that there are many ways you can foster a positive
climate in this important regard by your own emphasis
and example.

I also expect the highest standards of professional
and personal conduct from all United States Government
personnel. Public service is a trust requiring
government personnel to place public duties above
private interests. Accordingly, they must abide by
the highest ethical standards. To ensure that the
American people retain complete confidence in the
integrity of their government, government personnel
must abide not only by the letter of regulations but
also by the spirit of public service. You have the
authority and my full support to ensure that ethical
conduct is a hallmark of our presence overseas, both
on and off the job.

I am sure you will represent the United States with
imagination, energy, and skill. You have my full
personal confidence and best wishes.

Sincerely,

G. Bush

The Honorable Henry Lee Clarke
American Ambassador
Tashkent

Appendix B

PRINCIPLES FOR SECURITY AT NEW POSTS

The new embassies established following the collapse of the Soviet Union will not be the last new posts that the United States will need to open, or reopen after an extended closure. and security has become more important than ever. Our new post in Benghazi, Libya, was destroyed in 2012, with four Americans killed, including the ambassador. Based on the sequence of events that led to this disaster and on facts published afterward, it is clear to me that fundamental principles for security at overseas posts had been violated, principles that are especially critical for protecting vulnerable new posts.

The January 2014 unclassified report of the U.S. Senate Select Committee on Intelligence cites the State Department Accountability Review Board as concluding that "there appeared to be very real confusion over who, ultimately, was responsible and empowered to make decisions based upon both policy and security concerns" at the State Department and in Libya.[85] As described in this book's chapter 12, in 1992 and 1994 I received letters from Presidents George H. W. Bush and William J. Clinton that assigned direct responsibility for security of U.S. Embassy Tashkent and all of its personnel to me, as chief of mission, with no confusion or ambiguity, along with responsibility for pursuing other national objectives. From this basic responsibility, at least six further principles follow.

(1) Only the chief of mission can decide the level and type of security necessary for the overseas post. The chief of mission is, or should quickly become, the best-informed U.S. official about political, military, economic, and other conditions in the country, including terrorist and other threats, and be able to make judgments about how they affect all U.S. agencies there. That is especially true for new posts. That was the case in Tashkent in the early 1990s and in Benghazi in 2012. No one in Washington then had experience

in Uzbekistan or Libya greater than the assigned ambassadors. Although U.S. ambassadors have the authority, they are not alone in exercising it: they need advice from an experienced regional security officer, and they should also get candid views from the deputy chief of mission and others on the country team. They should ask for additional intelligence, technical information, and support from Washington, including from the Bureau of Diplomatic Security, especially if the threats could be originating outside the country of assignment.

(2) The State Department controls money, staffing positions, and other external resources that ambassadors may need to fulfill their responsibility for security. The State Department could also order an evacuation or post closing. Denying a chief of mission's requests for additional manpower for security in a dangerous situation like Libya's in 2012[86] was a fatal mistake. U.S. civilian and military resources for protecting lives are not so skimpy, and there must always be a backup capability for supporting overseas posts. If the State Department wishes to second-guess a chief of mission's security needs, it should first send the requested support on a temporary basis and a senior official to discuss the situation with the chief of mission. If the State Department cannot help, Defense Department resources should be enlisted, or in the worst case, an evacuation ordered.

(3) The chief of mission's authority over security is a burden, not a gift. It comes in exchange for the ambassador's obligation to consider objectively all the factors affecting security in the host country. Ambassadors must be prepared to change their decisions when security or other factors change substantially. As Ambassador to Uzbekistan in the early 1990s I was not a target for terrorism, but in most countries of the world now, including Uzbekistan, the U.S. ambassador *is* a target, as a symbol of the American presence. Personal bravery cannot be a consideration—in the age of suicide and vehicle bombs, the risk that an ambassador assumes extends to the staff and others who meet or accompany the ambassador. Vulnerability to attack can put at risk other U.S. goals in the country. When Ambassador Christopher Stevens chose to travel to the lightly defended compound in Benghazi, it was his call, and no Americans knew Benghazi better than he did. But he must have known

that the situation had changed. The security risks to foreigners in Benghazi had increased substantially,[87] the militia that was supposed to defend the compound went partially on strike,[88] and there was no increase in armed American protection to compensate for these adverse factors.[89] The diplomatic compound should have been evacuated when it lost its guards, or a new American guard force provided. If Ambassador Stevens could not make his trip safer, in its timing and with additional protection, the trip could have been canceled.

(4) The chief of mission must insist upon and personally review a written plan for the defense, reinforcement, and evacuation of each of the mission's posts. The plan must be reviewed by every agency present at the post, and every agency needed for support of that post's security. It should include alternative or fallback options under different scenarios. It needs to consider tactical choices, such as whether personnel should be kept together for their defense or dispersed to avoid creating a potential target. We had such a plan in Dushanbe, in Tashkent, and at every post at which I served.

(5) Nowadays every post requires designated backup support for its security, as part of the plan. Our American backup in Tashkent, 1992–95, was the U.S. Air Force in Germany, whose officers prepared to support us by studying our situation on the ground. I knew that if they flew those thousands of miles to Tashkent, it might mean that help would come too late to stop an attack on the Embassy, yet there was never a suggestion that being "late" after an attack could be a reason for not coming. Timely and effective support did not come to Benghazi, and yet the survivors still needed to be evacuated. If it were not for the armed contractors at the Annex, two of whom were killed, the loss of American lives could have been far greater.[90]

(6) Effective security depends upon being able to trust the people who provide it, regardless of the physical situation. High walls, mortar-resistant roofs, and strong gates help—unless someone on the inside opens them, or fails to defend them, as happened in Benghazi. Fortunately, in Tashkent in 1992 we were not tempted to trust a militia or a local contractor to guard the Embassy. Instead, we hired each guard to work directly for us as part of the embassy staff (see chapter 12), so he had no cause for divided loyalty. He was

part of our team and no other. In hindsight, when the 17 February Martyrs Brigade failed to protect either compound in Benghazi, that was not just a bad sign; it created an untenable situation, requiring either evacuation or immediate reinforcement by the U.S. military.

After the disaster in Benghazi, and after the misguided congressional reaction to it, I fear that the State Department will have a great aversion to even considering new posts that would start up without perfect security. I hope that will not be the case. Some day we will need to return to Benghazi, as we have returned to Dushanbe, Kabul, and other national or regional capitals that we left when the environment became too dangerous. Obviously, any new post must serve a sufficiently valuable U.S. purpose to outweigh the risks. That is a judgment call. But if the purpose is important, the real questions should become when and how it might be set up relatively safely, and the chief of mission in that country must exercise his or her authority and responsibility in answering them.

—Drafted by Henry L. Clarke, 2015, revised 2019

Appendix C

PRESS CONFERENCE, U.S. SECRETARY OF DEFENSE WILLIAM PERRY, TASHKENT, UZBEKISTAN, 6 APRIL 1995

SECRETARY: Good afternoon. I want to start by thanking Defense Minister Akhmedov for hosting this visit. We have been shown great warmth and wonderful hospitality by Defense Minister Akhmedov, Foreign Minister Kamilov, and President Karimov. This visit to Tashkent has been truly extraordinary in that respect. And this made the visit both pleasant and productive. Uzbekistan stands in an intersection of geography and history. Therefore it plays a critical role in regional stability and security. Indeed it plays a critical role in the stability and security of Eurasia. The United States, therefore, is interested in working with Uzbekistan to assist them in the regional stability and security issues. We applaud the vigor with which Uzbekistan has established its independence, and we support that independence. We urge Uzbekistan to continue to move toward democratization. And we expressed our concern that it's not happening fast enough. We applaud the movement in Uzbekistan toward economic reform. More than a hundred U.S. companies are visiting and investing in Uzbekistan, some of them with the support of the Overseas Private Investment Corporation. The United States is committed to a free, stable, prosperous, and independent Uzbekistan. And over the long run, free markets and democratic government hold the key to prosperity and stability.

Against this backdrop, we discussed a number of regional and bilateral issues, and I proposed ways to strengthen the ties between the United States and Uzbekistan. I invited General Akhmedov to visit me in Washington this fall to return the visit I've made here in Tashkent. I urged the prompt establishment of military attachés in our two capitals. To start, I proposed the establishment of a bilateral working group, whose first meeting would occur in the next month or two. We discussed the establishment of a number of exchange and military training programs. I urged that Uzbekistan become fully active in the Partnership for Peace, and both the defense minister and the president agreed to do that. I offered the United States' assistance in establishing defense conversion programs here in Uzbekistan. These represent small but important steps towards a stronger relationship between the United States and Uzbekistan. They show our commitment to Uzbekistan's sovereignty and stability. We believe that free markets and fair elections offer the surest road to strength and prosperity. I recognize, of course, that transitions to new economic and government structures are not easy and that not all countries can move quickly. Uzbekistan has a past of greatness and faces a future of greatness. And the United States is prepared to help.

I'll be happy to take questions.

BOB BURNS, AP: I want to ask you on the (inaudible) of political reform. Were you persuaded by the president's basic argument that economic reform has to come first in order to get rid of the mentality established in the people during the Soviet era.

SECRETARY: The president made a strong point to me both in our private meetings and to the press that economic reform comes first, [and] political reform has to follow it. We understand that economic reform is absolutely essential to effecting political reform but we argue that they can be done in parallel. And we will continue to urge that view on the Government of Uzbekistan to get the second path in line with the first path, which is the economic path. And when I told this to the president, I explained that we were being critical of some aspects of the Uzbek Government, but that we were doing it as a friend. The president replied there's an old Uzbek saying that friends criticize and enemies praise.

BILL GERTZ, WASHINGTON TIMES: Mr. Secretary, I want to ask you a question that relates to the regional security issues. As I understand it, the Russian Government wants to organize some sort of international peacekeeping operation in Tajikistan. And they want this operation, either OSCE or UN, to be Russian commanded and link their support for a U.S. commander in Haiti to that. What's your position on Russian peacekeeping, and should there be a Russian-led peacekeeping operation in Tajikistan?

SECRETARY: First of all, Bill, I reject any linkage between peacekeeping efforts in Haiti and peacekeeping efforts in Tajikistan. Secondly, we encourage the OSCE to play an active role in Tajikistan peacekeeping efforts. And I think that they should decide on the command of that operation on the basis of composition of forces. This is not an issue I discussed this morning with either the minister of defense, the minister of foreign affairs, or the president.

We have time for one more question.

SHAKHNOZA GANYEEVA, OSTANKINO T.V.: What happened today, what military technical areas of cooperation will you see as priority and most relevant between the U.S. and Uzbekistan?

SECRETARY: The cooperation areas which we discussed are primarily in the areas of training, doctrine, military structuring, and military education. We have offered to send a very senior retired military officer from the United States to consult and advise the Minister of Defense on the restructuring of the Uzbekistani military forces. We have a program in the United States that goes by the acronym IMET, I-M-E-T, which provides funding for this purpose. [It would?] support the sending of military officers from Uzbekistan to the United States to our academies and to our military training programs. It also supports English language training. We are also planning joint exercises, both on a bilateral basis and on a multilateral basis through Partnership for Peace.

Thank you.

Appendix D

REMARKS BY AMBASSADOR HENRY CLARKE ABOUT THE CENTRAL ASIAN–AMERICAN ENTERPRISE FUND, TASHKENT, FEBRUARY 3, 1995

It is a real pleasure to congratulate Richard Bernstrom and his team on the formal opening of the Tashkent office of the Central Asian–American Enterprise Fund. I'm honored to greet so many important officials of the Government of Uzbekistan and representatives of the private sector. Let me say a few words about why this occasion is so important to relations between the United States and Uzbekistan, and to Central Asia as a whole.

In the long run, I expect that economic ties between the United States and Uzbekistan will become the most important part of our relationship. I could be wrong. Economic ties between America and the Uzbek SSR did not develop during the Soviet period. Central planning was a major obstacle. Trade and investment from the U.S. will develop fully only if Uzbekistan succeeds in introducing a genuine market economy.

Privately owned enterprises, which are able to make fully independent business decisions, are essential to market economies. In most countries, including the United States, the growth of small and medium-sized businesses is the most important cause of increasing employment levels. Growth in small business is therefore vital to the economic health and stability of the whole country. Yet new and growing businesses need financial strength to succeed.

By providing financial support to small and medium-sized private businesses, the Central Asian–American Enterprise Fund will be strengthening the new private sector in Central Asia at one of its weakest but most important points. Moreover, by insisting on sound business plans before providing support, the Fund will help entrepreneurs develop the modern business judgment they need to succeed.

The Fund has come not a moment too soon—with the small business sector just starting to develop in Uzbekistan. President Karimov warmly welcomed this Fund, and the idea that it would open a main office in Tashkent, when we explained it to him last summer. Many other officials and private businessmen were pleased, as I was, with Chairman Solarz's determination to start operations quickly. The Fund has done just that.

At every beginning, no matter how optimistic we may be, it is useful to add a word of caution. Markets, and private businesses, can easily be destroyed by government interference. Political decisions and bureaucratic overregulation can prevent firms from functioning effectively. These will eventually hurt the entire economy. It is absolutely essential that businesses base their decisions solely on market factors.

The U.S. Government has tried to set a good example in the case of this Fund. Although the capital comes from American taxpayers, the Fund is an entirely independent body, with its own independent board of directors, and its own employees. It will make all—repeat all—of its financing decisions purely on the basis of commercial and financial considerations—that is, for the financial success of its clients and the Fund itself. Without official interference. We are asking for everyone's cooperation in making sure that the integrity of this objective decision-making process is respected.

As many of you know, I have a lot of confidence in Uzbekistan's economic potential. I also have great confidence in the management team of this new Fund. They know Uzbekistan, and they want to help the private sector here achieve its potential. For what they have already done, and for what they can do, I'd like to congratulate and thank them again.

Appendix E

REMARKS BY AMBASSADOR HENRY CLARKE AT THE KOKDUMALAK SIGNING CEREMONY, TASHKENT, APRIL 12, 1995

It is a great pleasure for me to represent the U.S. Export-Import Bank here today. And not only Eximbank: the United States Government as a whole strongly supports the Kokdumalak Gas Reinjection Project. It has been over 18 months since I called on Eximbank directors to urge their support for this project, and I am very happy to say that the U.S. Eximbank is very pleased with its role. This project is strongly supported in the Departments of State and Commerce and in the White House. So I would like to extend our official congratulations to Kellogg, Nissho Iwai, and Uzbekneftegas for launching this project.

The U.S. Government recognizes that this project will help Uzbekistan reach a strategic goal: self-sufficiency in oil. While no country in the world can be self-sufficient in everything, for Uzbekistan this project means a great step toward financial independence. With the foreign exchange it saves, by producing its own oil rather than importing it, Uzbekistan can invest in the equipment and technology it needs. As Uzbekistan's economy grows, we will see many more areas of cooperation among our companies, not only in oil and gas but also throughout the economy.

This loan marks a historic occasion for cooperation between the U.S.A. and Japan as well. We are especially pleased that the Eximbank of Japan has joined us in this pioneering venture in Uzbekistan and will finance such a large part of both American and Japanese exports for this project. Jexim's involvement encouraged our Eximbank, and I understand the reverse is also true. The Kokdumalak gas reinjection project is a tribute to multilateral economic cooperation, truly a sign that we are all much stronger together than separately. I hope it will not be the last occasion on which we celebrate such American-Japanese-Uzbekistan cooperation.

The potential for foreign business and economic development in Uzbekistan is enormous, but it is worth remembering that this potential will only be achieved if there is a very favorable climate for private business in Uzbekistan. There is still some work to do: speeding up visas and company registration, fewer obstacles in obtaining foreign exchange and local currency, more economic and business information available to businesses. But today is also a great step forward too: the best sign of a good business climate is the successful launching of a big project like this one.

Again, my congratulations: to the Governments of Uzbekistan, Japan, and the United States, to the National Bank of Uzbekistan, the two Eximbanks and Morgan Guaranty Trust, Uzbekneftegas, Nissho Iwai, and Kellogg.

Appendix F

REMARKS BY AMBASSADOR HENRY CLARKE AT THE MEETING OF EXPERTS ON SECURITY AND COOPERATION IN CENTRAL ASIA, TASHKENT, SEPTEMBER 5, 1995

Madam Chairman, I would like to point out the relationships between internal affairs and regional affairs and their effects on security in Central Asia. This relationship is by no means unique to Central Asia, but it is particularly important in Central Asia, where there are large ethnic minorities. We have seen ethnic conflict in Afghanistan; we have seen it reflected, in part, in Tajikistan. And as you mentioned in your statement, Madam Chairman, there is reason to fear similar conflict in the other states of Central Asia.

There are two main ideas about dealing with such conflicts: one is to use the power of the state to prevent ethnic or any other internal conflict. The second idea is to allow ethnic, communal, or any other groups to express their views and to have representatives elected to government.

The United States is strongly opposed to the use of violence to obtain political goals. We are especially opposed to terrorism and state-sponsored terrorism. It does not matter whether the violence is motivated by religious, national, or other secular reasons. Where there is a real threat of violence, the state has a responsibility to prevent it.

Yet in the long term this is insufficient. Groups that do not have the possibility of peaceful political expression will eventually resort to more extreme measures. Governments therefore increase the risk of instability in the long term if they engage in:

- censorship, or other restrictions on criticism or other forms of peaceful self-expression;
- restrictions on parties and candidates;
- denying free elections. This includes the holding of referenda in which opposition is not permitted.

Unfortunately, these various restrictions on peaceful political expression are now all too common in the Central Asian countries. In our view, the steady, progressive expansion of human and political rights will be necessary for the long-term stability of the Central Asian region.

Notes

Acknowledgments and Sources

*   Henry L. Clarke, oral history interview, Foreign Affairs Oral History Collection, Association for Diplomatic Studies and Training, Arlington, VA, www.adst.org, 1998, https://www.adst.org/OH%20TOCs/Clarke,%20Henry%20L.toc.pdf?_ga=2.104199360.1390069222.1553199447-1884321325.1398958943, pages 144–79.

Prologue: A New Path to Tashkent, without the Silk Route

1   Jack F. Matlock, Jr., *Autopsy on an Empire: The American Ambassador's Account of the Collapse of the Soviet Union* (New York: Random House, 1995), 441–44.
2   The Romanian language in Romania had long been written with the Latin alphabet. But the Cyrillic alphabet had been used in territories ruled by Tsarist Russia and in Soviet Moldova. The Soviets referred to it as a different language, called "Moldovan." The spoken language remained the same in both countries. With independence, Moldova quickly dropped the Cyrillic alphabet and installed the Latin alphabet.
3   Stan Escudero, destined for Tajikistan, spoke Farsi, a language closely related to Tajik. The rest of us—Bill Courtney, Joe Hulings, Ed Hurwitz, and I—spoke Russian and had served in Moscow or Leningrad.
4   According to Senate Foreign Relations Committee staff, no "committee print" of this hearing was published.

Chapter 1: Learning Karimov's System

5   *Time,* July 25, 1994, page 21.
6   The State Department's *Human Rights Report* to Congress for 1992, at the outset of the Uzbekistan section (page 970), stated, "The Na-

tional Democratic Party of Uzbekistan (NDPU), in many respects the successor organization to the Communist Party, controls the political system." The 1993 report repeated a similar statement (on page 1137)—yet we saw no evidence that by 1993 the NDPU acted like a Communist Party or that it controlled anything. The State Department finally accepted the embassy's view on political parties in its 1994 report.

7   On August 24, 1993, Mirsaidov's car was blown up. He was then severely beaten on September 18, 1993. Mirsaidov and his son were abducted, and he was drugged and again beaten, on April 18, 1995. See State Department's *Human Rights Report* for 1993, page 1138, and for 1995, page 1111.

8   *Human Rights Report* for 1992, page 973.

9   *Human Rights Report* for 1993, page 1143.

10   My interview with Muhammad Babur Malikov in Arlington, Virginia, March 21, 2015. See chapter 2 for more on the cotton fraud and its role in relations between Moscow and Uzbekistan.

11   Malikov, interview. The 1993 incident at the Tashkent airport did result in an investigation, discussed further in chapter 5.

12   Malikov, interview.

13   Malikov, interview. Nigina Malikova, Babur Malikov's daughter, participated in the interview and helped clarify this paragraph. I was not able to interview Mr. Ishankhodjaev for his view of the situation.

14   Malikov, interview.

15   Malikov, interview.

16   Malikov, interview.

Chapter 2: Why Should Uzbekistan Be Independent?

17   "Major Ethnic Groups in Central Asia," a map produced by the Office of the Geographer, U.S. Dept. of State, 1993. Only Turkmenistan, with a much smaller total population, had about 73 percent ethnic Turkmen.

18   Russians might call an Uzbek *churka* (block) or *chuchmek* (a reference to darker skin); Uzbeks called Russians *oq kuloq* (white ear).

19   New York: Harper & Row, 1981.

20   According to former Ambassador Babur Malikov, who was a judge in Uzbekistan in the 1980s, available land, water, and seed permitted a maximum output of 3.5 million tons at that time. Written comments to the author, April 14, 2015.

21   James Critchlow, *Nationalism in Uzbekistan: A Soviet Republic's Road to Sovereignty* (Boulder, CO: Westview Press, 1991), 41. I read this book

on the way to my assignment in Tashkent, so it became one of my many "first impressions" about Uzbekistan in 1992.

22   Malikov's written comments to the author on April 14, 2015.

23   James Critchlow, *Nationalism in Uzbekistan,* 42–45. Similarly, former U.S. ambassador to the USSR Jack Matlock writes that many Uzbeks considered the whole cotton affair "an imperialist trick to bring the area under tighter control by Moscow." *Autopsy on an Empire,* 163–64.

24   Malikov's comments to the author, April 14, 2015.

25   Critchlow, 157–65.

26   Martha Brill Olcott, *Central Asia's New States* (Washington: United States Institute of Peace Press), 1966, 45.

27   See chapter 3, "Dangerous Neighborhood."

28   See chapter 5, "Visitors..."

29   Also mentioned by President Karimov in the conversation with Ambassador Escudero and me, December 12, 1994.

Chapter 4: Islam—the Context or the Enemy?

30   Tashkent: Sharq Publishing, 1996.

31   Guests also received a beautiful book about the competing projects, James Steele, ed., *Architecture for a Changing World* (London: Academy Editions, 1992).

32   Critchlow,*Nationalism in Uzbekistan,* 175, 178.

33   Department of State *Human Rights Report* for 1993, 1142, based on Embassy Tashkent reporting.

34   Olcott, *Central Asia's New States,* 117.

35   Critchlow, *Nationalism in Uzbekistan,* 179–80.

36   95 Tashkent 03864, para 6, a telegram prepared after my departure.

37   95 Tashkent 03864, paras 7–8.

38   For example, a sign in English credits the reconstruction and restoration of Bahouddin Naqshiband's architectural complex near Bukhara to the initiative of President Karimov. Naqshiband was born, died, and founded a branch of Sufi Islam in Bukhara in the fourteenth century. Karimov's interest probably reflected not only that this sect originated in Bukhara, but also its reputation for being a contemplative rather than violent form of Islam. The Mufti would also have been a strong advocate for his sect. By 2009 the Naqshiband complex had become one of Bukhara's leading attractions for pilgrims and tourists.

Chapter 5: Visitors as Mixed Blessings, Yet Necessary for Bilateral Relations

39   One former Uzbek employee of the embassy informed me that she

had a friend at the airport who saw Yusupova violate the immigration control point. She said Yusupova was disruptive, yelling at and pushing the guards, and fell, causing her bruising. The witness did not see her taken away and beaten, which seems to have happened later and to have been confirmed by the official investigation.

40 I signed the Agreement on Trade Relations only two months later, on November 5, 1993. The Bilateral Investment Treaty was negotiated and signed in Washington on December 16, 1994. An agreement on double taxation was postponed.

41 93 Tashkent 03018, paras 5–8.

42 93 Tashkent 03018, paras 9, 10, 14.

43 93 Tashkent 03018, paras 17, 23, 27.

44 94 Tashkent 04371, paras 4, 5, 11.

45 94 Tashkent 04371, para 9.

46 94 Tashkent 04371 para 11.

47 94 Tashkent 04371 para 19.

48 94 Tashkent 04371, para 12.

49 94 Tashkent 04371, paras 13–17.

Chapter 6: Big Changes in U.S. Relations, Without Domestic Reform

50 Treaties and Other International Acts Series (T.I.A.S.), number 12083.

51 See chapter 9 on military contacts.

52 Traditional Uzbek courtesy and hospitality may have guided the way we were received, but the positive attitude toward the United States was not just our imagination. A poll taken in January 1992, before the U.S. Embassy opened, found 58 percent of Uzbekistan's residents viewed the U.S. favorably, versus 31 percent unfavorably. Office of Research, USIA, "People of Uzbekistan View the U.S. Positively," Washington, July 8, 1992, Table 1.

53 President Bush's letter of August 11, 1992 (Appendix A), was replaced by a similar letter to me from President William J. Clinton dated September 16, 1994, in which the first paragraphs on foreign policy goals were expanded and rewritten, for example to include a specific reference to the Universal Declaration of Human Rights. But the new instruction did not change what we were trying to do in Uzbekistan. Such presidential letters to U.S. ambassadors have been used for many years to provide general instructions, and they typically clarify the ambassador's authority with respect to the activities of all U.S. departments and agencies in each country.

54 American Councils for International Education, based in Washington,

D.C., implemented educational exchanges with the Soviet Union and its successor states.

55   In the 1992 poll, 58 percent of residents agreed with the question, "Should Western countries help build democracy in Uzbekistan?"; 34 percent said they should not be involved in this way. Office of Research, USIA, "People of Uzbekistan View the U.S. Positively," Table 4.

56   T.I.A.S. 12534. At the same time, Foreign Minister Saidkasymov and I signed "Implementation Memorandum Number One," linked to the assistance agreement, and dealing specifically with U.S. private organizations and their personnel, financed by the U.S. Government to implement assistance programs in Uzbekistan.

Chapter 7: Lost Economic Opportunities

57   For example, see Peter Hopkirk, *The Great Game: The Struggle for Empire in Central Asia* (New York: Kodansha, 1992), 278.

58   Republic of Uzbekistan, "Statement on Economic Reform," Tashkent, February 1995, 6.

59   Listed in *Treaties in Force* without T.I.A.S. number.

60   T.I.A.S. 12515.

61   I could hardly believe the irony of "continuing" the terms of an agreement with a country, the USSR, from which Uzbekistan had declared independence and which had not used the Tashkent–New York route. I assumed the State Department was too busy to negotiate a new agreement and wanted to help both Boeing and Uzbekistan. It worked.

62   Stalin had displaced Koreans from near the Soviet border with Korea to Uzbekistan in the 1930s.

Chapter 8: Water, Air, and Karakalpakstan

63   A northern remnant of the Aral Sea, in Kazakhstan, was cut off by a dam completed in 2005, reviving the northern remnant but speeding the disappearance of southern remnants of the former sea, until only one part was left in Uzbekistan by 2014. Mark Synnott, "Sins of the Aral Sea," *National Geographic,* June 2015, 115–29.

64   Camille Morse, "The Prevalence and Causes of Anemia in Muynak District, Karakalpakstan, Uzbekistan—Recommendations," Crosslink International, Tashkent, November 1994.

65   Project No. 110-0003. My copy of the MOU has no date, but it was probably signed in April 1993. USAID launched similar projects in areas of Kazakhstan and Turkmenistan near the Aral Sea, under con-

tract with CH2M–Hill International, Inc. USAID Briefing Paper, "U.S. Aral Sea Program," September 1995.

Chapter 11: "Club Med" and the "Best Little Embassy" in Central Asia

66 Stan Escudero, my successor as ambassador to Uzbekistan, surely found our building to be an improvement over his hotel floor in Dushanbe. But later successors found our building to be completely inadequate, and Ambassador Joe Presel is cited as calling it "the worst (U.S.) embassy building he had ever seen." The State Department eventually built a much larger and more secure embassy in another part of Tashkent.

Chapter 12: How Much Physical Security?

67 Some years later the situation changed completely in Tashkent, when a new embassy was built and Marine guards were assigned.
68 See Appendix A, page 3.
69 President William J. Clinton's letter to Ambassador Henry Lee Clarke, September 16, 1994, page 3.
70 U.S. General Accounting Office, *Peace Corps: New Programs in Former Eastern Bloc Countries Should be Strengthened,* Washington, D.C., December 19, 1994, 9–10.

Chapter 14: Language Hazards

71 Article 7, Investment Incentive Agreement, October 28, 1992, listed in T.I.A.S. without a number. No matter how difficult it might have been for Uzbekistan's ministries to draw up a conforming text in Uzbek, it would have been even harder for the United States and other English-speaking countries to certify an Uzbek text as conforming, which we would have to do to accept the Uzbek text as equally authoritative as the English text.

Chapter 15: Inspectors Have Their Say

72 Office of Inspector General, U.S. Department of State, *Report of Inspection: Embassy Tashkent, Uzbekistan,* Washington, D.C., January 1995, 9.

Epilogue: Will Independence Endure?

73 Charles Kurzman, "Uzbekistan: The Invention of Nationalism in an Invented Nation," *Critique,* No.15, Fall 1999.

74 In addition to Helene Carrere d' Encausse and James Critchlow, cit-
ed in chapter 2, see Edward A. Allworth, *The Modern Uzbeks, from the
Fourteenth Century to the Present, a Cultural History* (Stanford: Hoover
Institution Press, 1990).

75 Henry L. Clarke, "An American View of Uzbekistan," *Central Asian
Survey,* Vol.18, No.3 (Sept. 1999), 374–78.

76 From the title of chapter 6 in Olcott, *Central Asia's New States.* Many
observers shared this view in the early 1990s.

77 New York: Kodansha International, 1992.

78 Gerry Shih, "In Central Asia's Forbidding Highlands, a Quiet Newcomer: Chinese Troops," *Washington Post,* February 18, 2019, page 1 ff.

79 See Ambassador Collins's unambiguous statement to President Karimov, chapter 5.

80 For example, President Karimov's remarks to Ambassador Collins,
chapter 5, and to OSCE ambassadors, chapter 6.

81 Among the many reports of the sequence of events in Andijan, see
Nozima Kamalova, "The War on Terror and Its Implications for Human Rights in Uzbekistan," *Kennan Institute Occasional Papers No. 296*
(Washington, D.C.: Woodrow Wilson International Center for Scholars, 2007), 14–16; or Philip Shishkin, *Restless Valley: Revolution, Murder
and Intrigue in the Heart of Central Asia* (New Haven: Yale University
Press, 2013), 68–91; or Department of State, "Uzbekistan," *2005 Country Reports on Human Rights Practices.*

82 Chapter 6 in this book, and Kamalova, "The War on Terror and its
Implications for Human Rights in Uzbekistan."

83 Henry L. Clarke, "Privatization in Brčko District: Why It Is Different
and Why It Works," East European Studies Occasional Paper No. 72
(Washington: Woodrow Wilson International Center for Scholars,
April 2004).

84 For example, the Brčko Law Revision Commission (BLRC) undertook
such a comprehensive approach in Brčko District, described in the
Commission Chairman's Final Report, 31 December 2001, published
by the Office of the High Representative for Bosnia and Herzegovina. The criminal and civil codes that the BLRC introduced in Brčko
District became models for similar codes for all of Bosnia and Herzegovina, although the firing and rehiring process for judges and other
officials was unfortunately not followed elsewhere.

Appendix B: Principles for Security at New Posts

85 U.S. Senate Select Committee, "Review of Terrorist Attacks on U.S.

Facilities in Benghazi, Libya, September 11–12, 2012, Together with Additional Views," January 15, 2014, 16.

86 U.S. Senate Select Committee, "Review of Terrorist Attacks...," 15. Subsequently, the mission of a Defense Department Site Security Team (SST) in Tripoli changed, and Ambassador Stevens declined offers from General Carter Ham to "sustain" the SST in protecting the embassy, 20–21. According to Michael Zuckoff, in his *13 Hours, the Inside Account of What Really Happened in Benghazi* (New York: Twelve, Hachette Book Group), 64, Stevens "wouldn't buck the decision of State Department officials in Washington" and allowed the SST to depart Libya. In my view, the ambassador's personal responsibility to ensure the safety of his mission and personnel should have prevailed over any deference to the State Department, if he understood there was an increased threat.

87 Both the Select Committee and Zuckoff detail a series of incidents against U.S. and other Western countries' vehicles and facilities prior to the ambassador's trip, and the British Consulate in Benghazi had closed in response to them. Two armed militias in Benghazi, including Ansar al-Sharia, were known to be aligned ideologically with al-Qaeda. By September 11, an al-Qaeda anniversary, the ambassador's presence became publicly known in Benghazi. Zuckoff, *13 Hours*, 20, 69.

88 Zuckoff, *13 Hours*, 69.

89 According to Zuckoff, *13 Hours*, 66, Ambassador Stevens traveled with two American personal security guards, fewer than I did in Bosnia (2001–3) or Iraq (2007). The Special Mission Compound, with another three armed Americans, was also far less secure than American and international facilities in Bosnia or Iraq.

90 Both Zuckoff and the U.S. Senate Select Committee describe the sequence of events during the attacks similarly, at much greater length.

REFERENCES

Allworth, Edward A. *The Modern Uzbeks, from the Fourteenth Century to the Present, a Cultural History.* Stanford: Hoover Institution Press, 1990.

Baker, James A., III. *The Politics of Diplomacy, Revolution, War and Peace, 1989–1992.* New York: G. P. Putnam's Sons, 1995.

Beschloss, Michael R., and Strobe Talbott. *At the Highest Levels, the Inside Story of the End of the Cold War.* Boston: Little, Brown and Company, 1993.

Carrere d'Encausse, Helene. *Decline of an Empire: The Soviet Socialist Republics in Revolt.* New York: Harper & Row, 1981.

Clarke, Henry L. "An American View of Uzbekistan," *Central Asian Survey,* Vol. 18, No.3 (Sept. 1999), 373–83.

———. Oral History Interview, Foreign Affairs Oral History Collection, Association for Diplomatic Studies and Training, Arlington, VA, www.adst.org, 1998, https://www.adst.org/OH%20TOCs/Clarke,%20 Henry%20L.toc.pdf?_ga=22.104199360.1390069222.1553199447-1884321325.1398958943, 144–79.

———. "Privatization in Brčko District: Why It Is Different and Why It Works." East European Studies Occasional Paper No. 72. Washington: Woodrow Wilson International Center for Scholars, April 2004.

Critchlow, James. *Nationalism in Uzbekistan: A Soviet Republic's Road to Sovereignty.* Boulder, CO: Westview Press, 1991.

Gore, Al. *Earth in the Balance, Ecology and the Human Spirit.* Boston: Houghton Mifflin, 1992.

Hopkirk, Peter. *The Great Game: The Struggle for Empire in Central Asia.* New York: Kodansha, 1992.

Iriskulov, A., and other editors. *Amir Temur in World History.* Tashkent: Sharq Publishing, 1996.

Kamalova, Nozima. "The War on Terror and Its Implications for Human Rights in Uzbekistan." Kennan Institute Occasional Papers No. 296. Washington: Woodrow Wilson Center for Scholars, 2007.

Karnavas, Michael. *Brčko Law Revision Commission: Chairman's Final Report.* Office of the High Representative for Bosnia and Herzegovina, 31 December 2001.

Kreikemeyer, Anna. "Renaissance of Hegemony and Spheres of Influence — The Evolution of the Yeltsin Doctrine," in Hans-Georg Ehrhart, Anna Kreikemeyer, and Andrei V. Zagorsky (Eds.), *Crisis Management in the CIS: Whither Russia?* Baden-Baden: Nomos Verlagsgesellschaft, 1995.

Kurzman, Charles. "Uzbekistan: the Invention of Nationalism in an Invented Nation," *Critique*, No. 15, Fall 1999.

Matlock, Jack F. Jr. *Autopsy on an Empire: The American Ambassador's Account of the Collapse of the Soviet Union.* New York: Random House, 1995.

Odom, William E., and Robert Dujarric. *Commonwealth or Empire? Russia, Central Asia, and the Transcaucasus.* Indianapolis: Hudson Institute, 1995.

Office of Inspector General, U.S. Department of State. *Report of Inspection: Embassy Tashkent, Uzbekistan.* January 1995.

Office of Research, U.S. Information Agency. "People of Uzbekistan View the U.S. Positively." Washington, July 8, 1992.

Olcott, Martha Brill. *Central Asia's New States: Independence, Foreign Policy and Regional Security.* Washington: United States Institute of Peace Press, 1966.

Roth, Andrew. "Brutality Was Part of Uzbekistan President's Policy," *Washington Post*, September 3, 2016, B4.

Shih, Gerry. "In Central Asia's Forbidding Highlands, a Quiet Newcomer: Chinese Troops," *Washington Post*, February 18, 2019, 1.

Shishkin, Philip. *Restless Valley: Revolution, Murder, and Intrigue in the Heart of Central Asia.* New Haven: Yale University Press, 2013.

Steele, James. *Architecture for a Changing World.* London: Academy Editions, 1992.

Synnott, Mark. "Sins of the Aral Sea," *National Geographic*, June 2015, 115–29.

U.S. Department of State. "Uzbekistan." *Human Rights Reports to Congress* for 1992, 1993, 1994, 1995, and 2005.

U.S. General Accounting Office. *Peace Corps: New Programs in Former Eastern Bloc Countries Should be Strengthened.* Washington, December 19, 1994.

U.S. Senate Select Committee on Intelligence. "Review of the Terrorist Attacks on U.S. Facilities in Benghazi, Libya, September 11–12, 2012, together with Additional Views." January 15, 2014.

Zuckoff, Michael. *13 Hours, the Inside Account of What Really Happened in Benghazi.* New York: Twelve, Hachette Book Group, 2014.

INDEX

Abdullaev, Mukhtar, 52–53

Abdurazzakov, Ubaidulah, 23–24. 39–40

Accountability Review Board, U.S. State Department, 192

Aeroflot, 91–92, 149

Afghanistan, 5, 28, 31, 37–38, 42–44, 66, 106, 111, 119, 175–177, 181, 183–184, 203

Aga Khan, 50

Agency for International Development (USAID), 55–58, 75, 80–81, 85, 94–95, 99–101, 121–122, 161, 166, 209n65

Agreement on Trade Relations, U.S.–Uzbekistan, 91, 208n40

Agriculture, 13, 28, 92, 97–99,121

Agricultural equipment, 121

Airbus, 92

Air Force, Russian, 31–32

Air Force, Soviet, 105

Air Force, U.S. 39–41, 105, 155, 194

Air Force, Uzbekistan, 43

Air Force Academy, Uzbekistan 105

Akayev, Askar, 74, 103

Akhmedov, Rustam, 62, 64, 71, 105, 107, 109–112, 196

Al-Qaeda, 38, 140, 163, 183, 212n87

Aliev, Geydar, 27

Alimov, Timur, 22

Almaty, Kazakhstan. 80, 94, 121, 148

American Civil War, 98, 181

American Councils for International Education (ACCELS), 75, 208n54

Amir Temur (Tamerlane), 19, 49, 54, 133–134

Amu Darya river, 31, 37, 43, 97, 99, 103, 111

Andijan, Uzbekistan, 92, 183–184, 211n81

Andropov, Yuri, 27

Anniversary of Embassy opening (March 16), 171

Antonov aircraft (AN-2, AN-24), 98, 101, 149–150

Aral Sea, 96–99, 101–103, 209n63, 209n65

Army, Russian, 31, 37, 40

Army, U.S. 107–108

Army of Uzbekistan, 28, 43, 108

Askarov, Shukur, 120

Assistance Agreement, U.S.–Uzbekistan, 81, 185, 209n63, 209n65

Ataturk, Mustafa Kemal, 164

Aytun, Erdogan, 6

Azerbaijan 4, 5, 45,164

Azeri, language, 164

Azizkhodjaev, Alisher, 22

Babus, Bela, 121, 125–126, 142, 147

Babus, Sylvia, viii, 56, 62, 81, 105, 117, 121, 126, 142, 147, 165

Baker, James, 3

Baldersai, Uzbekistan, 102
Baltic Republics, 1–3, 16, 72, 87, 112, 173, 178
Barnohodjaeva, Delia (later Delia Valente), viii, 122, 166
Basmachi Rebellions, 26
Beer, 84, 130
Belarus, 2, 4, 5, 31
Belt and Road Initiative (of China), 177
Benghazi, Libya, 192–195, 211nn85–87
Bergne, Paul, 152
Bernstrom, Richard, 199
Biden, Joe, 5
Bilge, Kerem, 118
Birlik, political party, 5, 15, 18
Bishkek, Kyrgyzstan, 166
Boeing, 91–92, 109, 209n61
Border guards, 14, 21–22, 30–31, 38, 40, 58–59, 174
Botanical gardens, Tashkent, 144
Brasov, Romania, 102
Brčko District, Bosnia and Herzegovina, 186, 211nn83–84
Breidenstine, John, 121
Brown, Hank, 101
Bucharest, Romania, 2, 16, 57, 61, 63, 69, 84, 140, 152, 157
Buck, Craig, 80, 94
Bukhara, Uzbekistan, 27, 33, 38, 45–46, 49, 52–53, 65, 85–86, 207n38
Bukharan Jews, 46
Bureau of European Affairs, U.S. Dept. of State, 115
Burns, Bob, 197
Burns, Nicholas, 60
Bush, George H. W. 4, 11, 73, 139, 188–191, 192, 208n53

Campbell, Robert, Professor, 80
Carter, Ashton, 109, 113

Caspian Sea, 45
Caspian Sea Fleet, Russian, 31
Ceaușescu, Nicolae, 13, 19, 61, 69
Central Asia Horse Festival, Nukus, Karakalpakstan, 103
Central Asian–American Enterprise Fund (CAAEF), 9, 87, 199–200
Central Bank of Uzbekistan, 88–89
Central Planning Committee, USSR (GosPlan), 13, 98
Chernenko, Konstantin, 27
Chernomyrdin, Victor, 49
Chkalov aircraft factory, Tashkent, 28
Chilanzar *Rayon* or District, Tashkent, viii, 119, 130, 133
Chimgan, Uzbekistan, 102
China, 31, 45–46, 119, 160, 177–178, 180–181
Chirchik, Uzbekistan, 102, 108
Chzhen (or Chjen), Victor, 57, 94
CH2M–Hill International, Inc. 209n65
Citizenship, Dual, 32–33
Civil Air Transport Agreement, U.S.–Soviet, 92
Civil Service, U.S. State Department, 117
Clans, in Tajikistan 32, in Uzbekistan 174
Clarke, Christopher, ix
Clarke, Edwin "Dobby," iiiv, 128, 141–142, 148–149
Clarke, Kathleen "Kathy," 145
Clarke, Marie, 4
Clinton, William J. 41, 60–61, 65, 139, 192, 208n53, 210n69
Coca Cola, 30, 145
Cold War, 1, 13, 71–72, 76, 112, 118, 173
Collins, James, 64–67, 211nn79–80
Combined Arms Academy, Uzbekistan, 105

Commerce Department, U.S. 121
Commercial Attaché, U.S. 121, 134
Commodity Credit Corporation, 91
Commonwealth of Independent States (CIS), 2, 30, 32, 171
Communist Party of Soviet Union, 13, 15, 19, 27, 50, 84
Communist Party of Uzbekistan, 14–15, 26–27, 30, 50, 123, 157, 174, 206n6
Conboy, Teresa, 120
Consular Section, U.S. Embassy Tashkent, 117–118, 137, 166
Containment concept, 179
Cotton, viii, 15, 21, 26–27, 87–88, 92–93, 97–99, 206n10, 207n23
Cotton textile mills, 35, 88
Courtney, William, 101, 205n3
Crosslink International, 209n64
Currency Exchange, 89
Cyrillic alphabet, 163–165, 205n2

Daewoo, factory in Uzbekistan, 92
Dar es Salaam, Tanzania, U.S. Embassy, 140
Defense Attaché, Turkish, 106
Defense or Military Attaché, U.S. 64, 105–107, 109, 113, 118
Defense Department, U.S. 109, 111, 113, 118, 139, 183, 193, 212n86
Defense Intelligence Agency (DIA), U.S. 105
Defense Ministry, USSR, 102
Defense Ministry, Uzbekistan (incl. Protocol), 14, 105–107, 110, 196
Deputy Chief of Mission, U.S. 3, 22, 56, 61, 91, 103, 107, 115–116, 126, 139–140, 153 170, 193
Dollar payments, 69, 88–89, 135, 138, 158
Domodedovo airport, Moscow, 138
Dostum, Abdulrashid, Afghan General, 43–44, 176

Dukhovny, Victor, Professor, 99
Dushanbe, Tajikistan, 38–43, 45, 58, 60, 106, 111, 137, 194–195, 210n66
Dushanbe, U.S. Embassy, evacuation 38–41, reopening 41–42, 58, 106, 137

Economic Zone, Law of the Sea, 163
Egypt, 66
Energy, 9, 35, 92
Embassy, U.S. ambassador's residence – see Residence, U.S. ambassador's
Embassy building (or chancery) in Tashkent, U.S. 55, 108, 115, 122–123, 125, 128, 130–31, 133–34, 136–137, 210n66
Embassy guards in Tashkent, U.S. 135, 171
Embassy staffing, Tashkent, 55, 115, 122
Erk, political party, 15, 18
Escudero, Stan, 31, 39, 93, 205n3, 207n29, 210n66
Estonia, 26
Export-Import Bank (Eximbank), U.S. 91–92, 201
Export-Import Bank of Japan, 201

Fane, Daria, 13, 17, 43, 59, 91
Fazylbekov, Mayor of Tashkent, 133–34
Federal Aviation Administration (FAA), U.S. 92
Feeney, Paula, 101
Fergana Valley, Uzbekistan, ix, 36–37, 51–54, 60, 67, 90, 92, 94, 140, 146, 175–76, 183–184
Final Act, Helsinki Conference on Security and Cooperation in Europe, 34
Food, 30, 83–85, 87–88, 99, 102, 133, 153

Foreign Corrupt Practices Act, U.S. 93

Foreign Economic Relations, Ministry of Uzbekistan, 90–91, 165

Foreign investment in Uzbekistan, 90–93, 182, 186

Foreign Ministry of Israel, 4

Foreign Ministry of Uzbekistan, 11, 17, 41, 59, 78, 81, 163, 165

Foreign Relations Committee, U.S. Senate, 4–5, 205n4

Foreign Trade Bank, USSR, 138

Foreign Trade Bank, Uzbekistan, 138–39

Ford Scorpio, 141, 143

Fort, James and Catherine, 4–5

Fort Polk, Louisiana, 112

Ganyeeva, Shakhnoza, Ostankino TV, 198

General Services Officer (GSO), 101, 117, 125, 137

Georgia, former Soviet republic, 2, 4, 5, 45

Gertz, Bill, 197

Gold, 14, 35, 70, 72, 87, 90, 92–93, 110, 145

Gorbachev, Mikhail, 1, 30, 50, 69

Gore, Al, 101, 193

"Great game," 86, 175–179, 209n57

Hamidov, Bakhtiyar, 60

Hanauer, Larry, 118

Hartman, Arthur, 63

Health, 80, 99, 151–155, 161, 170

Health Ministry of Uzbekistan, 161

Hepatitis, 152–154

Hoagland, Richard, 120

Hulings, Joseph S. 205n3

Human rights, cases and policies, 5, 12–13, 15–19, 21–22, 34, 58–62, 66, 72–74, 79, 182–185, 205nn6–9, 207n33, 208n53, 211nn8–82

Human Rights Report, U.S. Dept. of State, 15, 205nn6–9

Hurwitz, Edward, 205n3

Independence for Uzbekistan, x, 1–2, 8–9, 14–15, 19, 25, 28, 30, 33, 35, 47, 50–51, 72, 84, 89, 92, 107, 110, 138, 164, 173–174, 177, 179, 180–181, 196, 201, 209n61

Independence Day, July 4, American holiday, 128, 133, 171

Independence Day, Sept 1, Uzbekistan holiday, 30

India, 42, 46, 61, 78–79, 158, 177

Information Agency, U.S. (USIA), 119–120, 134, 170, 208n52, 209n55

Information Service, U.S. (USIS), 57–59, 100, 147, 166

Inspector General's Office, U.S. Dept. of State, 138–39, 169–171, 210n72

International Monetary Fund (IMF), 34, 88

International Republican Institute (IRI), 76, 80

Interstate Council for the Aral Sea, 102

Intourist, 49, 71, 86

Investment Incentive Agreement, U.S.–Uzbekistan, 90–91, 165, 210n71

Iran, 31, 37–38, 45–46, 52, 60, 65–66, 84, 110, 119

Ishankhodjaev, Ulugbek, 22, 206n13

Islam, 8, 32, 37–38, 45, 49–54, 60, 207n38

Islamabad, Pakistan, U.S. Embassy, 42, 140

Islamic Center for Learning, Tashkent, 53

Islamic Movement of Uzbekistan, 54

Israel, 4, 45–46, 66, 79

Istanbul, Turkey, 6, 157

Jorgenson, Mary, 116

Kabul, Afghanistan, 42, 195

Kamalova, Nozina, 211nn81–82

Kamilov, Abdulaziz, 20, 31, 68, 109, 196

Karakalpak, ethnic group, 99, 100

Karakalpakstan, 88, 92, 96, 98–100, 102, 209n64

Kara Kum Canal, 103

Karshi, Uzbekistan, 147, 184

Karimov, Islam, 11–21, 23–24, 29–33, 38, 44–46, 49–50, 52–54, 59–63, 65–67, 72–74, 78, 80, 86–89, 94, 103, 107, 110, 113, 130. 133–134, 145, 158, 168, 174, 176, 182–186, 200, 207n29, 207n38, 211nn79–80

Kazakh, ethnic group, 46, 177

Kazakhstan, 2, 31–33, 35, 38, 45, 47, 56, 74–75, 80, 97–98, 103, 106–107, 110, 121, 148–49, 155, 166–167, 175, 179–180, 209n63, 209n65

Kellogg, M.W. U.S. company, 92, 201–202

Kent, George, 101, 118, 137

KGB (Committee for State Security), USSR, 1, 13–14, 27, 71, 78, 125, 131, 146

Khanabad airbase, Uzbekistan, 184

Khiva, Uzbekistan, 49

Khojand, Tajikistan, 176

Khorezm Oblast, Uzbekistan, 100–101

Kiev, U.S. Consulate General and Embassy, 116

Kirk, Roger, 57–58

Kokand, Uzbekistan, 53

Kokdumalak gas reinjection project, 92, 201

Koran, 51–52

Kravchuk, Leonid, 2

Kyrgyz ethnic group, 46, 176–177

Kyrgyz language, 166

Kyrgyzstan (or Kyrgyz Republic), 16, 32, 37–38, 51–52, 67, 74, 97, 103, 155, 175–176, 179–180, 184

Langan, Douglas, 115–117

Lankina, Tomila, 158

Leninabad Oblast, Tajikistan, 176

Lithuania, 1

Lubin, Nancy, 101

Malikov, Muhammad Babur, viii, 21–24, 27, 206nn10–16, 206n20, 207n22, 207n24

Malikova, Nigina, 206n13

Mandel, David, 122

Margilan, Uzbekistan, 51

Marine guards, U.S. 136–137, 210n67

Maqsudi, Farid, 145

Martin, Barbara, 126, 143

Martin, James, 167

Masood, Ahmed Shah, 66

Matera, Michael, 12, 56, 70, 91, 100, 153, 155, 170

McWilliams, Ed, 39, 41, 43

Medical program, U.S. Dept. of State, 151–154

Melli Majlis, "alternative parliament," 18

Memorandum of Understanding for a Senior Policy Advisor, 80

Memorandum of Understanding on Diplomatic and Consular Travel, 71

Memorandum of Understanding on Water Quality and Environmental Education, 100
Miller, Herb, 122
Mirsaidov, Shukrullo, 18, 206n7
Mirziyoyev, Shavkat, 187
Mohammad-Sadiq Mohamad-Yusuf, Mufti, 52
Moldova, 2–5, 164, 205n2
Monroe Doctrine, 175, 179
Morgan Guaranty Trust, or Morgan J,P, 92, 202
Morse, Camille, 209n64
Moscow, Russia, 2–3, 6–7, 13–16, 19, 23, 26–27, 30–31, 33, 35, 40–41, 58, 63, 78–79, 83–84, 102, 116, 136, 140 148, 151, 157–159, 205n3, 206n10, 207n23
Moscow, U.S. Embassy, 3, 64, 69, 105, 117, 125–126, 138, 154
Motorized Rifle Division, 201st Russian, 31
Mukhtorkhon, Mufti. See Abdullaev, Mukhtar
Museum of Applied Art, Tashkent, 141
Museum of the Arts, Karakalpakstan, 100
Muynak, Karakalpakstan, 96–101, 209n64

Nairobi, U.S. Embassy, 140
Namangan, Uzbekistan, 94
Naqshibandi Sufis, 52
Narodnoe Slova, newspaper, 113
National Democratic Institute (NDI), 76, 79
National Democratic Party of Uzbekistan (NDPU), 15, 205n6
National War College, U.S. 63–64, 105, 155, 175
Navoii, Uzbekistan, 167

Navruz holiday, 30
Navy, U.S. 47
Nazarbayev, Nursultan, 2, 103
Nelson, Dale, U.S. Brigadier General 107
Neva, automobile, 102, 142–143
New Post Support Unit, U.S. Embassy Bonn, viii, 122
Newly independent state(s) (NIS), 23, 34, 59–60, 64–65, 173, 178–180
Newmont Mining, U.S. company, 70, 72, 90, 92, 148
Niles, Thomas, 116
Nissho Iwai, Japanese company, 201–202
Niyazov, Saparmurad, 103
Nongovernmental organization(s) (NGOs), in Uzbekistan, 16, 80–82, 185
North Atlantic Treaty Organization (NATO), 72, 92, 106, 109, 112, 159
Nuclear weapons–free zone for Central Asia, 46–47
Nukus, Karakalpakstan, 98–103
Nukus Declaration on the Aral Sea Basin, 103

Oil, 35, 87, 201
Organization for Security and Co-operation in Europe (OSCE), 34, 73, 197–198
Osh, Kyrgyzstan, 67
Overseas Private Investment Corporation (OPIC), 90, 165, 196

Pakistan, 42, 46 78–79, 103, 177
Paris, 7, 88
Partnership for Peace (P4P), 72, 109, 109, 112, 197–198
Paul, Chris, 117, 135
Peace Corps, 70, 81, 85, 120, 145–146, 152, 154, 170, 210n70

Peace Corps agreement, U.S.–Uzbekistan, 70
Pepsi Cola, 144–145
Peres, Shimon, 79
Perry, William J. 9, 64, 107, 109–111, 183, 186, 196–198
Plov, 30
Pravda Vostoka, newspaper, 22
Presel, Joe, 210n66
Pressler, Larry, 5, 15, 17
Price controls, 87
Price Waterhouse, U.S. company, 94
Primakov, Yevgeny, Russian intelligence, 66
Privatization, 93–95, 186, 211n83
Pulatov, Abdurahim, 5, 15
Putin, Vladimir, 180

Radio Liberty, 71–72
Rafikov, Gani, 39, 91
Railroads, 35, 148
Rakhmonov, Imomali, 103
Rashidov, Sharaf, 27
Real estate market, 95
Regional Security Officer (RSO), 117, 135–136, 139–140, 142, 144, 193
Registan square, Samarkand, 48, 50, 110–111
Reid, Harry, 101
Residence, U.S. Ambassador's, 44, 61, 107, 109, 126–130, 140–141
Romanian language, 2, 157, 164, 205n2
Ruble zone, 34–35, 89
Rusoruzheniye, Russian arms export agency, 65
Russia, relations with Iran, 65–66, 110, with Ukraine, 173
Russian, language and ethnic group, ix, 2, 25–26, 28, 32–33, 157–160, 162–167, 175, 178–180, 205n3, 206n18

Safaev, Sadyk, 20, 22, 90–92,
Saidkasymov, Saidmukhtar, 22, 60, 71, 79, 81, 82, 185, 209n56
Salgo, Nicholas, 130, 133–134
Samarkand, Uzbekistan, 33, 38, 45–46, 48–50, 54, 65, 87, 105, 110–111,146
Saudi Arabia, 52, 66
Savitsky Collection of art, Nukus, Karakalpakstan, 100
Scotti, Jennifer, 117–118
Seabees, 55, 131
Senate Foreign Relations Committee, U.S. 4, 5, 205n4
Senate Select Committee on Intelligence, U.S. 192, 211nn85–86, 212n90
Shakhrisabz, Uzbekistan, 147–148
Sherwood, Elizabeth, 113
"Shock therapy," form of privatization, 65, 94
Shushkevich, Stanislav, 2
Silk Route, 6, 46, 49
Simon, Paul, 101
Simons, Thomas, 103
Smith, Timothy, 121
Solarz, Stephen, 87, 200
Solikh, Mohammad, 18
Som, currency of Uzbekistan, 34, 89
Soviet Union (or USSR), 1–4, 6, 13–14, 20, 25, 27, 42, 44, 51, 59, 72–73, 75, 78, 83–84, 88, 100–101, 121, 124, 131, 138, 146, 148, 154, 159, 166, 173–174, 178, 180, 192 205n1, 208n54
Sphere of influence, 47, 64–65, 175, 178–179
Specter, Arlen, 61–63
State Control Committee, Uzbekistan, 22

State Department, U.S. ix, 2–4, 7, 15–16, 22, 29, 39, 41–42, 59, 63, 65, 73, 88, 115, 117, 129, 131–132, 134, 136, 138, 141, 145, 151–154, 166, 167, 169–170, 179, 192–195, 205nn6–7, 209n61, 210n66, 212n86

State orders (for cotton and other crops in Uzbekistan), 88

Stevens, Christopher, 193–194, 212n86, 212n89

Sultanov, Utkur, 91

Summers, Lawrence, 57

Surkhandarya River, Tajikistan and Uzbekistan, 111

Sustainable Development of the Aral Sea Basin, International Conference in Nukus, 102

Sutton, Judy, 152, 154–155, 170

Syr Darya river, 36, 51, 97

Tamerlane. *See* Amir Temur

Tashkent, airport, 12, 21, 30–31, 39–40, 53, 58, 79, 91–92, 127, 168, 206n11, 207nn39

Tashkent International Health Clinic, 155, 170

Tax reform, 57, 85, 186

Tehran, Iran, 45, 65, 140

Termez, Uzbekistan, 31, 71, 111

Terterian, Anna, 120

Teshabaev, Deputy Foreign Minister, Uzbekistan, 21–23

Tel Aviv, 46, 58, 115–116

Tel Aviv, U.S. Embassy, 2–3, 6–7

Textile mills, 35, 88

Trade relations Agreement (see Agreement on Trade Relations, above)

Treasury Department, U.S. 56–57

Truck routes to Central Asia, 45

Turkey, 23, 45, 61, 145, 164, 177

Turkish Airlines, 6

Turkestan, 174

Turkmen ethnic group, 206n17

Turkmenistan, 31, 33, 35, 38, 45, 65–66, 74, 97–98, 74. 97–98, 103, 110, 155, 175, 180–181, 206n17, 209n65

Uighur (or Uyghur) ethnic group, 46, 160, 177

Ukraine, 2–4, 31, 110, 173, 180

Ulugbek, astronomer and ruler of Samarkand, 54

United Nations Educational, Scientific and Cultural Organization (UNESCO), 49–50

United Nations Mission to Uzbekistan, 34, 155, 159

University of World Economy and Diplomacy, Tashkent, 76, 79,

Urgench, Khorezm Oblast, Uzbekistan, 100–101, 150

Uzbek ethnic group, 25–30, 206nn18, 208nn52

Uzbek language, 157, 160, 164–168, 210n71

Uzbekistan Airways, 46, 91–92, 149

Uzbekistan-American Chamber of Commerce, 93

Uzbekneftegas, oil and gas company, 201–202

Verner, Jerry, 91, 119

Victory Day, May 9 holiday, 30

Voice of America, 71–72

Vozrozhdeniya Island (in former Aral Sea) 101

Wahabis, 38, 52–53

White, Sharon, 103, 107

World Bank, 34, 57, 88, 99, 187

World Bank Consultative Group Meeting, Paris, 88

World Vision, 81
World War II, 1, 27–28, 83, 112, 129

Xinjiang Province, China, 46, 177, 181

YAK-40 aircraft, 150
Yeltsin, Boris, 2, 33
Yusupova, Dildora, 58–59, 207n39

Zapinski, Chuck, 118
Zarafshan, Uzbekistan, 70, 167
Ziamov, Deputy Foreign Minister, Uzbekistan, 11–12
Zone of influence (see sphere of influence, above)

www.ingramcontent.com/pod-product-compliance
Lightning Source LLC
Chambersburg PA
CBHW071049280326
41928CB00050B/2141